1000 JOKES

You Could Tell Your Mother

Compiled by
Cameron Brown

Cartoons by

Niki

1000 JOKES You Could Tell Your Mother

Compiled by Cameron Brown
Cartoons by Niki

Originally published by
Facts, Figures & Fun, an imprint of
AAPPL Artists' and Photographers' Press Ltd.
Church Farm House, Wisley, Surrey, GU23 6QL   UK
info@ffnf.co.uk   www.ffnf.co.uk
info@aappl.com   www.aappl.com

This edition published 2007 for
Index Books Ltd.

ISBN 1-904332-61-7
ISBN 978-1-904332-61-9

You Could Tell Your Mother

A man walks into a doctor's surgery. He has a cucumber up his nose, a carrot in his left ear and a banana in his right ear.

"Ah! I can see what's the matter with you," says the doctor. "You're not eating properly."

❖

After a morning stroll the three bears head for the kitchen to see if their breakfast has cooled down.

"Somebody's eaten my porridge," cries the baby bear.

"And somebody's eaten my porridge," exclaims the mother bear.

"Stuff the porridge!" yells the father bear. "Where's the bloody DVD player?"

❖

A man was sent to Hell for his sins. As he was being taken to his place of eternal torment, he passed a room where a lawyer was having an intimate encounter with a beautiful young woman.

"What a rip-off," the man muttered. "I have to roast for all eternity, and that lawyer gets to spend it with a beautiful woman."

Jabbing the man with his pitchfork, the escorting demon snarled, "Who are you to question that woman's punishment?"

❖

A little boy at a wedding looks at his mother and says, "Mummy, why does the girl wear white?"

His mum replies, "The bride is in white because she's happy and this is the happiest day of her life."

The boy thinks about this, and then says, "Well then, why is the boy wearing black?"

A man went to visit a friend and was amazed to find him playing chess with his dog. He watched the game in astonishment for a while. "I can hardly believe my eyes!" he exclaimed. "That's the smartest dog I've ever seen."

"He's not so smart," the friend replied. "I've beaten him three games out of five."

Two tigers are prowling through the jungle in single file, and the one behind keeps licking the backside of the tiger in front.

"Will you stop that," says the first tiger. "It's getting really annoying."

"I'm sorry," says the second tiger, "but I just ate a lawyer and I'm trying to get the taste out of my mouth."

John went to visit his 90-year-old grandfather in a very secluded, rural area of Georgia. After spending a great evening chatting the night away, John's grandfather prepared breakfast of bacon, eggs and toast. However, John noticed a film-like substance on his plate, and questioned his grandfather asking, "Are these plates clean?"

His grandfather replied, "They're as clean as cold water can get them. Just you go ahead and finish your meal, sonny!" For lunch the old man made hamburgers.

Again, John was concerned about the plates as his appeared to have tiny specks around the edge that looked like dried egg and asked, "Are you sure these plates are clean?"

Without looking up the old man said, "I told you before,

sonny, those dishes are as clean as cold water can get them. Now don't you fret, I don't want to hear another word about it!"

Later that afternoon, John was on his way to a nearby town and as he was leaving his grandfather's dog started to growl, and wouldn't let him pass.

John yelled and said, "Grandfather, your dog won't let me get to my car!"

Without diverting his attention from the football game he was watching on TV, the old man shouted ... "Coldwater, go lay down!"

❖

Sam and John are at work in the timber yard when John accidentally chops off his arm with a saw. Sam wraps the arm in a plastic bag and takes John to a surgeon. Four hours later Sam is amazed to see John in the pub throwing darts. *Wow!* thinks Sam. *That surgeon is great.*

A few weeks later John accidentally cuts off his leg. Sam puts the leg in a plastic bag and takes John back to the surgeon. That evening he's amazed to see John playing football. *Wow!* thinks Sam. *That surgeon is amazing.*

A few weeks later John cuts off his head. Sam puts the head in a plastic bag and carries John to the surgeon. Next day the surgeon calls Sam and says, "I'm sorry, but John is dead."

"Don't blame yourself," says Sam. "I'm sure you did all you could."

"I'm not blaming myself," says the surgeon. "I'm blaming

you. If you'd put some holes in that plastic bag the poor bloke wouldn't have suffocated."

A snail was tired of his reputation for being so slow. He decided to get a fast car to make up the difference. After shopping around a while, he decided that the Datsun 240-Z was the car to get. So the snail goes to the nearest Datsun dealer and says he wants to buy the 240-Z, but he wants it repainted '240-S'.

The dealer asks, "Why 'S'?"

The snail replies, "'S' stands for snail. I want everybody who sees me roaring past to know who's driving."

Well, the dealer doesn't want to lose the unique opportunity to sell a car to a snail, so he agrees to have the car repainted for a small fee.

The snail gets his new car and spent the rest of his days roaring happily down the motorway at top speed. And whenever anyone saw him zooming by, they'd say, "Wow! Look at that S-car go!"

It was entertainment night at the old folks' home and the Amazing Claude was topping the bill. People came from miles around to see the famed hypnotist do his stuff. As Claude went to the front of the meeting room, he announced: "Unlike most hypnotists who invite two or three people up here to be put into a trance, I intend to hypnotize each and every member of the audience."

The excitement was almost electric as Claude withdrew a beautiful antique pocket watch from his coat. "I want you each to keep your eye on this antique watch. It's a very special watch. It's been in my family for six generations."

He began to swing the watch gently back and forth while quietly chanting, "Watch the watch, watch the watch, watch the watch ..."

The crowd became mesmerized as the watch swayed back and forth, light gleaming off its polished surface. Hundreds of pairs of eyes followed the swaying watch until, suddenly, it slipped from the hypnotist's fingers and fell to the floor, breaking into a hundred pieces.

"SHIT!" said the hypnotist. It took three days to clean up the old folks' home.

A French explorer, an English explorer and a New York explorer are captured by a fierce tribe. The chief says, "We're going to kill you, then use your skins to build a canoe. However, you get to choose how you die."

The Frenchman says, "I take ze poison." The chief gives him some poison, and the Frenchman drinks it down, shouting "Vive la France."

The Englishman says, "A pistol for me, please." The chief gives him a pistol. The Englishman shouts, "God save the queen," and blows his brains out.

The New Yorker says, "Gimme me a fork." The chief is puzzled, but he shrugs and gives him a fork. The New Yorker takes the fork and starts jabbing himself all over.

"What are you doing?" shouts the chief.

The New Yorker says, "So much for your canoe."

A widow decides to see if a pet will ease her loneliness and goes to the pet shop. She decides against puppies, kittens, etc., and is about to leave when she hears a voice saying, "My, do you look lovely this afternoon, madam."

She turns around quickly to see who has spoken, but there is no one. All she sees is a big green parrot, resting on his perch in his cage. "Did you say that?" she asks.

"Why, yes, I did!" he replies. "And may I add that dress colour really suits you."

The lady suddenly realizes how nice it would be to not

9

only have a talking parrot, but one that paid such nice compliments. So she pays for him and takes him home. On the way, she says, "You know, I am so proud of you that I believe I'll take you out for dinner! Would you like that?"

The parrot says, "Why yes, that would be delightful. I know a charming restaurant in Mayfair." They arrive home and the lady goes upstairs to her room to change for dinner, bringing the parrot along, of course, but when she starts getting ready the parrot begins complaining, swearing, and even bites her. Well, the woman is flabbergasted! She grabs the parrot by the throat, marches down the stairs into the kitchen and stuffs the parrot in the freezer. She leaves him there for five minutes before taking him back out. The parrot is very cold.

She says, "Well? Have you learned your lesson? I will not tolerate such language in my house!"

The parrot says, "Okay, okay, I promise it won't happen again. I am deeply sorry."

Within five minutes, he is cursing again and bites her once more on the arm and once on the finger. The lady is absolutely stunned. She rips the parrot out of his cage, goes down the stairs into the kitchen and slams him into the freezer. This time, she leaves him in there for fifteen minutes.

When she finally takes him out, the parrot is one step away from death. He is shivering and has frost on his beak. "I swear it will never, ever happen again! I will never insult you again! I promise!" As he thaws, he looks up at the lady and says, "I do have one question though. That turkey in there, what on earth did he do to you?"

A blonde, wanting to earn some money, decided to hire herself out as a handyman-type and started canvassing a wealthy neighbourhood. She went to the front door of the first house and asked the owner if he had any jobs for her to do.

"Well, you can paint my porch. How much will you charge?"

The blonde said, "How about $50?" The man agreed and told her that the paint and ladders that she might need were in the garage. The man's wife, inside the house, heard the conversation and said to her husband, "Does she realize that the porch goes all the way around the house?"

The man replied, "She should. She was standing on the porch."

A short time later, the blonde came to the door to collect her money.

"You're finished already?" he asked.

"Yes," the blonde answered, "and I had paint left over, so I gave it two coats." Impressed, the man reached in his pocket for the $50. "And by the way," the blonde added, "that's not a Porch, it's a Ferrari."

Two drunks stand on a cliff with their arms outstretched. One has some budgies lined up on each arm, the other has parrots lined up on his arms. After a couple of minutes, they both leap off the cliff and fall to the ground. Laying next to each other in intensive care at the hospital, one says to the other, "I don't think much of this budgie jumping."

The other replies, "Yeah, I'm not too keen on this parrot-gliding either."

An elderly lady goes to the bar on a cruise ship and orders a Scotch with two drops of water. As the bartender gives her the drink she says, "I'm on this cruise to celebrate my 80th birthday and it's today."

The bartender says, "Well, since it's your birthday, I'll buy you a drink. In fact, this one is on me."

As the woman finishes her drink, the woman to her right says, "I would like to buy you a drink, too."

The old woman says, "Thank you. Bartender, I want a Scotch with two drops of water."

"Coming up," says the bartender.

As she finishes that drink, the man to her left says, "I would like to buy you one, too."

The old woman says, "Thank you. Bartender, I want another Scotch with two drops of water."

"Coming right up," the bartender says.

As he gives her the drink, he says, "Ma'am, I'm dying of curiosity. Why the Scotch with only two drops of water?"

"Sonny, when you're my age, you've learned how to hold your booze. Holding your water, however, is a different matter altogether."

Some race horses are in a stable. One of them starts to boast about his track record. "In the last 15 races, I've won 8 of them!"

Another horse breaks in, "Well in the last 27 races, I've won 19!!"

"Well, in the last 36 races, I've won 28!" says another, flicking his tail.

At this point, they notice the greyhound which has been sitting there listening. "I don't mean to boast," says the greyhound, "but in my last 90 races, I've won 88 of them!"

The horses are clearly amazed. "Wow!" says one, after a hushed silence. "A talking dog."

What can a goose do, a duck can't and a lawyer should? Stick his bill up his rear.

A piece of string goes into a bar and orders a glass of whisky. When the drink arrives the string gulps it down in one go, then runs out without paying. Outside the string

12

ruffles itself and ties itself up, then goes back to the bar and orders another whisky.

"Here," says the bartender. "Aren't you that piece of string that just ran out without paying?"

The string replies, "No, I'm a frayed knot."

A junior partner in a law firm is sent to represent a client accused of murder. After a long trial the case is won and the client acquitted.

The young lawyer telegraphs his firm with the message "Justice prevailed". The senior partner telegraphs back, "Appeal immediately".

A man approaches a beautiful woman in a supermarket. "I've lost my wife somewhere," he says. "Do you mind if I talk to you for a moment?"

"Ok," says the woman, "but how's that going to help you find your wife?"

"Easy," replies the man. "She always turns up when I start chatting to strange women."

If it's true that girls are inclined to marry men like their fathers, it is understandable why so many mothers cry so much at weddings.

Three rats are sitting in a bar talking bragging about their bravery and toughness.

The first says, "I'm so tough, once I ate a whole bagful of rat poison!"

The second says, "Well I'm so tough, once I was caught in a rat trap and I bit it apart!"

The third rat gets up and says, "I'm off home to beat up the cat."

A fortune-teller tells a frog: "You are going to meet a beautiful young girl who will want to know everything about you."

The frog says, "This is great! Will I meet her at a party, or what?"

"No," says the fortune-teller. "In her biology class."

"Doctor, is there something wrong with my heart?"

"I've given you a thorough examination, and I can confidently say that your heart will last as long as you live."

A local charity realized that the organization had never received a donation from the town's most successful lawyer. The person in charge of contributions called him to persuade him to contribute.

"Our research shows that out of a yearly income of at least $500,000, you give not a penny to charity. Wouldn't you like to give back to the community in some way?"

The lawyer mulled this over for a moment and replied, "First, did your research also show that my mother is dying after a long illness, and has medical bills that are several times her annual income?"

Embarrassed, the charity rep mumbled, "Um ... no."

The lawyer interrupts, "Or that my brother, a disabled veteran, is blind and confined to a wheelchair?"

The stricken charity rep began to stammer out an apology, but was interrupted again.

"Or that my sister's husband died in a traffic accident," the lawyer said, his voice rising in indignation, "leaving her penniless with three children?!"

The humiliated charity rep, completely beaten, said simply, "I had no idea..."

On a roll, the lawyer cut him off once again, "So if I don't give any money to them, why should I give any to you?"

A couple made a deal that whoever died first would come back and inform the other of the afterlife. Their biggest fear was that there was no afterlife. After a long life, the husband was the first to go, and true to his word he made contact,

"Connie....Connie.!"

"Is that you, Joe?"

"Yes, I've come back like we agreed."

"What's it like?"

"Well, I get up in the morning and I have sex. I have breakfast, then it's off to the golf course. I have sex. I bathe in the sun, and then I have sex twice. I have lunch, another romp around the golf course, then sex pretty much all afternoon. After supper, to golf course again. Then I have sex until late at night. The next day it starts again."

"Oh, Joe, you surely must be in heaven."

"Not exactly; I'm a rabbit on a golf course in Arizona."

Joe suffers from very bad headaches and eventually finds a doctor who offers a solution. "The good news is that I can cure your headaches," says the doctor. "The bad news is that it will require castration. You have a rare condition that causes your testicles to press against the base of your spine. It's that pressure that causes the headaches."

Joe is shocked but decides he has no choice but to go

15

under the knife. After the operation Joe feels much better and decides to treat himself to a new suit. He goes into a tailor's to see what's on offer. The tailor looks at him and says, "Let's see. I'd guess you take a size 44 long."

Joe laughs, "That's right. How did you know my exact size?"

"It's my job to know," says the tailor. "How about a new shirt to go with it? I'd say you take a 34 sleeve and a 16 neck."

"Right again," says Joe. "How did you know?"

"It's my job," says the tailor. "How about some new underwear as well? Let's see. I'd say you're a size 36."

Joe laughs. "Got you that time. Actually I'm a 34. I've worn size 34 since I was eighteen."

The tailor tuts. "You shouldn't do that, sir. You see a size 34 would press your testicles against your spine and give you terrible headaches."

❖

My Darling,

I've been so desolate ever since I broke off our engagement; devastated! Won't you please consider coming back to me? You hold a place in my heart no other woman can fill. I can never find another woman like you. I need you so much. Won't you forgive me and let us make a new beginning? I love you so.

Yours always and truly,
John
P.S. Congratulations on your lottery win.

Two vampire bats wake up in the middle of the night, thirsty for blood. One says, "Let's fly out of the cave and get some blood."

"We're new here," says the second one. "It's dark out, and we don't know where to look. We'd better wait until the other bats go with us."

The first bat replies, "Who needs them? I can find some blood somewhere." He flies out of the cave.

When he returns, he is covered with blood.

The second bat says excitedly, "Where did you get the blood?"

The first bat takes his friend to the mouth of the cave. Pointing into the night, he asks, "See that black building over there?"

"Yes," the other bat answers.

"Well," says the first bat, "I didn't."

A couple send their dim son to a special tutor to help him catch up on his schoolwork. After a month they ask for a progress report.

"He's getting straight As," says the tutor.

"That's fantastic," say the parents.

"Yes, they're great," says the tutor. "But his Bs are still a little wonky."

A man goes into a barber's shop advertising David Beckham-style cuts. Half an hour later he's horrified to see his head half bald and covered in cuts.

"That's not how David Beckham has his hair," complains the man.

"It would be if he came in here," replies the barber.

An explorer comes across a pygmy standing by a dead elephant.

"Did you kill this beast?" asks the explorer.

"Yes," replies the pygmy.

"What did you use?" asks the explorer.

"A big club," replies the pygmy.

"That must have been an enormous club," says the explorer.

"Oh, it is," replies the pygmy. "There's about four hundred of us."

There were these two cows, chatting over the fence between their fields.

The first cow said, "I tell you, this mad-cow-disease is really pretty scary. They say it is spreading fast; I heard they've got it on the Johnson Farm."

The other cow replies, "I don't care. It can't be transferred to us ducks."

A lady was expecting the plumber; he was supposed to come at ten o'clock. Ten o'clock came and went; no plumber; eleven o'clock, twelve o'clock, one o'clock; no plumber. She concluded he wasn't coming, and went out to do some errands. While she was out, the plumber arrived. He knocked on the door; the lady's parrot, who was at home in a cage by the door, said, "Who is it?"

He replied, "It's the plumber."

He thought it was the lady who'd said, "Who is it?" and waited for her to come and let him in. When this didn't happen he knocked again, and again the parrot said, "Who is it?"

He said, "It's the plumber!"

He waited, and again the lady didn't come to let him in. He knocked again, and again the parrot said, "Who is it?"

He said, "It's the plumber!!!"

Again he waited; again she didn't come; again he knocked; again the parrot said, "Who is it?"

"Aarrrrrrggggggghhhhhhh!!!" he said, flying into a rage; he pushed the door in and ripped it off its hinges. He suffered a heart attack and he fell dead in the doorway.

The lady came home from her errands, only to see the door ripped off its hinges and a corpse lying in the doorway, "A dead body!" she exclaimed, "Who is it?!"

The parrot says, "It's the plumber."

A small boy is being tested on the kings and queens of England. "And who followed Edward VI?" asks the teacher.

"Mary," replies the boy.

"And who followed her?" asks the teacher.

The boy replies, "Her little lamb."

A woman is looking for a pet and tries the local pet shop. The shopkeeper says, "I've got just the thing for you madam. I'll just get him." With that, he disappears into the back of the shop, and returns a few seconds later with a cute little puppy. "This dog is a special dog," he tells her. "It can fly," he explains, and with that throws the dog into the air. It immediately begins to float gracefully around the shop. "There is one problem with him, however. Whenever you say 'my something', he'll eat whatever you've mentioned. Watch. "My apple!" The lady watches in astonishment as the dog zooms over to the shop attendant and furiously devours an apple he has produced from his pocket.

"I'll take him," she says, and a few minutes later she is on her way back home with the dog to show her husband. "Darling, look what a clever pet I bought today!" she exclaims when she gets back home. "He can fly!"

The husband peers at the dog, and then remarks, "Fly, eh? Ha! My foot!"

A little boy goes up to his father and asks what an ancestor is.

"Well," replies father. "I'm your ancestor and so is your granddad."

"Ok," replies the boy. "So why do people boast about them?"

A blind man with a guide dog walks into a shop. The man walks to the middle of the shop, picks up the dog by the tail, and starts swinging the dog around in circles over his head. The manager, who has seen all this, thinks it quite strange and says, "Pardon me. May I help you with something?"

The blind man says, "No thanks. I'm just looking around."

Little Thelma comes home from school and tells her father that they learned about the history of Valentine's Day. And, "Since Valentine's Day is for a Christian saint and we're Jewish," she asks, "will God get mad at me for giving someone a Valentine?"

Thelma's father thinks a bit, then says, "No, I don't think God would get mad. Who do you want to give a Valentine to?"

"Osama Bin Laden," she says.

"Why Osama Bin Laden?" her father asks in shock.

"Well," she says, "I thought that if a little American Jewish girl could have enough love to give Osama a Valentine, he might start to think that maybe we're not all bad, and maybe start loving people a little bit. And if other kids saw what I did and sent valentines to Osama, he'd love everyone a lot. And then he'd start going all over the place tell everyone how much he loved them and how he didn't hate anyone anymore."

Her father's heart swells and he looks at his daughter with newfound pride. "Thelma, that's the most wonderful thing I've ever heard."

"I know," Thelma says, "and once that gets him out in the open, the Marines could blow the shit out of him."

A lady calls a repairman because her dishwasher isn't working. He can't do an after-hours appointment and since she has to go to work, she tells him, "I'll leave the key under the mat. Fix the dishwasher, leave the bill on the counter, and I'll send you a cheque. By the way, I have a large rottweiler inside named Killer; he won't bother you. I also have a parrot, and whatever you do, do not talk to the bird!"

Well, sure enough the dog, Killer, totally ignores the repairman, but the whole time he is there, the parrot curses, yells, screams, and just about drives him nuts.

As he is ready to leave, he yells, "You stupid bird, why

don't you shut up?!"

To which the bird replies, "Killer, get him!!!"

A few days after Christmas, a mother was working in the kitchen listening to her young son playing with his new electric train in the living room. She heard the train stop and her son said, "All of you sons of bitches who want off, get the hell off now, 'cause this is the last stop! And all of you sons of bitches who are getting on, get your asses in the train, 'cause we're going down the tracks."

The mother went nuts and told her son, "We don't use that kind of language in this house. Now I want you to go to your room and you are to stay there for TWO HOURS. When you come out, you may play with your train, but I want you to use nice language."

Two hours later, the son comes out of the bedroom and resumes playing with his train. Soon the train stopped and the mother heard her son say, "All passengers who are disembarking from the train, please remember to take all of your belongings with you. We thank you for riding with us today and hope your trip was a pleasant one. We hope you will ride with us again soon." She hears the little boy continue, "For those of you just boarding, we ask you to stow all of your hand luggage under your seat. Remember, there is no smoking on the train. We hope you will have a pleasant and relaxing journey with us today."

As the mother began to smile, the child added, "For those of you who are pissed off about the TWO HOUR delay, please see the bitch in the kitchen."

The vicar is buying a parrot. "Are you sure it doesn't scream, yell, or swear?" asked the preacher.

"Oh, absolutely. It's a religious parrot," the storekeeper assures him. "Do you see those strings on his legs? When you pull the right one, he recites the lord's prayer, and when you pull on the left he recites the 23rd Psalm."

"Wonderful!" says the preacher, "but what happens if you pull both strings?"

"I fall off my perch, you stupid bloody idiot!" screeched the parrot.

❖

There was once a man from the city who was visiting a small farm, and during this visit he saw a farmer feeding pigs in a most extraordinary manner. The farmer would lift a pig up to a nearby apple tree, and the pig would eat the apples off the tree directly. The farmer would move the pig from one apple to another until the pig was satisfied, then he would start again with another pig.

The city man watched this activity for some time with great astonishment. Finally, he could not resist saying to the farmer, "This is the most inefficient method of feeding pigs that I can imagine. Just think of the time that would be saved if you simply shook the apples off the tree and let the pigs eat them from the ground!"

The farmer looked puzzled and replied, "What's time to a pig?"

❖

A young couple bring their new baby home, and the wife suggests that her husband tries his hand at changing a nappy.

"I'm busy," he says. "I'll do the next one."

Next time the baby's nappy needs changing she asks him again. The husband says, "I didn't mean the next nappy. I meant the next baby."

Aperitif: two French false teeth.
Apricots: beds for baby apes.
Assets: baby donkeys.
Derange: de place where de cowboys ride home to.
Disgruntled: a dumb pig.
Impale: to put in a bucket.
Inkling: a small bottle of ink.
Operator: a person who hates opera.
Pigtail: a story about a pig.
Politics: a parrot that has swallowed a watch.

How can you tell when a lawyer is about to lie?
His lips start moving.

Dear Child,

I am writing this slowly because I know that you can't read fast.

We don't live where we did when you left home.

Your dad read in the paper that most accidents happen within 20 miles from your home so we moved.

I won't be able to send you the address, as the last family that lived here took the house numbers when they left so that they wouldn't have to change their address.

This place is real nice. It even has a washing machine. I'm not sure if it works too well though.

Last week I put a load in, pulled the chain, and haven't seen them since.

The weather isn't too bad here; it only rained twice last week. The first time it rained for three days and the second

24

time for four days. The coat you wanted me to send you, your Uncle Steve said it would be a little too heavy to send in the mail with the buttons on, so we cut them off and put them in the pockets. We got another bill from the funeral home.

They said if we don't make the last payment on Grandma's grave, up she comes. John locked his keys in the car yesterday. We were worried because it took him two hours to get me and Shelby out.

Your sister had a baby this morning but I haven't found out what it is yet, so I don't know if you're an aunt or an uncle. If the baby is a girl, your sister is going to name it after me, she's going to call it Mom.

Uncle Pete fell in a whiskey vat last week. Some man tried to pull him out but he fought them off and drowned. We had him cremated and he burned for three days.

Three of your friends went off a bridge in a pick-up truck. Ralph was driving. He rolled down the window and swam to safety. Your two friends were in the back. They drowned because they couldn't get the tailgate down.

There isn't much more news at this time. Nothing much has happened.

PS I was going to send you some money but the envelope was already sealed.

Your Loving Mom

A burglar has just broken into a house, and he's looking around for stuff to steal. All of a sudden, a little voice pipes up, "I can see you, and so can Jesus!" Startled, the burglar looks around the room. No one there at all, so he goes back to his business. "I can see you, and so can Jesus!" The burglar jumps again, and takes a longer look around the room. Over in the corner by the window, almost obscured by curtains, is a cage in which sits a parrot, who pipes up again, "I can see you, and so can Jesus!"

"So what," says the burglar, "you're only a parrot!"

To which the parrot replies, "True, but Jesus is a rottweiler!"

Doctor to hospital patient: "Your coughing seems to be easier this morning."

Patient: "It should be. I've been practising all night."

A businessman was ordered to attend a conference for his company at such short notice that he didn't have time to write his speech, much less rehearse it. Once he'd arrived at his hotel he settled down to write it and found that it was after midnight before he had finished. Blinking back the urge to sleep, he began rehearsing his speech – over and over.

Finally, just after 2 a.m., he wearily began again with the opening words of his speech. But no sooner had he begun than someone in the next room cleared his throat emphatically and said in a loud, determined tone, "And finally... !"

"Doctor, doctor! How can I get this ugly mole off my face?"

"Get your dog to chase it back into its hole."

❖

"Doctor, doctor! I keep thinking I'm a pair of curtains."

"Well, pull yourself together."

A musician calls the orchestra office, asks for the conductor, and is told that he is dead.

The musician calls back 25 times more and gets the same message from receptionist.

She asks why he keeps calling. He replies, "I just like to hear you say it."

Q: What do you get when you play a new age song backwards?

A: A new age song.

Q: What do you get if Bach falls off a horse, but has the courage to get on again and continue riding?

A: Bach in the saddle again.

❖

"Doctor, doctor! I've swallowed a roll of film."

"Don't worry. Rest a bit, and we'll see what develops."

❖

"Doctor, doctor! I feel like a piano."

"Then I'd better take some notes."

A teacher asks her students what their parents do for a living. "What does your mother do all day, Billy?"

Billy replies, "My mummy is a doctor."

"That's wonderful," says the teacher. "How about you, Amy?"

Amy stands up and says, "My father is a postman."

"Thank you, Amy," says teacher. "And what about your father, Tim?"

Tim stands up and says, "My daddy plays piano in a whorehouse."

The teacher is aghast and promptly changes the subject. Later she phones Tim's mother to find out if it's true.

"No, it's not true," says Tim's mother. "His father's a lawyer, but how can I explain a thing like that to a seven-year-old?"

An English teacher says to her pupils, "There are two words I don't allow in my class. One is gross and the other is cool."

From the back of the room a voice calls out, "So, what are the words?"

A butcher is leaning on the counter minding his own business when a dog with a basket in its mouth comes through the door. "What can I do for you then?" he asks.

The dog knocks the basket sharply into the butcher's shins.

"You stupid dog." He says but as he reaches down to smack the dog, he notices a note and ten pounds in the basket. The scribble on the note asks for three pounds of his best mince. The butcher thinks this is too easy. He goes to the window and reaches for the dried up stuff that's been sitting out all day. The dog growls at him. The butcher turns around and, glaring at the pup, gets the best mince from the fridge. Weighing out about 2 1/2 pounds, he drops it on the scale and presses on it with his thumb. Again, the dog growls menacingly.

"Alright, alright," he says and throws on a generous half pound. He wraps it up, drops it in the basket, and drops in change from a fiver. The dog threatens to chew his ankles. Another fiver goes in the basket. The butcher is quite impressed and decides to follow the dog home. The dog soon enters a block of flats, pushes the lift button, enters the lift, and then pushes the button for the 12th floor. The dog walks down the corridor and smartly bangs the basket on the door. The door opens, and the dog's owner screams at the dog.

"Hey, what are you doing? That's a really smart dog you've got there," comments the butcher. "He's a stupid dog; that's the third time this week he's forgotten his key."

The self-important lawyer was called upon to make an impromptu speech at an exclusive occasion. After sitting down again the lawyer turned to the right and asked the person sitting there, "Now then, how would you have given that speech?"

"Probably under an assumed name," came the response.

A Texan goes into a pub in the outback of Australia and says, "Y'know, this country might be big, but back home I've got a horse that takes a whole week to ride round my ranch."

The bartender replies, "I know what y'mean, mate. I had a horse like that once – I had to shoot the lazy bastard."

"Old" is when: Your sweetie says, "Let's go upstairs and make love," and you answer, "Pick one; I can't do both!"

"Old" is when: Your friends compliment you on your new alligator shoes and you're barefoot.

"Old" is when: A sexy babe catches your fancy and your pacemaker opens the garage door.

"Old" is when: Going braless pulls all the wrinkles out of your face.

"Old" is when: You don't care where your spouse goes, just as long as you don't have to go along.

"Old" is when: You are cautioned to slow down by the doctor instead of by the police.

"Old" is when: "Getting a little action" means you don't need to take any fibre today

"Old" is when: "Getting lucky" means you find your car in the parking lot.

"Old" is when: An "all nighter" means not getting up to use the bathroom.

"Old" is when: You are not sure these are jokes.

A Marine was deployed to Afghanistan. While he was there he received a letter from his girlfriend. In the letter she explained that she had slept with two guys while he had been gone and she wanted to break up with him. AND, she wanted pictures of herself back. So the Marine did what any square-jawed Marine would do. He went around to his buddies and collected all the unwanted photos of women he could find. He then mailed about 25 pictures of women (with clothes and without) to his girlfriend with the following note: "I don't remember which one you are. Please remove your picture and send the rest back."

❖

The bat was very tired. It sank lower and lower until it did not have enough energy to flap its wings any more and so it flopped to the ground.

After a few minutes it crawled along the grass until it came to the old trees where it lived. Then it suddenly raced towards the trees, stopped when it almost hit them, then went backwards. Then it raced towards the trees again.

It did this so many times that I became curious.

"Why are you racing towards the trees, stopping, going backwards, then racing towards them again?" I asked.

The bat sighed, then said (for it was a talking bat), "I was very run down and so I needed to charge my bat-trees!"

A man is helping one of his cows give birth when he notices his four-year-old son watching from the fence. The man thinks, *Great. He's four and I'm going to have to start explaining the birds and bees. No need to jump the gun. I'll just let him ask, and I'll answer.* After everything is over the man walks over to his son and says, "Well, son, do you have any questions?"

"Just one," gasps the wide-eyed lad. "How fast was that calf going when he hit the cow?"

Heard the one about the man who wanted to be a tree surgeon but he couldn't stand the sight of sap?

Heard the one about the man who lost two hundred pounds of ugly fat? His wife left him...

Heard the one about the man who was sold a plot of land at the North Pole? He thought it was the ideal place to grow frozen peas.

Heard the one about the criminal who stole a ton of rubber bands? He was given a long stretch.

Heard the one about the woman with a very responsible job? If anything goes wrong, she's responsible.

A man comes home from an exhausting day at work, collapses on the couch in front of the TV and says to his wife, "Get me a beer before it starts." His wife gets him a beer. Fifteen minutes later he says, "Get me another beer before it starts." She looks cross but fetches another beer. A few minutes later he says, "Quick, get me another beer, it's going to start any minute."

His wife is furious and yells, "Is that all you're going to do tonight? Drink beer and sit in front of the TV? You've nothing but a lazy, drunken, fat slob, and furthermore ..."

The man sighs and says, "It's started."

A pregnant Irish woman falls into a coma after a car crash. After a year she wakes up to find she's given birth to twins, a boy and a girl.

"Where are they?" she asks.

"It's all right," says the doctor. "Your brother came and took them. He's had them baptised and everything."

"Oh God, not my brother," says the woman. "He's such an idiot. What did he call them?"

"Well, he named your daughter Denise … ," says the doctor.

"Oh, that's nice," says the mother.

"… and he called your son Denephew."

Bill Clinton, Al Gore, and George W. Bush were set to face a firing squad in a small Central American country. Bill Clinton was the first one placed against the wall. Just before the order was given he yelled out, "Earthquake!" The firing squad fell into a panic and Bill jumped over the wall and escaped in the confusion.

Al Gore was the second one placed against the wall. The squad was reassembled and Al pondered what he had just witnessed. Again before the order was given, Al yelled out, "Tornado!" Again the squad fell apart and Al slipped over the wall.

The last person, George W. Bush, was placed against the wall. He was thinking, *I see the pattern here; just scream out something about a disaster and hop over the wall.* He confidently refused the blindfold as the firing squad was reassembled. As the rifles were raised in his direction he grinned from ear to ear and yelled, "FIRE!!"

It was autumn, and the Indians on the remote reservation asked their new Chief if the winter was going to be cold or mild. Since he was an Indian Chief in a modern society, he had never been taught the old secrets and when he looked at the sky, he couldn't tell what the weather was going to be. Nevertheless, to be on the safe side, he replied to his tribe that the winter was indeed going to be cold and that the members of the village should collect wood to be prepared. But also, being a practical leader, he decided to seek advice from experts. He went to the phone booth, called the National Weather Service and asked, "Is the coming winter going to be cold?"

"It looks like this winter is going to be quite cold indeed," the meteorologist at the weather service responded.

So the Chief went back to his people and told them to collect even more wood in order to be prepared. A week later he called the National Weather Service again. "Is it still going to be a cold winter?" he asked.

"Yes," the man at the National Weather Service again replied, "it's going to be a very cold winter."

The Chief again went back to his people and ordered them to collect every scrap of wood they could find.

Two weeks later he called the National Weather Service again. "Are you absolutely sure that this winter is going to be very cold?" he asked for a third time.

"Absolutely," the weatherman replied. "In fact, it's going to be one of the coldest winters ever!"

"How can you be so sure?" the Chief asked.

The weatherman replied, "The Indians are gathering wood like crazy."

A diplomat was seated at an important banquet next to a Native American chief. He realised that it would be very rude if he did not speak to the chief but simply could not think of anything to say. The soup arrived and he said, "Likee soupee?" and the chief nodded in affirmation. That was the entire extent of their conversation.

After the coffee the chief was asked to say a few words,

which he did in perfect English, without any trace of accent. At the end of the speech he sat down and turned to the diplomat, "Likee speechee?"

As he lay on his deathbed, the man confided to his wife, "I cannot die without telling you the truth. I cheated on you throughout our whole marriage. All those nights when I told you I was working late, I was with other women. And not just one woman either, I've slept with dozens of them."

His wife looked at him calmly and said, "Why do you think I gave you the poison?"

A man dies and goes to heaven. He gets to meet God and asks God if he can ask him a few questions.

"Sure," God says, "Go right ahead."

"OK," the man says. "Why did you make women so pretty?"

God says, "So you would like them."

"OK," the guy says. "But how come you made them so beautiful?"

"So you would LOVE them," God replies.

The man ponders a moment and then asks, "But why did you make them so stupid?"

God says, "So they would love you!"

A man has just been found guilty of killing his very bossy and argumentative wife by pushing her out of the window on the 29th floor of a hotel.

"This is a very serious offence," says the judge. "If your wife had fallen on someone there could have been a very nasty accident."

What do you get if you throw a copy of *The Canterbury Tales* in the air? A flying Chaucer.

The defendant in one court case said that at the time the crime was committed he was in hospital, recovering from a vicious attack by a shark while swimming in the sea. He therefore had a water-bite alibi.

A San Francisco cabby picks up a nun. She gets into the cab and the driver won't stop staring at her in the rear view mirror. She asks him why he is staring and he replies, "I have a question to ask you, but I don't want to offend you."

She answers, "My dear son, you cannot offend me. When you're as old as I am and have been a nun as long as I have, you get a chance to see and hear just about everything. I'm sure that there's nothing you could say or ask that I would find offensive."

"Well, I've always had a fantasy to kiss a nun."

She responds, "Well, let's see what we can do about that: no.1, you have to promise you are single...and no.2, you must be Catholic."

The cab driver is very excited and says, "Yes, I am single and I'm Catholic too!"

"OK", the nun says, "Pull into the next alley."

He does and the nun fulfils his fantasy with a kiss that would make a hooker blush. But when they get back on the road, the cab driver starts crying.

"My dear child," said the nun, "why are you crying?"

"Forgive me sister, but I have sinned. I lied and I must confess, I'm married and I'm Jewish."

The nun says, "That's OK, my name is Kevin and I'm on my way to a Halloween Party!"

A man had survived the Johnstown flood and incorporated it into his after-dinner speeches whenever possible. Eventually he died and went to Heaven. Saint Peter said to him, "As it's your first day, the schedule is light. Dinner at eight, at which all those who arrived today will be welcomed. You can stand up and merely say thank you or, at the most, a few words."

The man answered, "I should like to speak on the subject 'How I survived the Johnstown flood'."

"Are you sure?" asked Saint Peter. "You do know that Noah will be in the audience?"

Harry and Tom are on the golf course. "I wish my wife had never taken up golf," says Harry. "She spends so much time practising that she's cut down our sex life to once a week."

"Count yourself lucky," replies Tom. "She's cut some of us out altogether."

"Now," said the prosecution counsel to the lady in the witness box, "at the time of the car crash what gear were you in?"

"Umm," mused the lady. "I think it was blue jeans and a tight white T-shirt."

A Jewish woman is sitting next to a business man on a plane. "Are you Jewish?" she asks.

"No, I'm not," he replies.

"You sure you're not Jewish?" she says.

"Yes, I'm not Jewish," replies the businessman.

"Admit it, you're Jewish," says the woman.

"No, I'm not," says the businessman.

"But you must be Jewish," says the woman.

"All right," says the businessman. "Just to make you happy – yes. Yes, I am Jewish."

"Funny," says the woman. "You don't look Jewish."

Nurse: "Doctor, the man you just gave a clean bill of health to dropped dead as he was leaving the surgery."

Doctor: "Turn him around. Make it look as if he was walking in."

A millionaire in Florida who collected live alligators kept them in the pool behind his mansion. The millionaire also had a beautiful daughter who was single. One day he decided to throw a huge party, and during the party he announced, "I have a proposition to every man here. I will give one million dollars or my daughter to the man who can swim across this pool full of alligators and emerge alive!"

As soon as he finished his last word, there was the sound of a large splash!! There was one guy in the pool swimming, splashing about and screaming out of fear. The crowd cheered him on as he kept stroking as though he was running for his life. Finally, he made it to the other side with only a torn shirt and some minor injuries. The millionaire was impressed.

He said, "My boy, that was incredible! Fantastic! I didn't think it could be done! Well I must keep my end of the bargain. Do you want my daughter or the one million dollars?"

The guy said, "Listen, I don't want your money, nor do I want your daughter! I want the bugger who pushed me into the water!"

A woman goes to her psychiatrist. "I can't sleep at night," she says. "When I'm in the next room I have this dreadful fear I won't hear the baby if he falls out of the crib. What can I do?"

"Easy," replies the doctor. "Take the carpet off the floor."

A man who smelled like a distillery flopped on a subway seat next to a priest. The man's tie was stained, his face was plastered with red lipstick, and a half empty bottle of gin was sticking out of his torn coat pocket. He opened his newspaper and began reading. After a few minutes, the dishevelled guy turned to the priest and asked, "Say, Father, what causes arthritis?"

"Mister, it's caused by loose living, being with cheap, wicked women, too much alcohol and a contempt for your fellow man."

"Well I'll be," the drunk muttered, returning to his paper. The priest, thinking about what he had said, nudged the man and apologised. "I'm very sorry. I didn't mean to come on so strong. How long have you had arthritis?"

"I don't have it, Father. I was just reading here that the Pope does."

A clever cannibal toasted his mother-in-law at the wedding dinner.

I think I have the perfect wife. Fortunately I'm not married to her.

❖

The young student was desperate for money, and so in his vacation decided to take a job in a local factory as it paid good wages.

"Now," said the supervisor, "your first job is to sweep the floor."

"But I've got a BA degree," said the student, "and I'm currently studying for a masters in business administration."

"Oh!" said the supervisor. "In that case I'd better show you how to hold the broom."

❖

The successful entrepreneur was constantly in demand for after-dinner speeches and could never find the time to prepare his own material. It would always be his assistant who wrote the speech.

It was at the annual conference that he was called upon to give encouragement to small businesses. After the meal, the entrepreneur stood up to address the audience.

"Ladies and Gentleman. There are three main areas of tension in today's small businesses. The first is the problem of not paying competitive salaries ..."

He then turned to the next page and read out, "From now on, you unappreciative pig, you're on your own ..."

People keep asking me if I mind that my husband chases after pretty young women. I tell them that it's a bit like dogs chasing after cars – they wouldn't know what to do if they caught one.

A cannibal wanted to become a detective so he could grill all his suspects.

Judge: "Is this the first time you've been up before me?"
Defendant: "I don't know, Your Honour. What time do you usually get up?"

A project manager, a software manager and a hardware engineer take a break from work and go to the beach for a walk. They find an old lamp, rub it, and a genie pops out.

"In return for rescuing me I'll grant you each one wish," says the genie.

The software manager says, "I'd like to be a millionaire who owns a luxury beach resort in the Caribbean."

Poof! He disappears.

The hardware engineer says, "I'd like to be a millionaire

too, but I want to own the world's greatest ski resort."

Poof! He disappears.

The genie turns to the project manager and says, "So, what do you want?"

The manager replies, "I want those two straight back after lunch."

One day a man came home and was greeted by his wife dressed in a very sexy nightie.

"Tie me up," she purred, "and you can do anything you want."

So, he tied her up and went golfing.

"Members of the jury, have you reached your decision?"

"Yes, we have, your honour. We find the gorgeously sexy woman who stole the jewellery not guilty."

A Minneapolis couple decided to go to Florida to thaw out during a particularly icy winter. They planned to stay at the same hotel where they spent their honeymoon 20 years earlier. Because of hectic lifestyles, it was difficult to coordinate their travel schedules. So, the husband left Minnesota and flew to Florida on Thursday, with his wife flying down the following day The husband checked into the hotel. There was a computer in his room so he decided to send an email to his wife. However, he accidentally left out one letter in her email address, and without realizing his error, sent the email. Meanwhile, somewhere in Houston, a widow had just returned home from her husband's funeral. He was a minister who was called home to glory following a heart attack. The widow decided to check her email expecting messages from relatives and friends. After reading the first message, she screamed and fainted. The widow's son rushed into the room, found his mother on the floor, and saw the computer screen which read:

To: My Loving Wife
Subject: I've Arrived
Date: October 16, 2004

I know you're surprised to hear from me. They have computers here now and you are allowed to send emails to your loved ones. I've just arrived and have been checked in. I see that everything has been prepared for your arrival tomorrow. Looking forward to seeing you then! Hope your journey is as uneventful as mine was. P.S. Sure is freaking hot down here

A vest is something a boy wears when his mother feels cold.

John got out at the 10th floor and nervously knocked on his blind date's door.

She opened it and was as beautiful and charming as everyone had said. "I'll be ready in a few minutes," she said. "Why don't you play with my dog, while you're waiting? He does wonderful tricks. He rolls over, shakes hands, sits up and if you make a hoop with your arms, he'll jump through."

The dog followed John onto the balcony and started rolling over. John made a hoop with his arms and the dog jumped through and over the balcony railing. Just then John's date walked out.

"Isn't he the cutest, happiest dog you've ever seen?"

"To tell the truth, " John replied, "he seemed a little depressed to me!"

If you have any advice to pass on to your children do it while they're still young enough to think you know what you're talking about.

The Browns were a wealthy middle-aged couple who lived in a large house in the country. All went well for many years until a new maid arrived. She was extremely attractive. Within six months of her arrival Mr Brown was starting to wake up every morning at 5 a.m. instead of his usual 7.30 a.m.

"Where are you going?" Mrs Brown would ask, as her husband got out of bed and slipped on his dressing gown.

"Once awake, I can't get back to sleep," Mr Brown replied, "so I think I'll do some work in my study or walk around the garden. You don't need to get up – just go back to sleep. You know how deep sleep keeps you beautiful."

Mrs Brown began to suspect that her husband was sneaking into the maid's room. What should she do? It was soon to be the maid's parents' wedding anniversary, so one Thursday afternoon, when Mr Brown was on a business trip to London, Mrs Brown suggested that the maid might like to pay a surprise visit to her parents.

"You can go now, if you like," suggested Mrs Brown, "and come back on Monday."

"Thanks very much," said the maid. "It's most kind of you." And she went off to pack for her trip.

Soon the maid had left the house. Mr Brown returned around 9 p.m. and, after watching TV for a while, went to bed.

Promptly at 5 a.m. Mr Brown woke up and said he

couldn't sleep any more and was going for a stroll around the garden.

As soon as her husband had left the room and she could hear him cleaning his teeth in the bathroom, Mrs Brown rushed to the maid's room and got into the maid's bed.

Mrs Brown had been lying in the dark for about five minutes when she heard the sash window of the room being slowly lifted, and a man climbed in through the window.

Mrs Brown tensed herself in the darkness, but relaxed as the man made tender, passionate love to her. She was ecstatic. Why could her husband make such wonderful love to the maid and be so boring in bed with her?

"Darling," whispered Mrs Brown, snuggling up to the man in the bed. "Let's do it again."

"Sorry, luv," replied the man. Mrs Brown was aghast. It was not her husband's voice. "No time for more now," continued the man, "but I can come back when I've finished the milk round."

Did you hear about the cannibal who passed his mother in the woods?

Last year, when I was on holiday in the USA, I bought my husband a lovely chair. Now all I've got to do is plug it in.

A little old lady answered a knock on the door one day, only to be confronted by a well-dressed young man carrying a vacuum cleaner.

"Good morning," said the young man. "If I could take a couple minutes of your time, I would like to demonstrate the very latest in high-powered vacuum cleaners."

"Buzz off!" said the old lady. "I haven't got any money," and she proceeded to close the door.

Quick as a flash, the young man wedged his foot in the door and pushed it wide open. "Don't be too hasty!" he said. "Not until you have at least seen my demonstration." And with that, he emptied a bucket of horse dung all over her hallway carpet. "If this vacuum cleaner does not remove all traces of this horse dung from your carpet, madam, I will personally eat the remainder."

"Well," she said, "I hope you've got a good appetite, because the electricity was cut off this morning!!!"

❖

Confident that her assistant had prepared yet another brilliant speech, the executive stood up and proceeded to give her hour's talk most eloquently. She went on and on reading, and after an hour and a half guests began to leave. The executive was most affronted and complained to the assistant. "That's because I gave you the duplicate copy of the speech as well," was the response.

❖

As the lawyer stood up to make her speech, the faces of the audience quickly fell. She began, "If you were to give me an orange you'd simply say, 'I give you this orange.' But when the transaction is entrusted to a lawyer they say, 'I hereby give and convey to you all and singular, my estate and interests in, rights, title, claim and advantages of and in said orange, together with all its rind, juice, pulp and pips and all rights and advantages with full power to bite, cut and otherwise eat the same or give away with and without the rind, skin, juice, pulp, everything herein before or herein after or in any other deed, or deeds, instruments of whatever nature or kind whatsoever to the contrary in anywise not withstanding …'"

A rat catcher walks into a doctor's office. "I was putting down some poison when one of the little buggers bit off my finger."

"Which one?" asks the doctor.

"How should I know?" says the rat catcher. "They all look the same to me."

"What can you do?" asked the personnel manager.

"Lots," replied the young man. "I can play golf, talk in a public school accent, make boring speeches, have affairs with secretaries without my wife finding out, go to sleep in the back of a Rolls Royce, and generally get publicity for working as hard as possible while in reality doing nothing at all."

"Excellent," said the personnel manager. "You can start tomorrow as managing director."

"I saw you! I saw what you got up to last night!" said little Emily when her big sister's boyfriend came to visit.

"Oh!" said the boy, blushing. "If you don't tell your parents I'll give you five pounds."

"That's very generous," replied Emily. "The others only gave me a pound."

Insurance agent: "Now, madam, this policy is a particularly good buy. Under it we pay up to £5,000 for broken arms or legs."

Woman: "But what do you do with them all?"

A pirate walked into a bar and the bartender said, "Hey, I haven't seen you in a while. What happened? You look terrible."

"What do you mean?" said the pirate, "I feel fine."

"What about the wooden leg? You didn't have that before."

"Well, we were in a battle and I got hit with a cannonball, but I'm fine now."

"Well, okay, but what about that hook? What happened to your hand?"

"We were in another battle. I boarded a ship and got into a sword fight. My hand was cut off and I got fitted with a hook. I'm fine, really."

"What about that eye patch?"

"Oh, one day we were at sea and a flock of birds flew over, I looked up and one of them pooped in my eye."

"You're kidding," said the bartender, "You couldn't lose an eye just from that!"

"It was my first day with the hook."

Religious knowledge teacher: "Where do naughty boys and girls go?"

Boy: "Behind the bicycle sheds."

A young couple were on their honeymoon. The husband was sitting in the bathroom on the edge of the bathtub saying to himself, 'Now how can I tell my wife that I've got really smelly feet and that my socks absolutely stink? I've managed to keep it from her while we were dating, but she's bound to find out sooner or later that my feet stink. Now how do I tell her?'

Meanwhile, the wife was sitting in the bed saying to herself, 'Now how do I tell my husband that I've got really bad breath? I've been very lucky to keep it from him while we were courting, but as soon as he's lived with me for a week, he's bound to find out. Now how do I tell him gently?'

The husband finally plucks up enough courage to tell his wife and so he walks into the bedroom. He walks over to the bed, climbs over to his wife, puts his arm around her neck, moves his face very close to hers and says, "Darling, I've a confession to make."

And she says, "So have I, love."

"Don't tell me, you've eaten my socks?"

Mothers of teenagers know why some animals eat their young.

The shy English girl on her first visit to Scotland nervously went up to a handsome young Scot who was wearing his national costume and asked, "Excuse me speaking to a stranger, but I've always been curious. Please can you tell me what is worn under the kilt?"

The Scotsman smiled and said, "Nothing's worn – everything's in excellent condition."

While waiting for a bus, the blind man's dog decided to go to the bathroom all over the blind man's legs.

A passer-by commented to the blind man, "What! That dog just went to the bathroom all over your legs, and you are petting him! Are you crazy?"

To which the blind man replied, "Madam, I am not petting him. I am feeling for his bottom, so I can kick him."

A guest speaker was talking to a member of the audience after his rather long speech.

"How did you find my speech?"

"Oh, very refreshing, very refreshing indeed."

"Did you really?" asked the delighted speaker.

"Oh yes. I felt like a new person when I woke up!"

There is a terrible bus accident. Unfortunately, no one survives the accident except a monkey which was on board and there are no witnesses. The police try to investigate further but they get no results. At last, they try to interrogate the monkey. The monkey seems to respond to their questions with gestures. Seeing that, they start asking the questions.

The policeman asks, "What were the people doing on the bus?"

The monkey shakes his head in a condemning manner and starts dancing around, meaning the people were dancing and having fun.

The policeman asks, "Yeah, but what else were they doing?".

The monkey uses his hand and takes it to his mouth as if holding a bottle.

The policeman says, "Oh! They were drinking, huh??!" The policeman continues, "Okay, were they doing anything else?"

The monkey nods his head and moves his mouth back and forth, meaning they were talking. The policeman loses his patience, "If they were having such a great time, who was driving the stupid bus then?"

The monkey promptly swings his arms out as if grabbing a wheel.

At the height of a political corruption trial, the prosecuting attorney attacked a witness. "Isn't it true," he bellowed, "that you accepted five thousand dollars to compromise this case?"

The witness stared out the window, as though he hadn't heard the question.

"Isn't it true that you accepted five thousand dollars to compromise this case?" the lawyer repeated. The witness still did not respond.

Finally, the judge leaned over and said, "Sir, please answer the question."

"Oh," the startled witness said, "I thought he was talking to you."

What's the definition of Australian aristocracy? A man who can trace his ancestry back to his father.

❖

A tribe of cannibals was converted by missionaries to becoming good Catholics. They ate fishermen only on Fridays.

A man goes to a fancy dress party with a woman draped over his shoulders and says he's come as a tortoise.

"Who's that on your back?" asks the host.

"That?" he says. "That's Michelle."

Two men are at the golf club bar discussing a recent murder. "Did you know that George Smith beat his wife to death with a five iron?" asks one of the men.

"Really?" says the other. "How many strokes?"

An Englishman was in a restaurant in Scotland when he was suddenly attacked by a severe bout of coughing and sneezing – and he sneezed so violently that his false teeth flew out of his mouth and dropped to the floor, where they broke at the feet of a Scotsman.

"Don't worry, sir," said the Scotsman. "My brother will soon get you a new pair and at far less cost than an English dentist would charge. And he can provide a suitable set almost immediately."

The Englishman couldn't believe his luck and gladly accepted the Scotsman's offer.

The Scotsman left the restaurant and returned nine minutes later with a pair of false teeth, which he handed to the Englishman.

"Fantastic," exclaimed the Englishman, trying the teeth. "They fit perfectly. Your brother must be a very clever dentist."

"Oh, he's not a dentist," replied the Scotsman. "He's an undertaker."

A lawyer bribed a man on the jury to hold out for a charge of manslaughter, as opposed to the charge of murder which was brought by the prosecution.

The jury was out for nearly a week before they returned to court with the manslaughter verdict. When the lawyer paid the juror, he asked him if it had been hard to persuade the other jurors to get the charge of manslaughter.

"Sure was," the juror replied, "all the others wanted to acquit him."

Two slugs are slithering along the pavement. They go round a corner and get stuck behind two snails. "Oh no!" says one. "Caravans."

A man was on holiday in Louisiana, where he tried to buy some alligator shoes. However he was not prepared to pay the high prices, and after having failed to haggle the vendor down to a reasonable price, ended up shouting, "I don't give two hoots for your shoes man, I'll go and kill my own croc!

To which the shopkeeper replied, "By all means, just watch out for those two 'good ole boys' who are doing the same!"

So the man went out into the Bayou, and after a while saw two men with spears, standing still in the water. 'They must be the 'ole boys' he thought. Just at that point he noticed an alligator moving in the water towards one of them. The guy stood completely passive, as the 'gator came ever closer. Just as the beast was about to swallow him, he struck home with his spear and wrestled the 'gator up onto the beach, where there were already several dead alligators. Together the two guys threw the 'gator onto its back, whereupon one exclaimed, "Darn! This one doesn't have any shoes either!"

Recently a teacher, a garbage collector, and a lawyer wound up together at the Pearly Gates. St. Peter informed them that in order to get into heaven, they would each have to answer one question.

St. Peter addressed the teacher and asked, "What was the name of the ship that crashed into the iceberg? They just made a movie about it."

The teacher answered quickly, "That would be the Titanic."

St. Peter let him through the gate, turned to the dustman and, figuring heaven didn't REALLY need all the smells that this man would bring with him, decided to make the question a little harder: "How many people died on the ship?"

Fortunately for him, the trash man had just seen the film, and answered, "1,503."

"That's right! You may enter."

St. Peter then turned to the lawyer. "And their names and addresses please …"

A man goes to the doctor and says, "Doctor, I can't pronounce my Fs, Ts or Hs."

"Well," says the doctor. "You can't say fairer than that."

Back in the days of ancient Rome, the Christians had been thrown to the lions to entertain the emperor and his guests.

One of the Christians, however, seemed to be whispering in the ear of the attacking lions, whereupon they turned and slunk off. This happened with each lion. Not pleased by the lack of sport, the emperor called for this particular Christian to come before him. "Tell me your magic secret of taming lions and I will spare your life," he said.

To which the Christian replied, "I have no magic power. I simply tell them that they will, of course, have to make a speech to the assembled audience once they have finished their dinner ..."

Barber: "Sir, how would you like your hair cut?"
Customer: "Off."

The Hollywood actress liked her tenth husband so much she decided to keep him for an extra fortnight.

Instructions for giving your cat a pill

1. Pick cat up and cradle it in the crook of your left arm as if holding a baby. Position right forefinger and thumb on either side of cat's mouth and gently apply pressure to cheeks while holding pill in right hand. As cat opens mouth, pop pill into mouth. Allow cat to close mouth and swallow.

2. Retrieve pill from floor and cat from behind sofa. Cradle cat in left arm and repeat process.

3. Retrieve cat from bedroom, and throw soggy pill away. Take new pill from foil wrap, cradle cat in left arm holding rear paws tightly with left hand. Force jaws open and push pill to back of mouth with right forefinger. Hold mouth shut for a count of 10.

4. Retrieve pill from goldfish bowl and cat from top of wardrobe. Call spouse from garden.

5. Kneel on floor with cat wedged firmly between knees, holding front and rear paws. Ignore low growls emitted by cat. Get spouse to hold cat's head firmly with one hand while forcing wooden ruler into mouth. Drop pill down ruler and rub cat's throat vigorously.

6. Retrieve cat from curtain rail, get another pill from foil wrap. Make note to buy new ruler and repair curtains. Carefully sweep shattered figurines from hearth and set to one side for gluing later.

7. Wrap cat in large towel and get spouse to lie on cat with its head just visible from below spouse's armpit. Put pill in end of drinking straw, force cat's mouth open with pencil and blow down drinking straw.

8. Check label to make sure pill not harmful to humans, drink glass of water to take taste away. Apply band-aid to spouse's forearm and remove blood from carpet with cold water and soap.

9. Retrieve cat from neighbour's shed. Get another pill. Place cat in cupboard and close door onto neck to leave head showing. Force mouth open with dessert spoon. Flick pill down throat with elastic band.

10. Fetch screwdriver from garage and put door back on hinges. Apply cold compress to cheek and check records for date of last tetanus shot. Throw T-shirt away and fetch new one from bedroom.

11. Ring fire brigade to retrieve cat from tree across the road. Apologize to neighbour who crashed into fence while swerving to avoid cat. Take last pill from foil wrap.

12. Tie cat's front paws to rear paws with garden twine

and bind tightly to leg of dining table. Find heavy duty pruning gloves from shed. Force cat's mouth open with small spanner. Push pill into mouth followed by large piece of fillet steak. Hold head vertically and pour 1/2 pint of water down throat to wash pill down.

13. Get spouse to drive you to emergency room; sit quietly while doctor stitches fingers and forearm and removes pill remnants from right eye. Stop by furniture shop on way home to order new table.

14. Arrange for vet to make a house call.

A farmer decides to breed his three sows with his neighbour's stud pig. The farmer drives the sows to his neighbour's farm, leaves them there for the day, then drives them back home in the evening. The next day the farmer looks at his sows to see if they're grazing on grass – a sure sign that they're pregnant. The sows aren't grazing, so the farmer puts them in his truck and drives them to the stud farm a second time. Next morning he looks at his sows and sees them sitting around as usual, so he loads them on the truck and drives them to stud a third time. This goes on for a fortnight, and the sows never seem to get pregnant. One morning the farmer decides to give up, stop driving his pigs around and have a lie-in instead. The farmer's wife hears a noise and looks out of the window.

"You ought to see this," says his wife. "Those sows are acting very strange."

"Are they grazing on grass?" asks the hopeful farmer.

"No," says his wife. "Two are sitting in the back of the truck, and the third is in the front honking the horn."

A jockey is about to enter an important race on a new horse. The horse's trainer meets him before the race and says, ''All you have to remember with this horse is that every time you approach a jump, you have to shout, 'ALLLLEEE OOOP!' really loudly in the horse's ear. Providing you do that, you'll be fine.''

The jockey thinks the trainer is mad but promises to shout the command. The race begins and they approach the first hurdle. The jockey ignores the trainer's ridiculous advice and the horse crashes straight through the centre of the jump.

They carry on and approach the second hurdle. The jockey, somewhat embarrassed, whispers 'Aleeee ooop' in the horse's ear. The same thing happens and the horse crashes straight through the centre of the jump.

At the third hurdle, the jockey thinks, it's no good, he'll have to do it, and yells, ''ALLLEEE OOOP!'' really loudly. Sure enough, the horse sails over the jump with no problems. This continues for the rest of the race, but due to the earlier problems the horse only finishes third.

The trainer is fuming and asks the jockey what went wrong. The jockey replies, ''Nothing is wrong with me; it's this bloody horse. What is he, deaf or something?''

The trainer replies, ''Deaf?? DEAF?? He's not deaf. He's BLIND!!!''

A man goes to a psychiatrist. "You've got to help me," says the man. "I can't stop deep-frying things in batter. I get up in the morning and deep-fry my boiled egg. I've deep-fried all my clothes and shoes. I've even deep-fried my bike and battered the cat. What's wrong with me?"

"It's obvious," replies the psychiatrist. "You're frittering your life away."

A man goes to the doctor with a long history of migraine headaches. When the doctor does his history and physical, he discovers that his poor patient has had practically every therapy known to man for his migraines and STILL no improvement.

"Listen," says the Doctor, "I have migraines too, and the advice I'm going to give you isn't really anything I learned in medical school, but it's advice that I've gotten from my own experience. When I have a migraine, I go home, get in a nice hot bathtub, and soak for a while. Then I have my wife sponge me off with the hottest water I can stand, especially around the forehead. This helps a little. Then I get out of the tub, take her into the bedroom, and even if my head is killing me, I force myself to make love to her. Almost always, the headache is immediately gone. Now, give it a try, and come back and see me in six weeks."

Six weeks later, the patient returns with a big grin.

"Doctor! I took your advice and it works! It REALLY WORKS! I've had migraines for 17 years and this is the FIRST time anyone has ever helped me!"

"Well," says the physician, "I'm glad I could help."

"By the way, Doctor," the patient adds, "you have a REALLY nice house."

❖

A man finds an old bottle. He rubs it and is astonished to see a pixie emerge from the bottle's mouth.

"You look tense," says the pixie. "Would you like a back rub?"

"Well, I'd prefer a million pounds," says the man.

"I can't give you any money," says the pixie. "But how about I rub your back?"

"Well, how about you fix me a date with a *Playboy* centrefold?" asks the man.

"Sorry," says the pixie. "But why don't I work on those shoulders of yours?"

"Can't you make me taller?" asks the man. "I'd prefer to be six foot six."

The pixie replies, "Lie down and I'll get started on your clavicles."

"Hang on a minute," says the man. "What's with the back rubs? I thought genies were meant to grant three wishes."

"Who said I was a genie?" replies the pixie. "I'm a massage in a bottle."

A woman tells her husband, "Jack, that young couple that just moved in next door seem such a loving twosome. Every morning, when he leaves the house, he kisses her goodbye, and every evening when he comes homes, he brings her a dozen roses. Now, why can't you do that?"

"Well," says Jack, "I hardly know the girl."

A carpet layer had just finished installing carpet for a lady. He stepped out for a smoke, only to realize he'd lost his cigarettes.

In the middle of the room, under the carpet, was a bump.

''No sense pulling up the entire floor for one pack of smokes,'' he said to himself. He proceeded to get out his hammer and flattened the hump.

As he was cleaning up, the lady came in. ''Here,'' she said, handling him his pack of cigarettes. ''I found them in the hallway. Now,'' she said, ''if only I could find my parakeet.''

A man answers a knock on his front door. Outside is a six-foot ladybird, which proceeds to head-butt him, kick him in the crotch and stamp on his head. The man wakes up in hospital, where he describes his ordeal to the doctor. "You're the sixth case like this we've had in today," says the doctor. "There's a rather nasty bug going around."

A bloke spent £10,000 on a little peace and quiet. His little piece wanted the ten thousand to keep it quiet from his wife.

A man goes into a pet shop where he sees a talking dog. After chatting to it for ten minutes he buys it. Later he goes to the pub and says, "I bet everyone £5 that this dog can talk."

A number of people take the bet, but the dog remains silent and the man is forced to pay out. Puzzled, the man takes the dog home, where it starts chatting away again. Next day the man returns to the pub and bets everyone £10 that the dog can talk. To the man's astonishment, the dog clams up and won't say a word. After paying out on his bets the man takes the dog outside and says, "I'm taking you back to the shop. You're absolutely useless."

"Wise up," says the dog. "Think of the odds we'll get tomorrow."

A police officer in a small town stopped a motorist who was speeding.

"But, Officer," the man began, "I can explain."

"Just be quiet," snapped the officer. "I'm going to let you cool your heels in jail until the chief gets back."

"But, Officer, I just wanted to say…"

"And I said to keep quiet! "

A few hours later the officer looked in on his prisoner and said, "Lucky for you that the chief's at his daughter's wedding. He'll be in a good mood when he gets back."

"Don't count on it," answered the fellow in the cell. "I'm the groom."

I wouldn't say my wife tells lies about her age – but does she really expect people to believe that she gave birth to our son at the age of three?

A man gets a job selling toothbrushes but doesn't do very well, whereas his mate, the top salesman, is selling thousands of toothbrushes a week. The man gets desperate and asks his mate for the secret of his success. After much pleading, his mate agrees to divulge his method and gets out a large pot of brown sludge and a plate of crackers. "What I do," says his mate, "is take this pot to the airport with a big sign reading 'Free crackers and dip', then I tell passengers to help themselves."

"How does that help you sell toothbrushes?" asks the man.

"Try it yourself," says his mate. The man takes a cracker and uses it to scoop some dip into his mouth. He spits it out straight away.

"Oh my God!" shouts the man. "It tastes like dog shit!"

"I know," says his mate. "Want to buy a toothbrush?"

A man goes shopping and sees a Thermos flask. He asks the sales assistant what it does.

"It keeps hot things hot and cold things cold," replies the assistant. He buys one and takes it to work the next day.

"Look at this," he says to his workmate. "It's a Thermos flask. It keeps hot things hot and cold things cold."

"What have you got in it?" asks his friend.

"Two cups of a coffee and a choc ice."

Senior civil servant: "Did you phone my wife as I asked you to?"

Secretary: "Certainly, sir. I told her you would be late home from the office because of an unexpected conference."

Senior civil servant: "And what did she say?"

Secretary: "Can I rely on that?"

A man complains to his friend that he's having trouble keeping his neighbour's free-range chickens out of his flowerbeds. A couple of weeks later his friend notices that the flowerbeds are looking great and asks how he managed to keep the birds away.

"It wasn't all that hard," says his friend. "One night I hid half a dozen eggs under a bush by my flowerbeds, and the next day I let me neighbour see me pick them up. I wasn't bothered after that."

The three bears go into their parlour.

"What's this?" says daddy bear. "I've no porridge. Who's been eating my porridge?"

The baby bear peers into its bowl and says, "Look, I've no porridge either. Who's been eating my porridge?"

Mummy bear shouts, "Shut up! I haven't made the damn porridge yet! Do we have to go through this every single morning?"

Taxiing down the tarmac, the jetliner abruptly stopped, turned around and returned to the gate.

After an hour-long wait, it finally took off.

A concerned passenger asked the flight attendant, "What was the problem?"

"The pilot was bothered by a noise he heard in the engine," explained the Flight Attendant, "and it took us a while to find a new pilot."

Why are lawyers buried 12 feet deep instead of just six?
Because deep down they really are good people

For three years, the young attorney had been taking his brief vacations at a country inn. The last time he'd finally managed an affair with the innkeeper's daughter.

Looking forward to an exciting few days, he dragged his suitcase up the stairs of the inn, then stopped short. There sat his lover with an infant on her lap!

"Helen, why didn't you write when you learned you were pregnant?" he cried. "I would have rushed up here, we could have got married, and the baby would have had my name!"

"Well," she said, "when my folks found out about my condition, we sat up all night talking and talking and decided it would be better to have a bastard in the family than a lawyer."

An elderly woman was on her first flight. Just before take-off, the stewardess came round with some boiled sweets and explained to the elderly woman that the sweets would help to reduce the pressure in her ears. Half an hour after take-off, the woman asked the stewardess if it was now all right to take the sweets out of her ears.

He'd give his right arm to be ambidextrous.

A junior soccer team is playing a match one Sunday. Just before the kick-off the team coach approaches one of his young players.

"Do you understand that you mustn't swear at the ref if he gives you a card and you mustn't attack an opponent if he fouls you?"

"Yes," replies the boy.

"Good," says the coach. "Now go and explain that to your mother."

An airliner was having engine trouble, and the pilot instructed the cabin crew to have the passengers take their seats and prepare for an emergency landing.

A few minutes later, the pilot asked the flight attendants if everyone was buckled in and ready.

"All set back here, Captain," came the reply, "except the lawyers are still going around passing out business cards."

A half-drowned man washes up on a beach outside a hospital. A medical team rushes out, gives him the kiss of life, then pumps out his stomach to get rid of any seawater. The pump brings up gallons of water, some seaweed, a number of small fish and some crabs. The medical team keeps pumping, but after five minutes the brine, the fish, the seaweed and the shellfish still keep coming in an endless stream.

Finally, a bystander taps one of the doctors on the shoulder and says, "Excuse me, but should you be doing that while he's still sitting in the water?"

Teacher: "If you stood facing due south, your back was north, what would be on your right hand?"
Pupil: "Fingers."

Teacher: "Can you tell me at which battle Nelson died?"
Pupil: "His last one!"

❖

Teacher: "Can you put 'defeat', 'deduct', 'defence' and 'detail' into a sentence?"
Pupil: "De feet of de duck gets under de fence before de tail."

Teacher: "Give me a sentence beginning with 'I'."

Pupil: "I is ..."

Teacher (angrily): "How many more times do I have to tell you?! You must *always* say 'I am'!"

Pupil: "All right, I am the letter in the alphabet after H."

"This is the captain of your aircraft speaking. On behalf of my crew I'd like to welcome you aboard flight 602 from New York to London. We are currently flying at a height of 35,000 feet midway across the Atlantic.

If you look out of the windows on the starboard side of the aircraft, you will observe that both the starboard engines are on fire.

If you look out of the windows on the port side, you will observe that the port wing has fallen off.

If you look down towards the Atlantic ocean, you will see a little yellow life raft with three people in it waving at you. That's me, your captain, the co-pilot, and one of the air stewardesses. This is a recorded message. Have a good flight!"

An old couple die in an accident and are transported to Heaven. The wife is amazed at the beauty of the place and the peace and contentment she feels. The husband, on the other hand, is furious.

"What's the matter?" she asks. "Don't you like it here?"

"Of course I like it here," snaps the husband. "And if wasn't for your damn health foods I'd have been here twenty years ago."

Doctor: Well, I have good news and bad news.

Patient: Go with the good news first.

Doctor: You have 24 hours to live.
Patient: What?! How about the bad news?
Doctor: I forgot to call you yesterday.

"Why," asked Mr White, "are you still overdrawn at the bank?"

"I don't know," replied his wife. "They sent me a bank statement last month and a letter saying I was £500 overdrawn. Then they sent me another letter insisting that I pay the £500 within seven days. So I paid it promptly. I immediately wrote them a cheque for the money."

A man went to a new barber and was horrified to find that a trim would be £20.

"But I'm practically bald," he says. "How can it cost £20?"

"To be honest, the cut is only £5. The other £15 is a search fee."

It was a few days before Christmas. The businessman's trip had gone reasonably well, and he was ready to go back home. The airport on the other hand had turned a tacky red and green, and loudspeakers blared annoying renditions of cherished Christmas carols.

Being someone who took Christmas very seriously, and being slightly tired, he was not in a particularly good mood. Going to check in his luggage he noticed the mistletoe; not real mistletoe, but very cheap plastic with red paint on some of the rounder parts and green paint on some of the flatter and pointier parts.

With a considerable degree of irritation and nowhere else to vent it, he said to the attendant, "Even if we were married, I would not want to kiss you under such a ghastly mockery of mistletoe."

"Sir, look more closely at where the mistletoe is."

"OK, I see that it's above the luggage scale which is the place you'd have to step forward for a kiss."

"That's not why it's there."

"OK, I give up. Why is it there?"

"It's there so you can kiss your luggage good-bye."

Angry employer to secretary: "Who told you that you could have the morning off just to go shopping? And now you have the cheek to ask for a pay rise – just because you came with me as my assistant to the conference in Brussels last weekend! Who gives you encouragement for such fantastic ideas?"

Secretary: "My lawyer, sir."

For months a little boy had been pestering his father to take him to the zoo. Eventually, Dad gives in and off they go. When they get back the boy's mother asks him if he had a good time.

"It was great," the boy replies. "And Daddy had fun too, especially when one of the animals came home at thirty to one."

Flight fifty has a pretty rough time above the ocean. Suddenly a voice comes over the intercom: "Ladies and gentlemen, please fasten your seat belts and assume crash positions. We have lost our engines and we are trying to put this baby as gentle as possible down on the water."

"Oh, stewardess! Are there any sharks in the ocean below?" asks a little old lady, terrified.

"Yes, I'm afraid there are some. But not to worry, we have a special gel in the bottle next to your chair designed especially for emergencies like this. Just rub the gel onto your arms and legs".

"And if I do this, the sharks won't eat me?" asks the little lady.

"Oh, they will eat you all right, but they won't enjoy it so much."

A man arrives at a football match midway through the second half.

"What's the score?" he asks.

"Nil-nil," is the reply.

"Oh," says the man, "and what was the score at half-time?"

I'm not feeling well," says a patient to his doctor. "Do you think it might be my diet?"

"What have you been eating?" asks the doctor.

"Snooker balls," replies the patient. "I have two reds for breakfast, three blues for lunch, and five browns and a pink for dinner."

"I think I see what the problem is," replies the doctor. "You're not eating enough greens."

After shopping for most of the day, a couple returns to find their car has been stolen. They go to the police station to make a full report. Then, a detective drives them back to the parking lot to see if any evidence can be found at the scene of the crime. To their amazement, the car has been returned.

There is an envelope on the windshield with a note of

apology and two tickets to a concert. The note reads, "I apologise for taking your car, but my wife was having a baby and I had to steal your car to rush her to the hospital. Please forgive the inconvenience. Here are two tickets for tonight's Garth Brooks concert."

Their faith in humanity restored, the couple attend the concert and return home late. They find their house has been robbed. Valuable goods have been taken from the house, from cellar to loft. And, there is a note on the door reading, "Well, you still have your car. I have to put my kid through school and university somehow, don't I?"

When I came home last night the wife complained that the cat had upset her – but she really shouldn't have eaten it in the first place.

A man is sitting on a train next to a vicar. The vicar is doing a crossword puzzle and is not looking happy.

"What's this one?" asks the vicar and reads out the clue. "Found on the bottom of a budgie's cage. Four letters. Ends in I-T."

"Grit?" suggests the man.

"Oh, yes," says the vicar. "Of course … you haven't got a rubber, have you?"

When Claude's wife was expecting their second child he told his three-year-old son that soon a giant stork would be arriving and it would land on the chimney of their house. In the stork's beak would be a wonderful present.

"Oh," said Claude's son. "I hope it will be quiet and won't upset mummy. A giant bird suddenly arriving like that might give her a shock. And that wouldn't be any good as you know you made her pregnant and she's expecting a baby."

❖

Aunt Bessie loved to visit her nieces and nephews. However, she had relatives all over the world.

The problem was that no matter how much she enjoyed seeing them, she hated flying. No matter how safe people told her it was, she was always worried that someone would have a bomb on the plane.

She read books about how safe it was and listened to the stewardess demonstrate all the safety features. But she still worried herself silly every time a visit was coming up.

Finally, the family decided that maybe if she saw the statistics she'd be convinced. So they sent her to a friend of the family who was an actuary.

"Tell me," she said suspiciously, "what are the chances that someone will have a bomb on a plane?"

The actuary looked through his tables and said, "A very small chance. Maybe one in five hundred thousand."

She nodded, then thought for a moment. "So what are the odds of two people having a bomb on the same plane?"

Again he went through his tables.

"Extremely remote," he said. "About one in a billion."

Aunt Bessie nodded and left his office.

And from that day on, every time she flew, she took a bomb with her.

❖

The two birds met for the first time in a tree, and one of them said: "Bred any good rooks recently?"

A major airline recently introduced a special half fare for wives who accompanied their husbands on business trips. Expecting valuable testimonials, the PR department sent out letters to all the wives of businessmen who had used the special rates, asking how they enjoyed their trip.

Letters are still pouring in asking, "What trip?"

While he is getting his hair trimmed Patrick tells his barber about a planned holiday to Rome. "Who knows," says Patrick. "I might even get to meet the Pope."

"You'll never meet the Pope," says the barber. "He's much too important to mix with the likes of you."

"But I might meet him," replies Patrick. "It's not impossible."

"Rubbish," says the barber. "I'll bet you £100 you don't meet him."

"OK," says Patrick. "You're on."

A month later Patrick comes back and says, "You owe me £100. I was walking around St Peter's Square when the Pope saw me from his balcony, invited me into the Vatican and asked me a question."

"My God," says the barber. "What did he say?"

Patrick replies, "He said, 'Where in Christ's name did you get that awful haircut?'"

Where does success come before work? In the dictionary.

Why are there so many Smiths in the phone book? They all have phones.

Why did Henry VIII put skittles on his lawn? So he could take Anne Boleyn.

Why did the Marxist only drink fake tea? Because all proper tea is theft.

What do you get if you divide the circumference of a

73

pumpkin by its diameter? Pumpkin pi.

What do you get if you put a canary in a food blender? Shredded tweet.

Why did the chicken run on to the football pitch? Because the ref blew for a foul.

What do you call a judge with no thumbs? Just his fingers.

Why did the raisin go out with the prune? Because she couldn't find a date.

What do you call people who ride on double-decker buses? Passengers.

What can you put in a wooden box that will actually make it lighter? Holes.

What did the grape say when it was trodden on? Nothing. It just let out a little wine.

What gets smaller the more you put in it? A hole in the ground.

What's big, green and can't fly? A field.

The secretary walks into her boss's office and says, "I'm afraid I've got some bad news for you."

"For heaven's sake," says her boss. "why do you always have to give me bad news? Try to be more positive."

"All right," replies the secretary. "The good news is that you're not sterile."

A man goes into a butcher's shop. The butcher points to some beef hanging from the rack and says, "I bet you £10 that you can't touch that meat."

"No thanks," replies the man. "The steaks are too high."

A father and his small son are standing in front of the tiger's cage at the zoo. Father is explaining how ferocious and strong tigers are, and the boy is taking it all in very seriously. In the end the little boy asks, "Dad, just one thing. If the tiger gets out of his cage and eats you up …?"

"Yes, son?" says the father.

"… which bus do I go home on?"

A man is disappointed with his wife. Almost every night she has a headache, or is too tired, or makes some other excuse not to make love. In desperation, knowing how much his wife loves money, he tells her, "I'll put a ten pound note in the top drawer of your dressing table every time we make love."

Soon he is happy, and his wife delighted in taking the ten pound notes from him for her passionate work. One day he happens to open the top drawer of the dressing table and sees a bundle of ten pound notes and another bundle of twenty pound notes – plus a number of fifty pound notes.

"Where did all this money come from?" he asks. "I only give you ten pound notes."

"Well, dear," said his wife, "not everyone is as mean as you."

In a record shop there was a notice stating "Mendelssohn's Organ Works". Underneath this notice someone had pinned a note on which was written "So does mine".

Two flies are having a game of football in a saucer. "Our game had better improve soon," says one. "Next week we're playing in the cup."

As a crowded airliner is about to take off, the peace is shattered by a 5-year-old boy who picks that moment to throw a wild temper tantrum. No matter what his frustrated, embarrassed mother does to try to calm him down, the boy continues to scream furiously and kick the seats around him.

Suddenly, from the rear of the plane, an elderly man in the uniform of an Air Force General is seen slowly walking forward up the aisle. Stopping the flustered mother with an upraised hand, the white-haired, courtly, soft-spoken General leans down and, motioning toward his chest, whispers something into the boy's ear.

Instantly, the boy calms down, gently takes his mother's hand, and quietly fastens his seat belt. All the other passengers burst into spontaneous applause.

As the General slowly makes his way back to his seat, one of the cabin attendants touches his sleeve. "Excuse me, General," she asks quietly, "but could I ask you what magic words you used on that little boy?"

The old man smiles serenely and gently confides, "I showed him my pilot's wings, service stars, and battle ribbons, and explained that they entitle me to throw one passenger out the plane door on any flight I choose."

In the early 1930s, a farmer and his wife went to a fair. The farmer was fascinated by the airplanes and asked a pilot how much a ride would cost.

"£10 for 3 minutes," replied the pilot. "That's too much," said the farmer.

The pilot thought for a second and then said, "I'll make you a deal. If you and your wife ride for 3 minutes without uttering a sound, the ride will be free. But if you make a sound, you'll have to pay £15."

The farmer and his wife agreed and went for a wild ride. After they landed, the pilot said to the farmer, "I want to congratulate you for not making a sound. You are a brave man."

"Maybe so," said the farmer, "But I have to tell you, I almost said something when my wife fell out."

A group of girlfriends is on vacation when they see a 5-storey hotel with a sign that reads: "For Women Only." Since they are without their boyfriends and husbands, they decide to go in.

The bouncer, a very attractive guy, explains to them how it works. "We have 5 floors. Go up floor by floor, and once you find what you are looking for, you can stay there. It's easy to decide since each floor has a sign telling you what's inside."

So they start going up and on the first floor the sign reads: "All the men on this floor are short and plain." The friends laugh and without hesitation move on to the next floor.

The sign on the second floor reads: "All the men here are short and handsome." Still, this isn't good enough, so the friends continue on up.

They reach the third floor and the sign reads: "All the men here are tall and plain."

They still want to do better, and so, knowing there are still two floors left, they continued on up.

On the fourth floor, the sign is perfect: "All the men here are tall and handsome."

The women get all excited and are going in when they realize that there is still one floor left. Wondering what they are missing, they head on up to the fifth floor.

There they find a sign that reads: "There are no men here. This floor was built only to prove that there is no way to please a woman."

The chief of staff of the US Air Force decided that he would personally intervene in the recruiting crisis. He directed that a nearby Air Force base be opened and that all eligible young men and women be invited. As he and his staff were standing near a brand new F-15 Fighter, a pair of twin brothers who looked like they had just stepped off a Marine Corps recruiting poster walked up to them. The chief of staff walked up to them, stuck out his hand and introduced himself.

He looked at the first young man and asked, "Son, what skills can you bring to the Air Force?"

The young man looks at him and says, "Pilot!"

The general gets all excited, turns to his aide and says, "Get him in today, all the paperwork done, everything, do it!"

The aide hustles the young man off. The general looks at the second young man and asks, "What skills can you bring to the Air Force?"

The young man says, "I chop wood!"

"Son," the general replies, "we don't need wood choppers in the Air Force; what do you know how to do?"

"I chop wood!"

"Young man," huffs the general, "you are not listening to me, we don't need wood choppers, this is the 21st century!"

"Well," the young man says, "you hired my brother!"

"Of course we did," says the general, "he's a pilot!"

The young man rolls his eyes and says, "So what! I have to chop it before he can pile it!"

As a survival test a German, an Australian and a Chinese man are to be abandoned on a desert island for a year. The German is put in charge of building the group's shelter, the Australian is put in charge of the group's power requirements, and the Chinese man is made responsible for the group's supplies. The men are unloaded on the desert island, and their equipment is checked. The German has brought lots of tools, nails and screws, the Australian has brought a wind turbine and solar generator, but the Chinese man can't be found anywhere. Everyone spends the rest of the day looking for him. At dusk they give up and head back to the boat. They get to the beach when the Chinese man jumps out from behind a tree and shouts, "Supplise!"

A statistician is a person who, if you've got your feet in the oven and your head in the refrigerator, will tell you that, on average, you're very comfortable.

A man sees a sign in front of a house, "Talking dog for sale". He rings the bell, and the owner takes him to the backyard where the dog is chained to a post.

"Can you talk?" asks the man.

"Yep," says the dog. "I discovered this gift when I was young. I decided to help the government, so I got in touch with the CIA. In no time they had me jetting from country to country, sitting in rooms with spies and world leaders, because no one would think that a dog would be eavesdropping. I was one of their most valuable spies for eight years running. The jetting around really tired me out, though. I wasn't getting any younger, and I wanted to settle down. So I signed up for a job at the airport to do some undercover security work, mostly wandering near suspicious characters and listening in. I uncovered some incredible dealings and was awarded a lot of medals. Later I got a wife and had some puppies, and now I'm retired."

The man is amazed and asks the owner what he wants for the dog.

"Ten dollars," replies the owner.

"That's a low price for such an amazing dog," says the man. "Why on earth are you selling him?"

The owner replies, "Because he's such a huge liar."

A little girl walks into a pet shop and asks in the sweetest little lisp: "Excuthe me, mithter, do you keep wittle wabbits?"

And the shopkeeper gets down on his knees, so that he's on her level, and asks: "Do you want a wittle white wabby or a soft and fuwwy bwack wabby or maybe one like that cute wittle bwown wabby over there?"

The little girl puts her hands on her knees, leans forward and says in a quiet voice: "I don't fink my pyfon really giveths a thit."

A blonde gets an opportunity to fly to a nearby country. She has never been on an airplane anywhere and was very excited and tense. As soon as she boarded the plane, a Boeing747, she started jumping in excitement, running over seat to seat and starts shouting, "BOEING! BOEING!! BOEING!!! BO....."

She sort of forgets where she is. Even the pilot in the cockpit hears the noise. Annoyed by the goings on, the pilot comes out and shouts, "Be silent!"

There was pin-drop silence everywhere and everybody is looking at the blonde and the angry pilot. She stared at the pilot in silence for a moment, concentrated really hard, and all of a sudden started shouting, "OEING! OEING! OEING! OE...."

The new doctor was making his round of the maternity ward and the first five women he saw were all expecting their babies on the same day: 28 March.

The doctor moved on to look at the sixth patient.

"And when is your baby expected?" he asked.

"I don't know," replied the woman. "I didn't go to the office party like the other women in here did."

Mary and Jane are talking. Mary declares that she's finally got pregnant after years of trying. "How did you manage it?" asks Jane.

"I went to that hypnotherapist on the High Street," replies Mary. "I got pregnant within two months."

"Oh, my husband and I tried seeing him years ago," says Jane. "It didn't work for us."

"Of course it wouldn't," replies Mary. "You have to go alone."

It's my wife's birthday tomorrow. Last week I asked her what she wanted as a present.

"Oh, I don't know," she said. "Just give me something with diamonds."

I'm giving her a pack of playing cards.

This farmer has about 200 hens, but no rooster, and he wants chicks. So he goes down the road to the next farmer and asks if he has a rooster which he would sell.

The other farmer says, "Yeah, I've this great rooster, named Randy. He'll service every chicken you got, no problem."

Well, Randy the rooster costs a lot of money, but the farmer decides he'd be worth it. So, he buys Randy and takes the rooster home.

He then sets him down in the barnyard and gives the rooster a pep talk, "Randy, I want you to pace yourself now. You've got a lot of chickens to service here, and you cost me a lot of money. Consequently, I'll need you to do a good job. So, take your time and have some fun," the farmer ended with a chuckle.

Randy seemed to understand, so the farmer points toward the hen house, and Randy takes off like a shot.

WHAM! Randy nails every hen in the hen house three or four times, and the farmer is really shocked.

After that the farmer hears a commotion in the duck pen. Sure enough, Randy is in there.

Later, the farmer sees Randy after the flock of geese down by the lake. Once again, WHAM! He gets all the geese.

By sunset he sees Randy out in the fields chasing quail and pheasants. The farmer is distraught, worried that his expensive rooster won't even last 24 hours.

Sure enough, the farmer goes to bed and wakes up the next day to find Randy dead as a doorknob, stone cold in the middle of the yard and buzzards are circling overhead.

The farmer, saddened by the loss of such a colourful and expensive animal, shakes his head and says, "Oh, Randy, I told you to pace yourself. I tried to get you to slow down; now look what you've done to yourself."

Randy opens one eye, nods toward the buzzards circling in the sky and says, "SHHHH, they're getting closer..."

Guest: "Why does your dog sit there and watch me eat?"

Hotel Host: "I can't imagine, unless it's because you have the plate he usually eats from."

After England draws Scotland in the Euro 2000 play-offs, Kev and the England team are chatting in the dressing room before the match.

"Look, guys, I know they're crap," says Kev. "But we have to play them to keep UEFA happy."

"Tell you what," pipes up Owen. "You guys go down to the pub, and I'll play Scotland on my own."

"Sounds good," replies Kev, and he and the rest of the team go for a drink. After an hour Kev turns on the pub TV and finds that the score is one-nil to England. The team go back to their beer and darts for an hour then switch on the TV again. The final score is a one-all draw. Horrified, they run back to the dressing room, where they find Owen sitting with his head in his hands.

"What the hell happened?" shouts Kev.

"Sorry," replies Owen, "but the ref sent me off in the eleventh minute."

The manager of a garden centre overhears one of his nurserymen talking to a customer. "No, we haven't had any of that in ages," says the nurseryman. "And I don't know when we'll be getting any more." The customer leaves, and the manager walks over to give the nurseryman a telling off.

"Never tell a customer we can't get them something," he says. "Whatever they want we can always get it on order and deliver it. D'you understand?" The nurseryman nods. "So what did he want?" asks the manager.

"Rain," replies the nurseryman.

A man walks into a bar, has a few drinks and asks what his tab was. The bartender replies that it is twenty dollars plus tip. The guy says, "I'll bet you my tab double or nothing that I can bite my eye." The bartender accepts the bet, and the guy pulls out his glass eye and bites it.

He has a few more drinks and asks for his bill again. The bartender reports that his bill now is thirty dollars plus tip.

He bets the bartender he can bite his other eye. The bartender accepts, knowing the man can't possibly have two glass eyes. The guy then proceeds to take out his false teeth and bite his other eye.

A man walks into a barber's shop and asks how many people are waiting to be served. "I've got three cuts and a shave booked this morning," replies the barber. The man leaves but comes back the next day.

"How many are waiting today?" he asks.

"I've got two cuts, a dye-job and a shave," replies the barber. Next day the man is back with the same question, and the barber tells him, "Four cuts and a wash."

This goes on for weeks until the barber gets suspicious – perhaps the man is a rival planning to open his own barber's shop in the area, or perhaps he wants to find out how much business he can expect. To solve the mystery he gets his assistant to follow the man the next time he drops by. Next day the man comes in, asks his question and leaves, this time trailed by the assistant.

When the assistant gets back the barber says, "Well? Who is he? Where did he go?"

The assistant replies, "I don't know who he is, but he seems to be a friend of your wife. He just went round to your house."

Why did the Irishman wear two condoms? To be sure, to be sure.

A man bumps into a friend who's been recovering from 'flu. The man asks how he's feeling.

"I'm better, thanks," replies his friend. "It was actually a wonderful experience."

"Wonderful?" says the man. "How can 'flu be wonderful?"

"I learned my wife really loves me," explains the friend. "She was so excited I was home. Every time the postman, milkman or dustman came by she'd run out, shouting, 'My husband's home! My husband's home!'"

Two policeman are walking the beat when one says, "When I get home, I'm going straight upstairs and tearing off the wife's underwear."

"Feeling randy?" asks the other.

"No," says the first. "The elastic is killing me."

Man to waitress in a Chinese restaurant: "Excuse me, but this chicken is rubbery."

Waitress: "Thank you, sir."

A man walks by a table in a casino and passes three men and a dog playing cards. "That's a very smart dog," says the man.

"He's not so clever," says one of the players. "Every time he gets a good hand he wags his tail."

A man with a nervous tic applies for a job in a store. Unfortunately, his tic makes it look as if he's winking all the time, and it starts to put customers off. The store manager calls him over and explains the situation. "It's not a problem," says the man. "I forgot to take my aspirin. All I need is a couple of pills, and the winking will stop all day." So saying, he reaches into his pockets to find some aspirin and starts dragging out handfuls of condoms.

"Why all the condoms?" asks the manager. "You're not some sort of sex maniac are you?"

"No," replies the man. "But they're what you get if you walk into a chemist winking and asking for a packet of aspirin."

Q: What do you call a brunette with a blonde on either side?
A: An interpreter.

The university lecturer was speaking to an audience of townspeople. He was attempting to prove that there was a definite connection between happiness and the amount of sex in people's lives.

To help prove his point he asked those in the audience who indulged every night to raise their hands. One five per cent did so, all laughing merrily.

He then asked how many indulged about once a week, and seventy per cent raised their hands, smiling contentedly as they did so.

Then the people who indulged once every month were asked to raise their hands, but it was noticeable that these people neither laughed nor smiled.

The lecturer felt that this proved his point – but to show how obvious this matter was he asked those who indulged only once every year to raise their hands. A tall man at the back of the hall leapt from his chair, waving his hand and laughing loudly.

The lecturer was astonished at this apparent contradiction to his theory, and he asked the man if he could explain why he was so happy.

The man replied, "Certainly. It's tonight! It's tonight!"

A visitor from Holland was chatting with his American friend and was jokingly explaining about the red, white and blue in the Netherlands flag.

"Our flag symbolizes our taxes," he said. "We get red when we talk about them, white when we get our tax bill, and blue after we pay them."

"That's the same with us," the American said, "only we see stars, too."

Johnny: Daddy, are caterpillars good to eat?

Father: Have I not told you never to mention such things during meals!

Mother: Why did you say that, Junior? Why did you ask the question?

Johnny: It's because I saw one on daddy's lettuce, but now it's gone.

A forester and a lawyer were in car accident and showed up at the pearly gates together.

St. Peter greets them at the pearly gates and takes them to the homes where they will spend all eternity. They get into St. Peter's holy vehicle and head on down a gold road, which turns into a platinum road, which turns onto an even grander road paved with diamonds, to a huge mansion where St. Peter turns to the lawyer and says, here is your home for the rest of eternity, enjoy! And if there is anything you need, just let me know.

Then St. Peter took the forester to his home, back down the diamond studded boulevard, down the platinum highway, down the street of gold, down an avenue of silver, along a stone alley and down an unpaved footpath to a shack. St Peter says, "Here you go."

He goes to leave when the forester says, "Wait a minute! How come the lawyer gets the big mansion and I get this shack?"

St. Peter says, "Well, foresters are a dime a dozen here but we have never had a lawyer before."

The Loch Ness Monster squeezes into a Soho bar and orders a shot of whisky for £8.

"You're quite an unusual sight, if you don't mind me saying so, sir," said the bartender. "We don't get many monsters in here."

The monster replies, "Aye, and at your prices I'm not surprised."

A chicken is playing in a football match and scores two early goals.

"You're very good," says the ref. "Do you train hard?"

"Yes," replies the chicken, "but it's not easy. I'm a lawyer so I don't get much free time."

Hearing this, the ref pulls out the red card and orders the chicken off the pitch.

"What's the matter?" says the chicken.

The ref replies, "Professional fowl."

A man walks into a bar and orders six whiskies. He lines them up in a row and knocks back the first, third and fifth glasses. Then he gets up to leave.

"Don't you want the others?" asks the bartender. "You've only had three of your whiskies."

"Best not," replies the man. "My doctor said it was only OK to have the odd drink."

An elderly man lies dying in his bed. In death's agony, he suddenly smells the aroma of his favourite chocolate biscuits wafting up the stairs. He gathers his remaining strength, lifts himself from the bed and slowly makes his way out of the bedroom. With laboured breaths, he staggers down the stairs into the hall and gazes into the kitchen. Here, spread out on racks on the kitchen table and worktops are literally hundreds of his favourite biscuits – a final act of love from his devoted wife, seeing to it that he leaves this world a happy man. Mustering one great final effort, the old man throws himself towards the table and lands on his knees. He reaches out a withered hand towards a tray of biscuits – when whack, it's suddenly struck with a spatula. "You stay out of those," says his wife. "They're for the funeral."

My books of prose may be bad, but they could be verse.

An old Indian lined up all of his 10 little Indian sons and stood in front of them.

He then asked, "Who push portaloo over cliff?"

Nobody answered him.

He then asked again, "Who push portaloo over cliff?"

Again nobody answered.

The old Indian said, "I tell story of Georgie and Georgie's

father. Georgie chop down cherry tree. Georgie tell truth. Big Georgie no punish." So the Indian asked again, "Who push portaloo over cliff?"

To which the littlest Indian replied, "I push portaloo over cliff."

The old Indian then shakes and spanks him, for his punishment. When he is done, the little Indian asks, "Georgie tell truth. Georgie no get punish. I tell truth, I get punished. Why you punish, father?"

The old Indian replied, "Big Georgie not in cherry tree when it got chopped down!!!"

Descartes walks into a bar. The bartender asks, "Can I get you a drink?"

Descartes replies, "I think not." … and disappears.

A doctor has come to see one of his patients in a hospital. The patient has had major surgery on both of his hands.

"Doctor," says the man excitedly and dramatically holds up his heavily bandaged hands. "Will I be able to play the piano when these bandages come off?"

"I don't see why not," replies the doctor.

"That's funny," says the man. "I wasn't able to play it before."

A leopard kept trying to escape from the zoo, but it was no good. He was always spotted.

An American cop pulls over a carload of nuns.

Cop: "Sister, this is a 65 MPH highway. Why are you going so slow?"

Sister: "Sir, I saw a lot of signs that said 22, not 65."

Cop: "Oh, Sister, that's not the speed limit, that's the name of the highway you're on!"

Sister: "Oh! Silly me! Thanks for letting me know. I'll be more careful."

At this point the cop looks in the backseat where the other nuns are shaking and trembling.

Cop: "Excuse me, Sister, what's wrong with your friends back there? They're shaking something terrible."

Sister: "Oh, we just got off of highway 119."

What goes, "Tick, tock, woof"?

A watch dog.

A man shows his friend a beautiful diamond ring he's bought for his girlfriend's birthday.

"I thought she wanted a four-wheel drive," says his pal.

"She did, but where am I going to find a fake Land Rover?"

❖

Three prisoners are locked in a cell. One takes out a harmonica and says, "At least I can play a little music to pass the time."

The second prisoner pulls out a pack of cards and says, "We can play games, too."

The third man pulls out a packet of tampons.

"Those aren't much use," says the first prisoner.

"Yes, they are," says the third prisoner. "On the packet it says we can use them to swim, play tennis and ski."

Harry has tickets for the World Cup final. As he sits in the stadium, a man comes over and asks if anyone is sitting in the seat next to him.

"No," says Harry. "That seat is empty."

"That's incredible!" says the man. "Who in their right mind would have a seat like this for the World Cup final and not use it?"

Harry replies, "Well, actually, I've got the tickets for both these seats. My wife was supposed to be here with me, but she passed away."

"I'm sorry to hear that," says the man, "but couldn't you find a friend or relative to take the seat?"

Harry shakes his head. "No, they're all at the funeral."

Shakespeare walks into a bar and asks the bartender for a beer.

"I can't serve you," says the bartender. "You're bard!"

A man goes into a pet shop and sees a duck tap-dancing on an upturned flowerpot. The man buys the duck for a fiver and takes it home. Next day he rings up the pet shop to complain.

"This duck has been sitting on my kitchen table for hours," says the man. "It hasn't danced a single step."

The pet shop owner replies, "Did you remember to light the candle under the flowerpot?"

❖

When I asked my boss for a pay rise because I was doing the work of three men, he said he couldn't increase my salary but if I told him the names of the three men he'd fire them.

Police Chief: As a recruit, you'll be faced with some difficult issues. What would you do if you had to arrest your mother?

New Recruit: Call for backup!

An American company and a Japanese company decided to have a competitive boat race. Both teams practiced hard and long to reach their peak performance. On the big day, they were as ready as they could be.

The Japanese team won by a mile.

Afterwards, the American team became discouraged by the loss and their morale sagged. Corporate management decided that the reason for the crushing defeat had to be found. A Continuous Measurable Improvement Team of "Executives" was set up to investigate the problem and to recommend appropriate corrective action.

Their conclusion: The problem was that the Japanese team had 8 people rowing and 1 person steering, whereas the American team had 1 person rowing and 8 people steering. The American Corporate Steering Committee immediately hired a consulting firm to do a study on the management structure.

After some time and millions of dollars, the consulting firm concluded that "too many people were steering and not enough rowing." To prevent losing to the Japanese again next year, the management structure was changed to "4 Steering Managers, 3 Area Steering Managers, and 1 Staff Steering Manager" and a new performance system for the person rowing the boat to give more incentive to work harder and become a star performer. "We must give him empowerment and enrichment." That ought to do it.

The next year the Japanese team won by two miles.

The American Corporation laid off the rower for poor performance, sold all of the paddles, cancelled all capital investment for new equipment, halted development of a new boat, awarded high performance awards to the consulting firm, and distributed the money saved as bonuses to the senior executives.

Last night I discovered why my boss hired *me* rather than all the other candidates to be his deputy. Over a lengthy business dinner he admitted that when he interviewed all the other candidates, they seemed to be the cleverest, most dynamic people in the world. Yet when he interviewed me, I managed to convince him that *he* was the cleverest, most dynamic person in the world.

A blonde, a brunette and a redhead go on holiday to a tropical island. The brunette takes a beach umbrella, the redhead takes a crate of suntan oil, and the blonde takes a car door.

"What are you doing with a car door?" asks the redhead.

The blonde replies, "If it gets too hot we can roll down the window."

Tom had this problem of getting up late in the morning and was always late for work. His boss was mad at him and threatened to fire him if he didn't do something about it. So Tom went to his doctor who gave him a pill and told him to take it before he went to bed. Tom slept well and in fact beat the alarm in the morning by almost two hours. He had a leisurely breakfast and drove cheerfully to work.

"Boss," he said. "The pill actually worked!"

"That's all fine," said the boss. "But where were you yesterday?"

A class has been photographed, and teacher is trying to persuade them to buy a copy of the group picture. "Just think how nice it will be to look at it when you are all grown up and say 'There's Jennifer – she's a lawyer' or 'That's Michael – he's a doctor'."

A small voice calls out, "And there's teacher – she's dead!"

Heard the one about the author who changed his name to biro because he wanted a pen name?

A man goes to the doctor with a painful leg. The doctor hears a tiny voice coming from the man's kneecap and listens with his stethoscope. The kneecap keeps saying, "Lend us a tenner. Lend us a tenner …"

"My ankle hurts, too," says the man, so the doctor listens there and hears another little voice saying, "Lend us a tenner. Lend us a tenner …"

The doctor tuts and says, "This is worse than I thought. Your leg is broke in two places."

A husband and wife were driving down a country lane on their way to visit some friends. They came to a muddy patch in the road and the car became stuck.

After a few minutes of trying to get the car out by themselves, they saw a young farmer coming down the lane, driving some oxen before him. The farmer stopped when he saw the couple in trouble and offered to pull the car out of the mud for £50. The husband accepted and minutes later the car was free.

The farmer turned to the husband and said, "You know, you're the tenth car I've helped out of the mud today."

The husband looks around at the fields incredulously and asks the farmer, "When do you have time to plough your land? At night?"

"No," the young farmer replied seriously, "Night is when I put the water in the mud-hole."

The boss returned from lunch in a good mood and called the whole staff in to listen to a couple of jokes he had picked up. Everybody but one girl laughed uproariously.

"What's the matter?" grumbled the boss. "Haven't you got a sense of humour?"

"I don't have to laugh," she replied. "I'm leaving on Friday."

A Jewish grandmother is walking home after a long day at a garment factory. Suddenly a flasher jumps out and opens his coat in front of her. The lady looks at him and says, "You call that a lining … ?"

Dear Sir,

I am writing in response to your request for additional information for block number 3 of the accident reporting form. I put "poor planning" as the cause of my accident. You said in your letter that I should explain more fully and I trust the following detail will be sufficient.

I am an amateur radio operator and on the day of the accident, I was working alone on the top section of my new

80 foot tower. When I had completed my work, I discovered that I had, over the course of several trips up the tower, brought up about 300 pounds of tools and spare hardware. Rather than carry the now un-needed tools and material down by hand, I decided to lower the items down in a small barrel by using a pulley, which fortunately was attached to the gin pole at the top of the tower.

Securing the rope at ground level, I went to the top of the tower and loaded the tools and material into the barrel. Then I went back to the ground and untied the rope, holding it tightly to insure a slow descent of the 300 pounds of tools. You will note in block number 11 of the accident reporting form that I weigh only 155 pounds.

Due to my surprise of being jerked off the ground so suddenly, I lost my presence of mind and forgot to let go of the rope. Needless to say, I proceeded at a rather rapid rate of speed up the side of the tower. In the vicinity of the 40 foot level, I met the barrel coming down. This explains my fractured skull and broken collarbone.

Slowed only slightly, I continued my rapid ascent, not stopping until the fingers of my right hand were two knuckles deep into the pulley. Fortunately, by this time, I had regained my presence of mind and was able to hold onto the rope in spite of my pain.

At approximately the same time, however, the barrel of tools hit the ground and the bottom fell out of the barrel. Devoid of the weight of the tools, the barrel now weighed approximately 20 pounds. I refer you again to my weight in block number 11. As you might imagine, I began a rapid descent down the side of the tower.

In the vicinity of the 40 foot level, I met the barrel coming up. This accounts for the two fractured ankles and the lacerations to my legs and lower body. The encounter with the barrel slowed me enough to lessen my injuries when I fell onto the pile of tools and fortunately only three vertebrae were cracked.

I am sorry to report, however, that as I lay there on the tools, in pain, unable to stand and watching the empty barrel 80 feet above me, I again lost my presence of mind and let go of the rope.

Customer: Do you have any cockroaches?
Clerk: Yes, we sell them to the fisherman.
Customer: I would like 20,000 of them.
Clerk: What would you want with 20,000 cockroaches?
Customer: I'm moving tomorrow and my lease says I must leave my apartment in the condition in which I found it.

Two cannibals are having dinner. "Your wife makes a great roast," says one.

"I know," says the other, "but I'm going to miss her."

Two cannibals are relaxing after a big meal. One turns to the other and says, "Y'know, that missionary we had has given me terrible indigestion."

The other replies, "You know what they say – you can't keep a good man down."

A man really loved a woman, but he was just too shy to propose to her. Now he was getting on and neither of them had ever been married. Of course, they went out together about once a week and had done for years, but he was so timid he just never got around to suggesting marriage, much less living together. One day, he became determined to ask her the question. So he called her on the phone, "Jean."

"Yes, Jean here."

"Will you marry me?"

"Of course I will! Who's calling?"

A man is driving through the Welsh mountains when he's stopped by a policeman for speeding. "I was only going at 40 miles an hour, officer," he says.

"That's all very well," says the policeman, "but what if Mister Fog comes down?"

"Well," says the driver, sarcastically, "if Mister Fog comes down I'll take Mister Foot off Mister Accelerator and put it on Master Brake."

"No, sir," says the policeman. "What I actually said was, 'What if mist or fog comes down?'"

An old man visits his doctor and after a thorough examination the doctor tells him: "I have good news and bad news. What would you like to hear first?"

Patient: "Well, give me the bad news first."

Doctor: "You have cancer. I estimate that you have about two years left."

Patient: "Oh no! That's awful! In two years my life will be over! What kind of good news could you probably tell me after this??"

Doctor: "You also have Alzheimer's. In about three months you are going to forget everything I told you."

Why do seagulls fly over the sea? Because if they flew over the bay they'd be bagels.

A mine collapses near a small town. An engineer survives the disaster and goes to the local bar. The bar is empty except for one other customer.

"Hey, bartender," says the engineer. "I'll have a beer and pour another for my friend over there."

The bartender replies, "I'm sorry, sir, but that guy's Irish, and we don't serve his kind here."

"Well, you'd better, because if it weren't for that guy I wouldn't be here," says the engineer. "You know the mine that caved in? Well, I was in that mine and so was that guy. When the last of us were escaping, he held the roof of the mine up with his head. So get him a beer. If you don't believe me look at the top of this head. You'll see it's flat from holding the roof up."

The bartender serves the Irishman his beer, then comes back to talk to the engineer. "I saw the flat spot on his head, but I also noticed some bruising under his chin. What's that all about?"

The engineer replies, "Oh, that's where we put the jack."

❖

A Yorkshire man orders a headstone for the grave of his dead wife. He asks for a simple inscription saying 'She was thine'. A week later he returns to the stonemason and sees that he's carved 'She was thin'.

"That's no good t'me," says the Yorkshire man. "You've left off the 'e'."

The stonemason agrees to rectify the error. A week later the Yorkshire man returns. The inscription now reads, 'E she was thin'.

Give a man a fish and he will eat for a day. Teach him how to fish and he will sit in a boat and drink beer all day.

A Catholic priest, a Methodist preacher and a rabbi are discussing how they divide their collection money.

The priest says, "I draw a line down the centre of the room and throw the money up in the air. Whatever lands on the left is God's, whatever lands on the right is mine."

The preacher says, "I draw a circle in the middle of the room. Whatever lands in the circle is mine, and the rest belongs to God."

The rabbi says, "I take the money, throw it up in the air and ask God to take what he wants. Whatever comes back down is mine."

While cruising at 36,000 feet, the airplane shuddered, and a passenger looked out the window.

"Oh no!" he screamed, "One of the engines just blew up!"

Other passengers left their seats and came running over; suddenly the aircraft was rocked by a second blast as yet another engine exploded on the other side.

The passengers were in a panic now, and even the stewardesses couldn't maintain order. Just then, standing tall and smiling confidently, the pilot strode from the cockpit and assured everyone that there was nothing to worry about. His words and his demeanour made most of the passengers feel better, and they sat down as the pilot calmly walked to the door of the aircraft. There, he grabbed several packages from under the seats and began handing them to the flight attendants.

Each crew member attached the package to their backs.

"Say," spoke up an alert passenger, "Aren't those parachutes?"

The pilot confirmed that they were.

The passenger went on, "But I thought you said there was nothing to worry about?"

"There isn't," replied the pilot as a third engine exploded. "We're going to get help."

Paddy is going through customs at Dublin airport when he's asked to identify a bottle in his luggage.

"That's holy water I've brought back from Lourdes," says Paddy.

The customs officer opens it and it and says, "This smells more like whisky."

"Isn't that fantastic," says Paddy. "Another bloody miracle!"

Murphy applied for an engineering position at an Irish firm based in Dublin. An American applied for the same job and, both applicants having the same qualifications, they were asked to take a test by the department manager. Upon completion of the test, both men only missed one of the questions. The manager went to Murphy and said: "Thank you for your interest, but we've decided to give the American the job."

Murphy: "And why would you be doing that? We both got nine questions correct. This being Ireland and me being Irish I should get the job!"

Manager: "We have made our decisions not on the correct answers, but on the question you missed."

Murphy: "And just how would one incorrect answer be better than the other?"

Manager: "Simple, the American put down on question 5, 'I don't know.'. You put down, 'Neither do I'."

A man enters a little country store and sees a sign reading, "Danger! Beware of dog". He then sees an old dog lying asleep on the floor.

"Is that the dog people are supposed to beware of?" says the man to the shopkeeper.

"Yes," replies the shopkeeper. "Before I put up the sign everyone kept falling over him."

One Monday evening a tourist visits a brothel in Paris and, on leaving, is very surprised to be handed 5,000 Euros. The next evening he goes back and the same thing happens. He goes back on the third night, but doesn't get a single cent. Upset, he complains to the concierge.

The concierge says, "Why should we pay you? We don't film on Wednesdays."

Birdie, birdie in the sky,
Dropped some white stuff in my eye,
I'm a big girl I won't cry,
I'm just glad that cows don't fly.

A Jewish man living in Florida rings his son in New York and tells him he's divorcing his mother after fifty years of marriage.

"That's terrible," says the son. "Are you sure you've thought it through?"

"I've thought it through," replies the father. "My mind's made up."

"Don't do anything rash," says the son. "Postpone the meeting with your lawyers and for God's sake don't tell mother what you're thinking. I'll ring up my sis and cousin Jacob. We'll come down with all the children and try to sort something out."

"All right," says his father and puts down the phone. Then he turns to his wife and says, "It's working, but how the hell do we get them all down next year?"

A Chihuahua, an Alsatian and a bulldog are sitting in a park when an attractive collie comes along. The collie tells them that the one who constructs the best sentence using the words "liver" and "cheese" can take her out.

"I love liver and cheese," says the Alsatian. The collie is not impressed.

"I hate liver and cheese," says the bulldog. The collie doesn't think this is very good either.

Finally, the Chihuahua says, "Liver alone. Cheese mine."

A drunk stumbles across a baptismal service by the river. The minister notices him and says, "Sir, are you ready to find Jesus?"

The drunk replies, "Yesh, Your Honour, I shur am."

The minister pushes the drunk under the water and pulls him up. "Have you found Jesus?" he asks.

"No, I shur dint," says the drunk.

The preacher dunks him and says, "Brother, have you found Jesus yet?"

"No, I shur dint!" the drunk slurs again.

The preacher holds the drunk under for half a minute and brings him up again. "Sinner, have you still not found Jesus?"

The drunk wipes his eyes and says, "Nope. Are you sure this is where he fell in?"

The Smiths were shown into the dentist's office, where Mr. Smith made it clear he was in a big hurry.

"No fancy stuff, Doctor," he ordered. "No gas or needles or any of that stuff. Just pull the tooth and get it over with."

"I wish more of my patients were as stoic as you," said the dentist admiringly. "Now, which tooth is it?"

Mr. Smith turned to his wife: "Show him, my dear."

The big difference between sex for money and sex for free is that sex for money usually costs a lot less.

In a trial, a southern small-town prosecuting attorney called his first witness, a grandmotherly, elderly woman, to the stand. He approached her and asked, "Mrs. Jones, do you know me?"

She responded, "Why, yes, I do know you, Mr. Williams. I've known you since you were a young boy, and frankly, you've been a big disappointment to me. You lie, you cheat on your wife, you manipulate people and talk about them behind their backs. You think you're a big shot when you haven't the brains to realize you never will amount to anything more than a two-bit paper pusher. Yes, I know you."

The lawyer was stunned! Not knowing what else to do, he pointed across the room and asked, "Mrs. Jones, do you know the defence attorney?"

She again replied, "Why, yes, I do. I've known Mr. Bradley since he was a youngster, too. He's lazy, bigoted, and he has a drinking problem. He can't build a normal relationship with anyone and his law practice is one of the worst in the entire state. Not to mention he cheated on his wife with three different women. One of them was your wife. Yes, I know him."

The defence attorney almost died. The judge asked both lawyers to approach the bench, and in a very quiet voice, said, "If either of you bastards asks her if she knows me, I'll throw your sorry asses in jail for contempt."

A Catholic couple trying for a baby ask their priest to pray for them. "I'm going to Rome for a few months," says the priest. "While I'm there I'll light a candle for you at the altar of Saint Peter."

The priest comes back nine months later and finds that the woman has given birth to quintuplets. "Praise be to God," says the priest. "But where has your husband gone? I heard he left the country."

"So he did, Father," says the woman. "He flew to Rome to blow your bloody candle out."

There once was this blonde riding a horse. After a while it began to speed up. She was hanging on by the tail and cut her forehead open.

After a long struggle, she was able to climb back onto the horse. She then fell off the side and got her foot caught. The horse was now dragging her.

She finally got back on the horse with a broken ankle, bruises all over, and she was bleeding from three different spots. Finally, the horse came to a complete stop.

Luckily the supermarket manager had come out and shut the machine off.

This is the story of four people named Everybody, Somebody, Anybody, and Nobody. There was an important job to be done and Everybody was asked to do it. Anybody could have done it, but Nobody did it. Somebody got angry about that, because it was Everybody's job. Everybody thought Anybody could do it, but Nobody realized that Everybody wouldn't do it. Consequently, it wound up that Nobody told Anybody, so Everybody blamed Somebody.

A policeman is staking out a bar, looking for drunk drivers. At closing time he sees a man stumbling out of the bar, trip on the kerb and fumble for his keys for five minutes. When he finally gets into his car, it takes the man another five minutes to get the key in the ignition.

Meanwhile, everybody else leaves the bar and drives off. When the man finally pulls away, the policeman is waiting for him. He pulls him over and gives him a breathalyser test. The test shows he has a blood alcohol level of zero.

"That can't be right," says the policeman.

"Yes, it can," says the man. "Tonight I'm the designated decoy."

A young man asked a rich old American man how he made his money.

The old man fingered his waistcoat and said, "Well, son, it was 1932, the depth of the Great Depression. I was down to my last nickel. I invested that nickel in an apple. I spent the entire day polishing the apple and, at the end of the day, I sold the apple for ten cents. The next morning, I invested those ten cents in two apples. I spent the entire day polishing them and sold them at 5:00 pm for 20 cents. I continued this system for a month, by the end of which I'd accumulated a fortune of $1.37."

"And that's how you built an empire?" the boy asked.

"Heavens, no!" the man replied. "Then my wife's father died and left us two million dollars."

Somewhere in the world a woman gives birth to a child every minute. We have to find this woman and stop her.

A man was so excited about his promotion to manager of the company he worked for and kept bragging about it to his wife for weeks on end.

Finally she couldn't take it any longer, and told him, "Listen, it means nothing, they even have a manager of peas at the supermarket!"

"Really?" he said. Not sure if this was true or not, he called the supermarket."Can I please talk to the manager of peas?"

"Canned or frozen?"

Jack was living in Arizona during a heat wave when the following took place.

"It's just too hot to wear clothes today," complained Jack as he stepped out of the shower. "Honey, what do you think the neighbours would think if I mowed the lawn like this?"

"Probably that I married you for your money," his wife replied.

A man walks into a bar and finds a drunk playing with a small ball of gloop. The drunk mutters to himself, "It looks like plastic, but it feels like rubber." Interested, the man looks over the drunk's shoulder and takes a peek at the strange substance. "It's weird stuff," says the drunk. "It looks like plastic, but it feels like rubber."

"That's unusual," says the man. "I'm a chemist, perhaps I can tell what it is."

The drunk hands the man the gloop, and he rolls it between his fingers. "You're right," he says. "It does look like plastic but feel like rubber. Do you know where it came from?"

"Sure," replies the drunk. "It just fell out of my nose."

A person receives a telegram informing him about his mother-in-law's death. It also enquires whether she should be buried or burnt.

He replies, "Don't take chances. Burn the body and bury the ashes."

A guy phones the local hospital and yells, "You've got to send help! My wife's in labour!"

The nurse says, "Calm down. Is this her first child?"

"No!" he replies. "This is her husband."

❖

A mother and baby camel are talking one day when the baby camel asks, "Mum why have I got these huge three-toed feet?"

The mother replies, "Well, son, when we trek across the desert your toes will help you to stay on top of the soft sand."

"OK," says the son. A few minutes later the son asks, "Mum, why have I got these great long eyelashes?"

"They are there to keep the sand out of your eyes on the trips through the desert."

"Thanks, mum," replies the son.

After a short while, the son returns and asks, "Mum, why have I got these great big humps on my back??"

The mother, now a little impatient with the boy replies, "They are there to help us store water for our long treks across the desert, so we can go without drinking for long periods."

"That's great, mum, so we have huge feet to stop us sinking, and long eyelashes to keep the sand from our eyes and these humps to store water in the desert. So, mum",

"Yes, son?"

"Why the heck are we in the zoo?"

A young husband with an inferiority complex insisted he was just a little pebble on a vast beach. The marriage counsellor, trying to be creative, told him, "If you wish to save your marriage, you'd better be a little boulder."

A man walks into a bar and orders twenty pints of Guinness. He lines them up on the bar and announces that he'll give £100 to the man who can drink all of them. Patrick sticks up his hand and says he'd like a go if the man can wait half an hour. Patrick then leaves the pub, comes back thirty minutes later and downs the twenty pints, one after another. The man is impressed and hands over the money. "But tell me," he asks. "Where did you go to for that half hour?"

"Ah, well," says Patrick. "Before I took your bet I popped to the pub next door to see if I could do it."

A really huge muscular bloke with a bad stutter goes to a counter in a department store and asks, "W-w-w-where's the m-m-m-men's dep-p-p-partment?"

The assistant behind the counter just looks at him and says nothing.

The man repeats himself: "W-w-w-where's the m-m-m-men's dep-p-p-partment?" Again, the assistant doesn't answer him.

The guy asks several more times: "W-w-w-where's the m-m-m-men's dep-p-p-partment?"

And the assistant just seems to ignore him. Finally, the guy storms off.

The customer who was waiting in line behind the guy asks the assistant, "Why wouldn't you answer that bloke's question?"

The assistant answers, "And g-g-g-get b-b-b-beaten up?"

A young man is wandering through China when he comes across a house in the mountains. He knocks on the door and is greeted by an ancient Chinese man. "I'm lost," says the young man. "Can you put me up for the night?"

"Certainly," says the old man. "But on one condition. If you so much as lay a finger on my young daughter I will inflict upon you the three worst Chinese tortures known to man."

The young man agrees and is invited to sit at the dinner table. The old man's daughter turns out to be young and beautiful, and later that night the man creeps into her room for a night of passion. At dawn he creeps back to his room, exhausted, and goes to sleep. A short while later he wakes

111

to feel a weight on him. He opens his eyes and sees a large rock on his chest with a note reading, "Chinese Torture 1: Large rock on chest."

"That's pretty crappy," thinks the man. "If that's the best he can do I don't have much to worry about."

The man gets up, walks to the window and throws the boulder out into a ravine. As he does so, he notices another note stuck to the window frame. It reads, "Chinese Torture 2: Rock tied to left testicle." The man looks down and sees that his testicle is indeed tied to the falling rock. The man jumps out of the window and is hoping for a soft landing that will save his testicle, when he sees a third note pinned to the rope. As he falls, he reads, "Chinese Torture 3: Right testicle tied to bedpost."

A man walks into a bar with a lump of tarmac under his arm.

"What would you like?" asks the bartender.

The man replies, "A pint of beer and one for the road."

A wealthy man was having an affair with an Italian woman for a few years.

One night, during one of their rendezvous, she confided in him that she was pregnant.

Not wanting to ruin his reputation or his marriage, he paid her a large sum of money if she would go to Italy to have the child. If she stayed in Italy, he would also provide child support until the child turned 18.

She agreed, but wondered how he would know when the baby was born. To keep it discrete, he told her to mail him a postcard, and write 'Spaghetti' on the back. He would then arrange for child support.

One day, about 9 months later, he came home to his confused wife.

"Darling," she said, "you received a very strange postcard today."

"Oh, just give it to me and I'll explain it later," he said.

The wife obeyed, and watched as her husband read the card, turned white, and fainted.

On the card was written 'Spaghetti, Spaghetti, Spaghetti. Two with meatballs, one without.'

A private doctor says to a patient, "I'll examine you for £20."

"OK," replies the patient. "If you can find it, you can have it."

Each evening a bird lover stood in the backyard, hooting like an owl, and, one night, an owl finally called back to him. For a year the man and his feathered friend hooted back and forth. He even kept a log of their "conversations". Just as he thought he was on the verge of a breakthrough in interspecies communication, his wife had a chat with her next-door neighbour. "My husband spends his nights calling out to owls," she said.

"That's odd," the neighbour replied. "So does mine."

An Englishman is applying to emigrate to Australia. "Do you have a criminal record?" asks the emigration official.

"No," says the Englishman. "Do I need one?"

An Australian applies for a job as a royal footman. Taking his references from his last job, he goes to the interview, where they ask him to drop his trousers.

"It's a formality," says the interviewer. "Some footmen are required to wear kilts, so we like to examine the knees of applicants for blemishes."

The Aussie drops his trousers, and his knees are inspected.

"Excellent," says the interviewer. "Now could you show me your testimonials."

A few minutes later the Aussie is thrown out into the street.

"Strewth," he says, picking himself up off the pavement. "If I knew the lingo a bit better I reckon I might've got that job."

A public school raises its fees but sends out letters mistakenly saying that the new fees will be paid "per anum" rather than the correct "per annum". One parent writes back to say that he agrees to the new fees but would rather continue paying through the nose.

❖

A man goes on vacation to a tropical island. As soon as he gets off the plane, he hears drums. He thinks, *Hmmm, this is cool.* He goes to the beach, he hears the drums, he eats lunch, he hears drums, he goes to a luau, and hears drums. He tries to sleep, but he hears drums.

This goes on to the point where he hasn't slept for several nights because of the drums. Finally, he goes down to the front desk.

When he gets there, he asks the manager, "Hey! What's with these drums. Don't they ever stop? I can't get any sleep."

The manager says, "No! Drums must never stop. It's very bad if drums stop."

"Why?"

"When drums stop...bass solo begins."

Father (at hospital looking through glass at newly arrived babies): "Kitchy kitchy koo. Look, she smiled...isn't she adorable?"

Friend: "But your baby didn't smile."

Father: "I was talking about the nurse."

According to inside contacts, the Japanese banking crisis shows no signs of ameliorating. If anything, it's getting worse.

Following last week's news that Origami Bank had folded, we are hearing that Sumo Bank has gone belly up, and Bonsai Bank plans to cut back some of its branches. Karaoke Bank is up for sale, and it is (you guessed it!) going for a song.

Meanwhile, shares in Kamikaze Bank have nose-dived, and 500 back-office staff at Karate Bank got the chop. Analysts report that there is something fishy going on at Sushi Bank, and staff there fear they may get a raw deal.

❖

A man goes to a rabbi and asks if he can bury his pet racing pigeon in the Jewish cemetery.

"A pigeon in our cemetery?" says the rabbi. "Of course you can't."

"Oh dear," says the man. "I really want my favourite bird to be buried in sacred soil. Do you think the Methodists would let me use their cemetery for five hundred pounds?"

"Five hundred pounds?" says the rabbi. "Why didn't you tell me it was a Jewish pigeon?"

Two deaf men were in a coffee shop discussing their wives. One signs to the other, "Boy was my wife mad at me last night. She went on and on and wouldn't stop!"

The other one says, "When my wife goes on at me I just don't listen."

"How do you manage that?"

"It's easy! I turn off the light!"

A wealthy investor walked into a bank and said to the bank manager, "I would like to speak with Mr. Reginald Jones, who I understand is a tried and trusted employee of yours."

The banker said, "Yes, he certainly was trusted. And he will be tried as soon as we catch him."

A man who lived in a block of flats thought it was raining and put his hand out the window to check. As he did so a glass eye fell into his hand. He looked up to see where it came from in time to see a young woman looking down.

"Is this yours?" he asked.

She said, "Yes, could you bring it up?" and the man agreed.

On arrival she was profuse in her thanks and offered the man a drink. As she was very attractive he agreed. Shortly afterwards she said, "I'm about to have dinner. There's plenty; would you like to join me?"

He readily accepted her offer and both enjoyed a lovely meal. As the evening was drawing to a close the lady said, "I've had a marvellous evening. Would you like to stay the night?"

The man hesitated then said, "Do you act like this with every man you meet?"

"No," she replied, "only those who catch my eye."

What do you call a Frenchman in sandals?
Philippe Philoppe.

A man buys his grandfather the services of a call girl on his ninetieth birthday. The girl arrives and says, "Hi! I'm here to give you super sex."

"Oh, thank you," replies the old man. "I'll have the soup, please."

A man walks into a bar, sits down on a bench and orders a cold one. He swigs down the beer, looks in his pocket, cringes and orders another.

He gulps down that one, looks in his pocket again, cringes and orders yet another one. This goes on for at least an hour and a half.

Finally the bartender, bursting with curiosity, says, "I know it's none of my business, buddy, but I have to ask. Why the whole 'drink, look in pocket, cringe and order another one' routine?"

"Well," slurred the man, "There's a picture of my wife in my pocket. When she starts to look good, then it's time for me to go home."

Showing his friend around his home, Jennings pointed out all of the knickknacks his wife had acquired over their long years of marriage.

"The day before I die, I'd like to sell every piece we've got just to see how much it's all worth."

"Well," his friend replies, "since you couldn't possibly know the day before you were going to die, you'll never be able to sell!"

"And that's where you're wrong," the man smiled. "If I sell it, my wife will kill me!"

Two Israeli politicians are discussing how to restore the economy. "I've got an idea," says one. "As a last resort we'll declare war on the USA. After we lose they'll give us enough economic aid to get us back on our feet."

"That's true," says the other. "But what if we win?"

A man is in a bar talking to his friend. "Last night, while I was out drinking, a burglar broke into my house."

"Did he get anything?" asks his friend.

"Yes," says the man. "A broken jaw, six teeth knocked out and a pair of broken ribs. My wife thought it was me coming home drunk."

A man takes his rottweiler to the vet. "My dog's cross-eyed. Is there anything you can do for him?"

"All right," says the vet. "Let's have a look at him." So he picks up the dog, examines his eyes and checks his teeth.

Finally, he says, "I'm going to have to put him down."

"What? Because he's cross-eyed?" asks the man.

"No," replies the vet. "Because he's really, really heavy."

A man travelling through Arizona stops at a small town and goes into a bar. He stands at the end of the bar and lights up a cigar. As he sips his drink, he stands there quietly, blowing smoke rings.

After he's blown nine or ten smoke rings an angry Indian comes up to him and says, "Listen, buddy, quit calling me names or I'll smash your face in."

After a few days, the Lord called to Adam and said, "It is time for you and Eve to begin the process of populating the earth so I want you to kiss her."

Adam answered, "Yes, Lord, but what is a 'kiss'?"

So the Lord gave a brief description to Adam who took Eve by the hand and took her to a nearby bush.

A few minutes later, Adam emerged and said, "Thank you, Lord, that was enjoyable."

And the Lord replied, "Yes, Adam, I thought you might enjoy that and now I'd like you to caress Eve."

And Adam said, "What is a 'caress'?"

So the Lord again gave Adam a brief description and Adam went behind the bush with Eve.

Quite a few minutes later, Adam returned, smiling, and said, "Lord, that was even better than the kiss."

And the Lord said, "You've done well, Adam. And now I want you to make love to Eve."

And Adam asked, "What is 'make love', Lord?'"

So the Lord again gave Adam directions and Adam went again to Eve behind the bush, but this time he reappeared in two seconds.

And Adam said, "Lord, what is a 'headache'?"

A boy is about to go on his first date, and is nervous about what to talk about. He asks his father for advice.

The father replies: "My son, there are three subjects that always work. These are food, family, and philosophy."

The boy picks up his date and they go to a soda fountain. Ice cream sodas in front of them, they stare at each other for a long time, as the boy's nervousness builds.

He remembers his father's advice, and chooses the first topic.

He asks the girl: "Do you like spinach?"

She says, "No," and the silence returns.

After a few more uncomfortable minutes, the boy thinks of his father's suggestion and turns to the second item on the list. He asks: "Do you have a brother?"

Again, the girl says, "No," and there is silence once again.

The boy then plays his last card. He thinks of his father's advice and asks the girl the following question: "If you had a brother, would he like spinach?"

"For Heaven's sake, Chris, why can't you talk to me once in a while?" Julie whined.

"What?" Chris replied.

"Look around!" Julie yelled, as she pointed around the room. "Look at all these books! You always have your head buried in a book! You don't even seem to know I'm alive!"

"I'm sorry, honey," Chris said.

"Sometimes I wish I were a book. Maybe then you'd at least look at me!" Julie exclaimed.

"Hmmmm," Chris mumbled, "that's not such a bad idea. Then I could take you to the library every few days and change you for something more interesting."

Two little girls were busy boasting to each other about how great their respective fathers were.

"My father had lunch with Shakespeare yesterday," said Sally.

"But Shakespeare is dead," commented Clare.

"Oh," replied Sally, unperturbed. "No wonder Dad said he was quiet."

A man goes into a bar looking glum.

"What's the matter?" asks the bartender.

"I've just discovered that my eldest son is gay," says the man. A week later the man is back looking even more miserable. He says to the bartender, "I've just discovered my second son is gay." A week later he's back looking extremely depressed. "Today my youngest son told me he is gay as well."

"Heck," says the bartender. "Does anyone in your family like women?"

"Yes," says the man. "It turns out my wife does."

An old man goes to a school reunion where he finds that his surviving classmates are only interested in talking about their ailments: kidney stones, heart murmurs, liver pains, etc. When he gets home his daughter asks him how it went. "It wasn't much of a reunion," he replies. "It was more like an organ recital."

A new manager is saying goodbye to the man he's replacing.

The departing manager says, "I've left three numbered envelopes in the desk drawer. Open an envelope if you encounter a crisis you can't solve."

Three months later there's an emergency, and the manager

finds he can't cope. He opens the first envelope, and the message inside says, 'Blame your predecessor!' Six months later there's another crisis, and the manager opens the second envelope. The message inside reads, 'Blame your staff!' Three months later, yet another disaster strikes the company, and the manager opens the third envelope. The message is, 'Prepare three envelopes.'

Three Marines were walking through the forest when they came upon a set of tracks.

The first Marine said, "Those are deer tracks."

The second Marine said, "No, those are elk tracks."

The third Marine said, "You're both wrong, those are moose tracks."

The Marines were still arguing when the train hit them.

The psychology instructor had just finished a lecture on mental health and was giving an oral test.

Speaking specifically about manic depression, she asked, "How would you diagnose a patient who walks back and forth screaming at the top of his lungs one minute, then sits in a chair weeping uncontrollably the next?"

A young man in the rear raised his hand and answered, "A football manager?"

When little Reggie was inducted into the army, he was advised to act tough.

"That's the only way to command respect in the army," his friends said.

So Reggie did his best to carry out the advice. He swaggered all around camp, bragging, blustering and talking out of the corner of his mouth.

"Show me a sergeant and I'll show you a dope," Reggie shouted.

No sooner had he spoken than a brawny, battle-hardened figure appeared.

"I am a sergeant!" he bellowed.

"I am a dope," whispered Reggie.

A man is walking with his friend, who happens to be a psychologist. He says to this friend, "I'm a walking economy."

The friend asks, "How so?"

"My hair line is in recession, my stomach is a victim of inflation, and both of these together are putting me into a deep depression!"

A priest, a vicar and a rabbi are asked the question "When does life begin?"

The priest says, "The moment of conception."

The vicar replies, "The moment of birth."

The rabbi replies, "The moment the kids are married and the mortgage has been paid off."

In a small town in the US, there is a rather sizeable factory that hires only married men.

Concerned about this, a local woman called on the manager and asked him, "Why is it you limit your employees to married men? Is it because you think women are weak, dumb, cantankerous or what?"

"Not at all, Ma'am," the manager replied. "It is because our employees are used to obeying orders, are accustomed to being shoved around, know how to keep their mouths shut and don't pout when I yell at them."

Lucy is playing in the garden when she spots two spiders mating. "Daddy, what are those two spiders doing?" she asks.

"They're mating," says Dad.

"What do you call the spider on top, Daddy?" asks Lucy.

"That's daddy longlegs," replies Dad.

Lucy replies, "So if one's a daddy longlegs, the other must be mummy longlegs?"

"No, dear," says Daddy. "Both of them are daddy longlegs."

Lucy thinks for a moment, then stamps the arachnids flat. "Well," she says. "We're certainly not having *that* sort of thing in our garden!"

A student comes to a young professor's office. She glances down the hall, closes his door, kneels pleadingly.

"I would do anything to pass this exam."

She leans closer to him, flips back her hair, gazes meaningfully into his eyes.

"I mean..," she whispers, "..I would do ANYTHING!!"

He returns her gaze. "Anything??"

"Yes. Anything!" she says.

His voice turns to a whisper. "Would you... study??"

Three old ladies are discussing the problems of old age. One says, "Sometimes I find myself with a loaf of bread in my hand and can't remember whether I need to put it away or start making a sandwich."

The second lady says, "Sometimes I find myself on the stair landing and can't remember whether I was going up or down."

The third one says, "Well my memory is perfect – knock on wood." She raps her knuckles on the wooden table, then says, "Just wait till I answer the door."

With the help of a fertility specialist, a 65-year-old woman has a baby.

All her relatives come to visit and meet the newest member of their family.

When they ask to see the baby, the 65-year-old mother says, "Not yet."

A little later they ask to see the baby again.

Again the mother says, "Not yet."

Finally they say, "When can we see the baby?"

And the mother says, "When the baby cries."

They ask, "Why do we have to wait until the baby cries?"

The new mother says, "Because I forgot where I put it."

An American manufacturer is showing his factory to a potential customer from Albania. At noon, when the lunch whistle blows, two thousand men and women immediately stop work and leave the building.

"Your workers, they're escaping!" cries the visitor.

"You've got to stop them."

"Don't worry, they'll be back," says the American. And indeed, at exactly one o'clock the whistle blows again, and all the workers return from their break.

When the tour is over, the manufacturer turns to his guest and says, "Well, now, which of these machines would you like to order?"

"Forget the machines," says the visitor. "How much do you want for that whistle?"

"My mother made me a homosexual."

"If I bought her the wool would she make me one too?"

A young man professed a desire to become a great writer. When asked to define 'great' he said, "I want to write stuff that the whole world will read, stuff that people will react to on a truly emotional level, stuff that will make them scream, cry, howl in pain and anger!" He now works for Microsoft writing error messages.

An old farmer went to town to see a movie. The ticket girl said, "Sir, what is that on your shoulder?"

The old farmer said, "That is my pet rooster, Chuckie. Wherever I go, Chuckie goes."

"I'm sorry, sir," said the ticket girl. "We can't allow animals in the theatre. Not even a pet chicken."

The old farmer went around the corner and stuffed the

chicken down his pants. He returned to the booth, bought a ticket and entered the theatre. He sat down next to two old emergency room nurses named Mildred and Marge.

The movie started and the chicken began to squirm. The old farmer unzipped his pants so Chuckie could stick his head out and watch the movie.

"Marge," whispered Mildred.

"What?" said Marge.

"I think the guy next to me is a pervert."

"What makes you think so?" asked Marge.

"He unzipped his pants and he has his thing out," whispered Mildred.

"Well, don't worry about it," said Marge. "At our age it isn't anything we haven't seen before."

"Yes," said Mildred. "But this one's eating my popcorn!"

Notice on a spiritualist's door: "To avoid confusion, please use bell."

An old lady buys a parrot, but it refuses to say a word. Three years pass, and the parrot remains silent until, one day, the old lady gives it an apple.

"Oh my God!" shouts the parrot. "There's a bloody maggot in it!"

"Good heavens," says the old lady. "All these years without speaking. Why have you started now?"

"Well," replies the parrot, "until today the food has been quite passable."

Outraged customer: "This cat you sold me is absolutely useless!"

Pet shop owner: "What's wrong with it? It looks perfectly all right to me."

Outraged customer: "When you sold it to me you promised it would be a good cat for mice. Yet every time it sees a mouse it runs away and hides."

Pet shop owner: "Well, isn't that a good cat for mice?"

A hangover is the wrath of grapes.

A man had been feeling down for so long that he finally decided to seek the aid of a psychiatrist.

He went there, lay on the couch, poured his heart out, then waited for the profound wisdom of the psychiatrist to make him feel better.

The psychiatrist asked him a few questions, took some notes then sat thinking in silence for a few minutes with a puzzled look on his face.

Suddenly, he looked up with an expression of delight and said, "Um, I think your problem is low self-esteem. It is very common among losers."

A writer dies and Saint Peter offers him the choice of heaven or hell. To see what he has in store Saint Peter takes him to hell, where rows of writers are chained to their desks and are being whipped by demons in a steaming dungeon. However, when they get to heaven the writer is astonished to see that nothing has changed: rows of writers are chained to their desks in a steaming dungeon being whipped. "Hey!" says the writer. "This is just as bad as hell."

"No, it's not," replies Saint Peter. "Up here you get published."

Doctor to patient: "Don't forget to stick out your tongue when the nurse comes."

Patient: "Why?"

Doctor: "I don't like her."

A man hasn't been feeling well, so he goes to his doctor for a complete check-up.

Afterward the doctor comes out with the results.

"I'm afraid I have some very bad news," the doctor says. "You're dying, and you don't have much time left."

"Oh, that's terrible!" says the man. "How long have I got?"

"Ten," the doctor says sadly.

"Ten?" the man asks. "Ten what? Months? Weeks? What?!"

"Nine..."

A man walks into a fishmonger's carrying a salmon under his arm. "Do you make fishcakes?" he asks.

"Of course," says the fishmonger.

"Oh good," says the man. "It's his birthday."

The only time a fisherman tells the truth is when he calls another fisherman a liar.

A man walks into a bar and says, "Bartender, give me two beers. One for me and one for my best buddy here." So saying, he pulls a three-inch man from his pocket.

"Wow!" says the bartender. "You mean to say that that little guy can drink a whole beer?"

"Sure," he says, so the bartender pours a beer, and the little guy drinks it all up.

"What else can he do?" asks the bartender. "Can he walk?"

"Sure," the man says and flicks a coin to the end of the bar. The little guy runs to the end of the bar, picks up the coin and runs back.

"That's amazing," says the bartender. "What else can he do? Can he talk?"

"Sure," he says, turning to the little guy. "Hey, Dad, tell him about time you were in Africa and really pissed off that witch doctor."

A sandwich walks into a bar. The bartender says, "Sorry, we don't serve food in here."

An elderly woman returns home and finds her husband in bed with a young girl. Enraged, she flings him out of the window and watches him plummet to his death. At her trial she pleads not guilty to murder.

"How can you plead not guilty?" asks the prosecuting lawyer. "You threw your husband to his death."

"I didn't know he was going to die," replies the woman. "I reckoned if he could still commit adultery aged ninety-eight there was a good chance he could fly too."

If two's company, and three's a crowd, what are four and five? Nine.

Say "coast" five times quickly then answer this question: "What do you put in a toaster?" (No, you put bread in a toaster.)

Say "silk" fives times quickly then answer this question: "What do cows drink?" (No, they drink water.)

What do you call a deaf monster? Whatever you like – he can't hear you.

What do you call a sheep with no legs? A cloud.

What do you call an underground train full of professors? A tube of smarties.

What do you call an unemployed jester? Nobody's fool.

What do you call a dead tractor collector? An ex-tractor fan.

What's green and looks like a bucket? A green bucket.

What do you call an igloo without a toilet? An ig.

What goes Moooooooz? A jet flying backwards.

What cheese is made backwards? Edam.

What do you call a pair of ants at Gretna Green? An ant-elope.

What do you call the costume of a one-legged ballerina? A one-one.

What do you call a sleepwalking nun? A roamin' Catholic.

What do you call a deer with no eyes? No idea.

What do you call a deer with no eyes and no legs? Still no idea.

Where do you find the most fish? Between the head and the tail.

What word is always pronounced incorrectly? Incorrectly.

What has forty feet and sings? A choir.

What's brown and sticky? A stick.

What's green and would kill you if it fell out of a tree? A pool table.

What is Cole's Law? Mostly it's thinly sliced cabbage.

What's the quickest way to make anti-freeze? Hide her nightie.

What happens when you throw a green stone into the Red Sea? It gets wet.

What lies on its back a hundred feet in the air? A centipede.

What is half of infinity? Nity.

Why did the tiny ghost join the football squad? He heard they needed a little team spirit.

The Wolf Man comes home after a long day at the office. "How was work, dear?" his wife asks.

"I don't want to talk about work!" he shouts.

"All right," she says. "So would you like to sit down and have dinner?"

"I'm not hungry!" he yells. "I don't want to eat. Can't I come home from work and do my own thing with you forcing food down my throat?"

The wife sighs and says, "Well, I guess it's that time of the month again."

Research shows that most men sleep on the right side of the bed. Even when they're asleep they have to be right.

Two cannibals meet one day. The first cannibal says, "You know, I just can't seem to get a tender missionary. I've baked 'em, I've roasted 'em, I've stewed 'em, I've barbequed 'em, I've even tried every sort of marinade. I just cannot seem to get them tender."

The second cannibal asks, "What kind of missionary do you use?"

The other replied, "You know, the ones that hang out at that place at the bend of the river. They have those brown cloaks with a rope around the waist and their sort of bald on top with a funny ring of hair on their heads."

"Ah ha!" he replies. "No wonder, those are friars!"

An estate agent is trying to sell a very old man a new home. "It would be a marvellous investment," says the agent.

"You've got to be joking," says the old man. "At my age I don't even buy green bananas."

When I wake up in the morning I just can't get started until I've had that first, piping hot pot of coffee. I've tried other enemas ...

A woman was walking in the park with eleven children following her.

"Good afternoon," called a friendly gardener. "Are all the children yours or is it a picnic?"

"Unfortunately," replied the woman, "the children are all mine – and it's certainly no picnic."

Good King Wenceslas rings up his local pizza parlour. "The usual please. Deep pan, crisp and even."

A child is born in Boston, Massachusetts, to parents who were both born in Boston, Massachusetts. The child is not a citizen of the United States. How is this possible?

The child was born before 1776.

When the famous chef was cremated the service lasted for thirty minutes at gas mark 6.

Red meat may be bad for you, but fuzzy green meat is even worse.

A man and his wife were making their first visit to the ante-natal clinic, the wife being pregnant with their first child.

After everything checked out, the doctor took a small stamp and stamped the wife's stomach with indelible ink.

The couple was curious about what the stamp was for, so when they got home, the husband got out his magnifying glass to try to see what it was.

In very tiny letters, the stamp said, "When you can read this, come back and see me."

"Mum," asked the small girl, "do you mind if my exam results are like a submarine?"

"What do you mean?" asked the mother.

"Below C-level."

A man walked into a therapist's office looking very depressed. "You've got to help me. I can't go on like this."

"What's the problem?" the doctor enquired.

"Well, I'm 35 years old and I still have no luck with the ladies. No matter how hard I try, I just seem to scare them away."

"My friend, this is not a serious problem. You just need to work on your self-esteem. Each morning, I want you to get up and run to the bathroom mirror. Tell yourself that you are a good person, a fun person, and an attractive person. But say it with real conviction. Within a week you'll have women buzzing all around you."

The man seemed content with this advice and walked out of the office a bit excited. Three weeks later he returned with the same downtrodden expression on his face.

"Did my advice not work?" asked the doctor.

"It worked alright. For the past several weeks I've enjoyed some of the best moments in my life with the most fabulous looking women."

"So, what's your problem?"

"My wife is getting fed up!"

An art collector is walking down the road when he notices a mangy cat in a shop doorway lapping milk from a saucer. He realises that the saucer is extremely old and valuable, so he walks into the shop and offers to buy the cat for two pounds. The store owner replies, "I'm sorry, but the cat isn't for sale."

The collector says, "Please. I need a cat around the house to catch mice. I'll pay you twenty pounds."

The store owner says, "OK. Sold." And he hands over the cat.

The collector continues, "Hey, for the twenty pounds I wonder if you could throw in that old saucer. The cat's used to it and it'll save me from having to buy a dish."

The store owner says, "Sorry, chum. That's my lucky saucer. So far this week I've sold sixty-eight cats."

God is chatting to the Archangel Gabriel. "Y'know, I just created a twenty-four-hour period of alternating light and darkness."

"Wow," replies Gabriel. "What are you going to do now?"

"I think I'll call it a day," replies God.

A successful businessman has a meeting with his new son-in-law. "To welcome you to the family," says the father-in-law, "I'm making you a 50-50 partner in my business. All you have to do is go to the factory and learn the ropes."

The son-in-law interrupts, "Sorry. I hate factories. I can't stand the noise."

"I see," replies the father-in-law. "Well, then, you'll work in the office and take charge of some of the operations."

"No. I hate office work," says the son-in-law. "I can't stand being behind a desk."

"Wait a minute," says the father-in-law. "I make you half-owner of a money-making organisation, but you tell me that you don't like factories and won't work in an office. What am I going to do with you?"

"Easy," says the son-in-law. "Buy me out."

A blonde and a brunette are watching an evening news story about a man about to jump off a bridge. The brunette turns to the blonde and says, "I bet you £50 the man is going to jump." The blonde accepts the bet, and, sure enough, the man jumps. The blonde gives the brunette £50.

"I can't accept your money," says the brunette. "I watched the midday news and saw the man jump then."

"I watched the midday news, too," replies the blonde. "I didn't think he'd do it twice in one day."

A sniper takes a pot-shot at a general visiting the front line. "We know exactly where he is, sir," says one of the soldiers. "He's been up there for weeks."

"Then why don't you see him off?" asks the general.

The soldier replies, "Because if we got rid of him they might replace him with someone who can actually shoot straight."

An old man and an old woman are talking in an old folks' home. The man says, "I'm so old I forgot how old I am."

"I'll tell you how old you are," says the old woman. "Take off your clothes and bend over." The man does so and the woman says, "You're seventy-four."

The man is astonished. "How can you tell?" he asks.

The woman replies, "You told me yesterday."

A blonde has her hair dyed brown. A few days later she's out driving through the countryside when she stops her car to let a flock of sheep pass. Admiring the cute woolly creatures, she says to the shepherd, "If I can guess how many sheep you have, can I take one?" The shepherd agrees, so the blonde thinks for a moment and says "352".

The shepherd is amazed. "You're right. Which sheep do you want?"

The blonde picks the cutest animal.

The shepherd says to her, "All right. How's this for a bet? If I can guess your real hair colour, can I have my dog back?"

A man goes into a pub and points at a beer tap.

"Do you want a pint?" asks the bartender.

The man nods, and the bartender notices that he has a huge scar across his throat. "Where did you get that?" asks the bartender.

The man manages to croak, "Falklands."

"Blimey," says the bartender. "Well, have this one on the house, mate. You boys did a great job over there."

The man croaks, "Muchas gracias."

A Jewish boy goes to a new school where his first lesson is religious instruction. The teacher says to the class, "I've got a bar of chocolate for the boy or girl who can tell me who the greatest man who ever lived was."

A boy puts up his hand and says, "Winston Churchill."

"He was great," says the teacher, "but he's not the person I'm thinking of."

A girl sticks up her hand. "Abraham Lincoln?" she asks.

"He too was great but is not the person I'm thinking of," says the teacher.

The Jewish boy puts up his hand and says, "The greatest man who ever lived was Jesus Christ." The teacher is surprised, but it's the name she was after so she gives the

138

boy the chocolate. After the lesson is over the teacher asks the boy how he knew the right answer.

The boy replies, "Lady, you know the answer was Moses, and I know the answer was Moses, but business is business."

A bloke is chatting to his friend in the pub. He looks at his watch and says, "My wife will be on the plane by now."

"Is she going on holiday?" asks his friend.

"No. She's taking half an inch off the bottom of the kitchen door."

A ventriloquist is telling blonde jokes in a bar when one of his audience, a young blonde lady, stands up and complains. "I've heard just about enough of your lousy blonde jokes!" she shouts. "What makes you think you can stereotype women this way? What does a person's hair colour have to do with their worth as a human being?"

The ventriloquist is very embarrassed and starts to apologise.

The blonde interrupts. "Stay out of it, mister. I'm talking to the little bastard on your knee."

A group of psychiatrists were attending a convention. Four of them decided to leave, and walked out together.

One said to the other three, "People are always coming to us with their guilt and fears, but we have no one that we can go to when we have problems." The others agreed.

Then one said, "Since we are all professionals, why don't we take some time right now to hear each other out?"

The other three agreed.

The first then confessed, "I have an uncontrollable desire to kill my patients."

The second psychiatrist said, "I love expensive things and so I find ways to cheat my patients out of their money whenever I can so I can buy the things I want."

The third followed with, "I'm involved with selling drugs and often get my patients to sell them for me."

The fourth psychiatrist then confessed, "I know I'm not supposed to, but no matter how hard I try, I can't keep a secret..."

An electrician and a plumber are shopping in a hardware store. One of them is the father of the other's son. How can this be possible?

They are husband and wife.

Two crisps were walking down the road. One was assaulted.

A man goes out and buys the best car available in the US or Europe, a 2006 Turbo BeepBeep. It is the best and most expensive car in the world, and it costs him $500,000. He takes it out for a spin and, while doing so, stops for a red light. An old man on a moped, both looking about 90 years old, pulls up next to him.

The old man looks over the sleek, shiny surface of the car and asks, "What kind of car ya got there, sonny?"

The dude replies, "A 2006 Turbo BeepBeep. They cost $500,000."

"That's a lot of money!" says the old man, shocked. "Why does it cost so much?"

"'Cause this car can do up to 320 miles an hour!" states the cool dude proudly.

The old man asks, "Can I take a look inside?"

"Sure," replies the owner.

So the old man pokes his head in the window and looks around. Leaning back on his moped, the old man says, "That's a pretty nice car, alright!"

Just then the light changes, so the guy decides to show the old man what his car can do. He floors it, and within 30 seconds the speedometer reads 320. Suddenly, the guy notices a dot in his rear view mirror. It seems to be getting closer!

Whhhooooooooooossssshhhhhh! Something whips by him! Going maybe three times as fast! The guy wonders what on earth could be going faster than his Turbo BeepBeep. Then, ahead of him, he sees a dot coming towards him.

Whooooooooooosh! It goes by again! And, it almost looked like the old man on the moped! Couldn't be, thinks the guy. How could a moped outrun a Turbo BeepBeep? Again, he sees a dot in his rear-view mirror! WhooooooooshhhhhhhhhKa-BbbbblaMMMMM! It ploughs into the back of his car, demolishing the rear end.

The guy jumps out and discovers it is the old man! Of course, the moped and the old man are hurting, for certain. The guy runs up to the dying old man and says, "You're hurt bad! Is there anything I can do for you?"

The old man replies, "Yeah. Unhook my braces from the side-view mirror on your car!"

A boss accosts his employee coming through the door at ten o'clock in the morning. "You should have been here at nine," he says.

"Why?" asks the employee. "What happened?"

A blonde comes home to find her husband in bed with a redhead. She grabs a gun and holds it to her own head. The husband begs her not to shoot herself. The blonde shouts at her husband, "Shut up! You're next!"

I went to a school reunion the other day. Sadly all my friends had become so fat and old that no one could recognise me.

Every morning a man passes a house in his street, and every morning he sees a woman in her front garden beating her husband over the head with a French loaf. This goes on for months, until one morning he passes the house and sees the woman beating her husband with a large éclair. Later that day he meets the woman in the street. "Aren't you the woman who beats her husband with a French loaf?" asks the man. "Only today I could have sworn you were hitting him with a giant cake."

"Oh, I was," replies the woman. "Today is his birthday."

When I die, I want to go peacefully like my grandfather did, in his sleep - not screaming like the passengers in his car.

A Frenchman with a parrot perched on his shoulder walks into a bar. The bartender says, "Wow, that's really lovely. Where did you get him?"

"In France," says the parrot. "They've got millions of 'em."

A very ugly person walked into the doctor's office and said, "Doctor, I'm so depressed and lonely. I don't have any friends, no one will come near me, and everybody laughs at me. Can you help me accept my ugliness?"

"I'm sure I can." the psychiatrist replied. "Just go over and lie face down on that couch."

Did you know that Hannibal was the first man to experiment with genetics? He crossed a mountain with an elephant.

The aspiring spy was being interviewed in Whitehall by a secret service chief, who was explaining the sort of men he looked for.

"We need people who are more than just involved," he said. "In this game you have to be committed. It is rather like the difference between bacon and eggs. So far as the chicken is concerned with the production of this marvellous start to the day – well, she *is* involved, but the pig, *he* is committed!"

❖

A little old lady gets home after a game of bridge with her friends and discovers that she has nothing in the larder for her husband's dinner. All she can find is a tin of cat food, an egg and a lettuce leaf. There's no time to go shopping, so she stirs the egg into the cat food, quickly cooks it in a pan, puts it on a plate and garnishes it with the lettuce leaf.

Her husband comes home, eats the meal and declares that it's the best thing he's ever tasted. Next week the old lady is playing bridge with her friends, and she tells them about her culinary experiment.

"He seems to love cat food," she tells them. "He's had egg and cat food every day this week. He can't get enough of it."

"You can't feed your husband cat food!" declares one of her friends. "You'll kill him."

Sure enough, next week the old lady informs her friends that her husband had passed away.

"We told you cat food would kill him," says one.

"It had nothing to do with it," replies the old lady. "He died when he fell off the fence."

"What was he doing up there?" asks the friend.

The old lady replies, "He was trying to lick his backside."

The hard-pressed managing director had just returned from a gruelling overseas trip and was relaxing at home when the telephone rang. When he hung up almost at once his wife inquired who it was.

"Someone with the wrong number, my love," he said. "He wanted to know if the coast was clear, so I suggested he telephone the Met. Office."

The only reason the railways in Britain print timetables is so that passengers know how late their trains have been.

Bob and Joe went hunting. This was Joe's first time ever hunting, so he was following Bob's lead. Bob saw a small herd of deer and told Joe to stay in the exact spot he was and to be quiet! After a few minutes, Bob heard a loud scream.

He ran back and asked Joe what had happened. Joe said, "There was this snake and he slithered across my feet, but I never screamed. Then there was this bear that came up to me and snarled, but I never screamed."

"So then what did make you scream," Bob asked.

"Well," Joe continued, "two squirrels crawled up my pants and I overheard them say, 'Should we take them home or eat 'em now?'"

Q: Before Mount Everest was discovered, what was the highest mountain on earth?

A: Mount Everest.

Tailor: "Your suit will be ready in six weeks, sir."

Customer: "Six weeks! But God made the whole world in only six days!"

Tailor: "Quite true, sir. But look what a state the world is in."

❖

An old man is sitting on a park bench crying his eyes out. A young jogger comes by and asks him what is the matter.

The old man says, "I'm a multi-millionaire, I have a great big house, the fastest car in the world and I just married a beautiful blonde bombshell who satisfies me every night in bed whether I like it or not (sob)."

The young jogger says, "Man, you have everything I have ever dreamed for in my life. What could be so wrong in your life that you are sitting here in the park crying?"

The old man says, "I can't remember where I live."

Two men got out of their cars after they collided at an intersection. One took a flask from his pocket and said to the other, "Here, maybe you'd like a nip to calm your nerves."

"Thanks," he said, and took a long pull from the container. "Here, you have one, too," he added, handing back the whiskey.

"Well, I'd rather not," said the first man. "At least not until after the police have been here."

Did you hear about the Scotsman who died of a broken heart? He was tired of reading jokes about how mean the Scots are so he went into his nearest pub and ordered a round for everyone.

"That's very kind of you, sir," commented the bartender. "There are almost fifty people in here. I didn't know you Jews were so generous."

A student was in his college campus bookstore. Questioned about a book for one of his classes, the assistant responded, "This book will do half the job for you."

"Good," the student replied, "I'll take two."

❖

An old man goes to a church and makes a confession. "Father, I'm seventy-five years old. I've been married for fifty years. All these years I had been faithful to my wife, but yesterday I was intimate with an eighteen-year-old model."

The priest replies, "I see, my son. And when was your last confession?"

The old man says, "Never, I'm Jewish."

"So why are you telling me?" asks the priest.

"I'm not just telling you," says the old man. "I'm telling everyone."

A woman walks up to a wrinkled old man sitting on a park bench. "You look very contented," she says. "What's your secret for a long, happy life?"

"I smoke sixty cigarettes a day," replies the man. "I drink a crate of beer a week, eat nothing but fatty meat and never exercise."

"That's amazing," says the woman. "And how old are you?"

The man replies, "Twenty-six."

"Hello," said the school teacher, answering the phone. "This is Miss Smith of Form Two of the Junior School."

"Hello," said the voice on the phone. "I'm phoning to tell you that Jim Brown is sick and won't be coming to school today."

"Oh, I *am* sorry to hear that," commented the teacher. "Who is that speaking?"

The voice on the telephone replied, "This is my father."

Little boy to mother: "Mummy, can I go swimming?"

Mother: "Certainly not. The sea's too rough, there's a terrible rip tide and a dangerous offshore current, and I've heard that this coast in infested with jellyfish and sharks."

Little boy: "But daddy's gone swimming."

Mother: "Yes, I know, but he's got excellent life insurance."

❖

A man was driving along and saw a rabbit hopping across the middle of the road. He swerved to avoid hitting the rabbit, but unfortunately the rabbit jumped in front of the car and was hit. The driver, being a sensitive man as well as an animal lover, pulled over to the side of the road and got out to see what had become of the rabbit. Much to his dismay, the rabbit was dead. The driver felt so awful he began to cry.

A woman driving down the highway saw the man crying on the side of the road and pulled over. She stepped out of her car and asked the man what was wrong.

"I feel terrible," he explained. "I accidentally hit this rabbit and killed it."

The woman told the man not to worry. She knew what to do. She went to her car trunk and pulled out a spray can. She walked over to the limp, dead rabbit, and sprayed the contents of the can onto the rabbit. Miraculously, the rabbit came to life, jumped up, waved its paw at the two humans and hopped down the road. 50 feet away the rabbit stopped, turned around, waved at the two again, hopped down the road another 50 feet, turned, waved, and hopped another 50 feet. The man was astonished. He couldn't figure out what substance could be in the woman's spray can! He ran over to the woman and demanded, "What was in your spray can? What did you spray onto that rabbit?"

The woman turned the can around so that the man could read the label. It said:

'Hare Spray. Restores Life to Dead Hare. Adds Permanent Wave.'

Heard the one about the man who decided to go into the cement business?

He'd always been a good mixer.

148

"Susan!" said the teacher. "Why did you just let out that awful yell?"

"Please, miss," said Susan, "I've just hit my fumb wiv a 'ammer."

"Susan," responded the teacher, "the word is 'thumb' not 'fumb'."

"Yes, miss," said Susan, "but as well as 'itting my thumb I also 'it my thinger."

A little boy asks the gardener, "What do you put on your rhubarb?"

"Well, usually rotted horse manure," says the gardener.

"We have custard," says the boy.

The son of a builder is approaching his sixth birthday, and his father asks him what he'd like as a present. "What I really want is a baby brother," says the boy.

"Sorry, son," says the father. "Your birthday is five days away. I can't get you a baby brother in that time."

The son replies, "Can't you do what you do at work and put more men on the job?"

A boss is carpeting one of his employees for persistent lateness. "Do you know when we start work in the office?" he asks.

"No," replies the employee. "They're usually hard at it by the time I get here."

A man goes into a bar with a lamp. After he's had a few drinks the man says to the bartender, "This lamp is magic, y'know. If you rub it a genie comes out and grants you a wish."

"Oh yes?" replies the bartender. "Let's have a go then." He rubs the lamp with a bar cloth, and out pops a genie. "Fantastic," says the bartender. "It works. Can I have a million bucks, please?"

"As you wish," replies the genie, and the bar is suddenly full of ducks.

"I forgot to mention," says the man. "He's a little deaf."

A Scotsman and an Englishman are strolling along the beach when they find a lamp. They clean it up and out pops a genie. "I'll give you each one wish for freeing me," says the genie.

The Englishman says, "I'm sick and tired of Scots coming into England. I wish there was a huge wall around England to keep them out."

Poof! It's done.

The Scotsman says, "So tell me about this wall, genie."

"Well," says the genie. "It's 500 feet high and a third of a mile thick. Nothing can get in and nothing can get out."

"Right," says the Scotsman. "Fill it with water."

A golfer is bemoaning his lack of skill to his caddie. "I'm awful. There can't be any golfers worse than me," he says.

"Oh there are," replies the caddie. "It's just that they don't play any more."

A golfer is taking a long time teeing off, and his friend asks him what's the matter.

"My wife is watching from the clubhouse," he says. "So I want to make sure this is a good one."

"You're crazy," replies the friend. "The clubhouse has to be 500 yards away. You'll never hit her from this distance."

Some cannibals get a job in a big corporation on condition that they don't eat any of the other staff. Things go very well until their boss calls them into his office one day and gives them some bad news: an office cleaner is missing in mysterious circumstances and the cannibals are under suspicion. The cannibals get together after work, and their leader says, "Which of you idiots had the cleaner?" One of the cannibals raises his hand. "You idiot! For weeks we've been feasting on team leaders, project managers and human resources staff, then you go and eat someone they'll actually miss!"

A young man was sitting in the cinema when a very fat lady got up during the interval and stepped painfully on his toes while squeezing past him into the aisle.

A short time later the same fat lady returned, carrying an ice cream and a large packet of popcorn.

"Did I tread on your toes, young man?" she asked.

"I'm afraid you did. And you didn't apologise."

"Good," snapped the woman. "Then this *is* my row."

❖

A small-time jewel thief came home after robbing a nearby country house and began to saw the legs off his bed. When his wife asked him what he was doing he replied that he wanted to lie low for a while.

❖

Interviewer to job applicant: "You start at £100 a week, and after six months it goes up to £130."

Applicant: "All right then. I'll come back in six months."

❖

A lady approaches her priest and tells him, "Father, I have a problem. I have two female talking parrots, but they only know how to say one thing."

"What do they say?" the priest inquired.

"They only know how to say, 'Hi, we're prostitutes. Want to have some fun?'"

"That's terrible!" the priest exclaimed, "but I have a solution to your problem. Bring your two female parrots over to my house and I will put them with my two male talking parrots whom I taught to pray and read the bible. My parrots will teach your parrots to stop saying that terrible phrase and your female parrots will learn to praise and worship."

"Thank you!" the woman responded. The next day the woman brings her female parrots to the priest's house.

His two male parrots are holding rosary beads and praying in their cage.

The lady puts her two female parrots in with the male parrots and the female parrots say, "Hi, we're prostitutes, want to have some fun?"

One male parrot looks over at the other male parrot and exclaims, "Put the beads away. Our prayers have been answered!"

A man rings his local hospital. "How is Mr Jackson in Ward B?" he asks.

"Mr Jackson is out of danger," replies the nurse on duty. "His test results were normal. Can I ask who's calling?"

"Yes, it's Mr Jackson in Ward B," says the man. "No one tells me anything."

Does the name Pavlov ring a bell?

Two men are approaching each other on the pavement. Both are dragging their right foot as they walk.

As they meet, one man looks at the other knowingly, points to his foot and says, "Falklands, 15 years back?"

The other points his thumb behind him and says, "Dog pooh, 20 feet back."

A man stopped at a rural petrol station and, after filling his tank, he paid the bill and bought a soft drink. He stood by his car to drink his coke and he watched a couple of men working along the roadside. One man would dig a hole two or three feet deep and then move on. The other man came along behind and filled in the hole. While one was digging a new hole, the other was about 25 feet behind filling in the old. The men worked right past the fellow with the soft drink and went on down the road. "I can't stand this," said the man tossing the can away and heading down the road toward the men.

"Hold it, hold it," he said to the men. "Can you tell me what's going on here with this digging?"

"Well, we work for the council," one of the men said.

"But one of you is digging a hole and the other is filling it up. You're not accomplishing anything. Aren't you wasting the council's money?"

"You don't understand, mister," one of the men said, leaning on his shovel and wiping his brow. "Normally there's three of us: me, Rodney and Mike. I dig the hole, Rodney sticks in the tree and Mike here puts the soil back."

"Yeah," piped up Mike. "Now just because Rodney's sick, that don't mean we can't work, does it?"

❖

Mrs Smith: "Doctor, please can you help me? I've had twelve children and I'm pregnant again and I don't want any more kids after this one. I desperately need a hearing aid."

Doctor: "A hearing aid? What do you want a hearing aid for? Surely you want some birth control pills or some form of contraceptive device?"

Mrs Smith: "No, Doctor, I definitely want a hearing aid. You see, my husband gets drunk every Friday night and comes lumbering into my bed and says to me, 'Do you want to go to sleep or what?' Me being a bit deaf, I always say, 'What?'"

Two old men hobble into the pub. One says, "I've heard Guinness puts lead in your pencil. Shall we try some?"

"All right," says the other. "But to be honest, I've got nobody to write to."

An applicant was filling out a job application.

When he came to the question, "Have you ever been arrested?" he wrote: No.

The next question, intended for people who had answered in the affirmative to the previous question, was, "Why?"

The applicant answered it anyway: Never got caught.

A Jewish man collapses on a Dublin street. A priest rushes to his side to administer the last rites. "Tell me, my son," says the priest. "Do you believe in the Father, the Son and the Holy Ghost?"

The man looks up at him and says, "Wonderful. Here I am dying on the ground and all he does is ask me riddles."

A man was driving down a local street one day and approached a stop sign. He barely slowed down and ran right through the stop sign after glancing for traffic.

What the driver didn't know was that a policeman was

watching the intersection. The policeman pulled out after him and stopped the car two blocks away.

Policeman: "License, registration and proof of insurance, please."

Driver: "Before I give it to you, tell me what the heck you stopped me for, man."

Policeman: "Watch your tone, sir; you ran the stop sign back there!!"

Driver: "Man, I slowed down, what the heck is the difference!?!"

The police officer pulled out truncheon and began smashing it over the man's head and shoulders.

Policeman: "Now, do you want me to just slow down or stop?"

Heard the one abut the man who wanted to go to Jeopardy?

He'd heard there were thousands of jobs there.

❖

A man went to a psychiatrist. "Doctor," he said, "I've got trouble. Every time I get into bed, I think there's somebody under it. I get under the bed, I think there's somebody on top of it. You must help me, I'm going crazy!"

"Just put yourself in my hands for two years," said the shrink. "Come to me three times a week, and I'll cure your fears."

"How much do you charge?"

"A hundred pounds per visit."

"I'll sleep on it," he says.

Six months later the doctor met the man on the street. "Why didn't you ever come to see me again?" asked the psychiatrist.

"For a hundred pounds a visit? A bartender cured me for ten quid."

"Is that so? How?"

"He told me to cut the legs off the bed!"

Farmer Joe decided his injuries from his recent accident were serious enough to take the trucking company responsible for the accident to court.

In court, the trucking company's fancy lawyer was questioning farmer Joe.

"Didn't you say, at the scene of the accident, that you were fine?"

"Well, I'll tell you what happened. I had just loaded my favourite mule Bessie into the…"

"I didn't ask for any details," the lawyer interrupted. "Just answer the question. Did you not say, at the scene of the accident, that you were fine?"

"Well I had just got Bessie into the trailer and was driving down the road…"

"Judge, I am trying to establish the fact that, at the scene of the accident, this man told the Highway Patrolman on the scene that he was just fine.

Now, several weeks after the accident, he is trying to sue my client. I believe he is a fraud. Please tell him to simply answer the question."

By this time the Judge was fairly interested in Farmer Joe's answer and told the lawyer so.

"Well," said the farmer, "as I was saying, I had just loaded Bessie, my favourite mule, into the trailer and was driving her down the highway when this truck and trailer ran the stop sign and smacked my truck right in the side. I was thrown into one ditch and Bessie was thrown into the other. I was hurting real bad and didn't want to move. However, I could hear ol' Bessie moaning and groaning. I knew she was in terrible shape just by her groans. Shortly after the accident a Highway Patrolman came on the scene. He could hear Bessie moaning and groaning so he went over to her. After he looked at her he took out his gun and shot her between the eyes.Then the Patrolman came across the road with his gun in his hand and looked at me. He said, 'Your mule was in such bad shape I had to shoot her. How are you feeling?'

Sally and Sarah were talking about the wonderful party they had just attended.

"That bloke was really hunky," said Sally.

"I know," sighed Sarah.

"He and I got on really well," said Sally. "He wants to see me again and asked for my phone number."

"Did you give it to him?" asked Sarah.

"I told him my number was in the phone book."

"Does he know your name?" asked Sarah.

"I told him that was in the phone book too. I can't wait until he phones ..."

A salesman out touring his territory has a heart attack in his hotel room and dies. The hotel owner calls the salesman's company and relates the tragedy to the sales manager. The sales manager says, "Return his samples by post and search his pockets for orders."

How about the two old men, one a retired professor of psychology and the other a retired professor of history.

Their wives had talked them into a two week stay at a hotel in the country. They were sitting around on the porch of the hotel watching the sun set. The history professor said to the psychology professor, "Have you read Marx?"

To which the professor of psychology said, "Yes, I think it's the wicker chairs."

Which is correct to say, "The yolk of the egg are white" or "The yolk of the egg is white"? Neither. The yolk of the egg is yellow.

In the office restroom the boss placed a sign about the sink. It had a single word on it: "Think!" The next day he found another sign above the dispenser. This one said "Thoap!"

❖

The maker doesn't want it, the buyer doesn't use it, and the user doesn't see it. What is it?

A coffin.

❖

Jones came into the office an hour late for the third time in one week and found the boss waiting for him. "What's the story this time, Jones?" he asked sarcastically. "Let's hear a good excuse for a change."

Jones sighed, "Everything went wrong this morning, boss. The wife decided to drive me to the station. She got ready in ten minutes, but then Tower Bridge got stuck. Rather than let you down, I swam across the Thames - look, my suit's still damp - then ran all the way here."

"You'll have to do better than that, Jones," said the boss, obviously disappointed. "No woman can get ready in ten minutes."

A number of girls at a posh boarding school were beginning to use lipstick and would put it on in the bathroom. That was fine, but after they put on their lipstick they would press their lips to the mirror leaving dozens of little lip prints.

Every night, the maintenance man would remove them and the next day, the girls would put them back. Finally the headmistress decided that something had to be done. She called all the girls to the bathroom and met them there with the maintenance man. She explained that all these lip prints were causing a major problem for the maintenance man who had to clean the mirrors every night.

To demonstrate how difficult it had been to clean the mirrors, she asked the maintenance man to show the girls how much effort was required. He took out a long-handled squeegee, dipped it in the toilet, and cleaned the mirror with it.

Since then, there have been no lip prints on the mirror.

There are teachers, and then there are educators.

A man in his nineties is watching a group of teenage girls. He turns to his friend and says, "I wish I was twenty years older."

"Don't you mean twenty years younger?"

"No, twenty years older. That way I wouldn't give a damn one way or another."

While crossing the US-Mexican border on his bicycle, the man was stopped by a guard who pointed to two sacks the man had on his shoulders. "What's in the bags?" asked the guard.

"Sand," said the cyclist.

"Get them off - we'll take a look," said the guard.

The cyclist did as he was told, emptied the bags, and, proving they contained nothing but sand, reloaded the bags, put them on his shoulders and continued across the border.

Two weeks later, the same thing happened. Again the guard demanded to see the two bags, which again contained nothing but sand. This went on every week for six months, until one day the cyclist with the sand bags failed to appear.

A few days later, the guard happened to meet the cyclist downtown. "Say, friend, you sure have us all fooled," said the guard. "We know you're smuggling something across the border. I won't say a word - but what is it ?"

"Bicycles!"

❖

A bald man sees a sign outside a barber's shop saying: 'Baldies! Instant treatment! A head of hair just like mine for £5,000.' Underneath the sign is a picture of the barber with a fine mane of luxuriant hair.

The bald man goes in and says, "Can you guarantee my head will look like yours, instantly, for £5,000?"

"I sure can," says the barber. "It'll only take a few seconds for us to look exactly alike." So the bald man hands over the £5,000, and the barber shaves off his own hair.

Prince Charles arrives in Iran on an official visit. He says to the president: "Where's the shah?"

"What do you mean?" says the president. "There is no shah. We got rid of the shah years ago."

"All right," says Prince Charles. "In that case I'll have a bath."

A seriously ill man is lying in his hospital bed on a ventilator. The man's family and the hospital chaplain gather round to comfort him. The man gestures for a pen and paper, writes a brief note, hands it to the chaplain and passes away. The chaplain reads out the man's dying words. "Help! You're standing on my oxygen tube."

A man announces his plan to marry a nineteen-year-old stripper on his seventy-fifth birthday. His doctor says to him, "I think you ought to reconsider. Prolonged sex with a girl that young could be fatal."

The man shrugs and says, "If she dies, she dies."

What do you get if you cross a chicken with a clock? An alarm cock.

What do you call a plump pet cat that has eaten a duck? A duck-filled fatty puss.

What did the policeman say to his stomach? I've got you under a vest.

What is small, round, smells and giggles? A tickled onion.

Where was the Declaration of Independence signed? At the bottom.

What says "Oom, oom"? A backward cow.

What game do mice like to play? Hide and squeak.

Why was the young glow worm a bit sad? Because it had glowing pains.

What do you do when your nose goes on strike? Picket.

Where do very young fish go to be educated? Plaice school.

What do you get if a witch gets 'flu? Cold spells.

What slithers along the ground and works for the government? A civil serpent.

Where did the major general keep his armies? Up his sleevies.

Why do storks lift only one leg? Because if they lifted the other leg they would fall over.

An ageing playboy visits his doctor after a lifetime of wine, women and song. "Well," says the doctor, "the good news is that you don't have to give up singing."

Deep within a forest a little turtle began to climb a tree. After hours of effort he reached the top, jumped into the air waving his front legs and crashed to the ground.

After recovering, he slowly climbed the tree again, jumped, and fell to the ground. The turtle tried again and again while a couple of birds sitting on a branch watched his sad efforts.

Finally, the female bird turned to her mate. "Dear," she chirped, "I think it's time to tell him he's adopted."

❖

It's a beautiful, warm spring morning and a man and his wife are spending the day at the zoo. She's wearing a cute, loose-fitting, pink spring dress, sleeveless with straps. He's wearing his normal jeans and a T-shirt. The zoo is not very busy this morning.

As they walk through the ape exhibit, they pass in front of a very large hairy gorilla. Noticing the girl, the gorilla goes crazy.

He jumps up on the bars, and holding on with one hand (and 2 feet), he grunts and pounds his chest with his free hand. He is obviously excited at the pretty lady in the wavy dress. The husband, noticing the excitement, thinks this is funny. He suggests that his wife teases the poor fellow some more. The husband suggests she pucker her lips, wiggle her bottom at him, and play along.

She does, and Mr. Gorilla gets even more excited, making noises that would wake the dead.

Then the husband suggests that she let one of her straps fall to show a little more skin.

She does, and Mr. Gorilla is about to tear the bars down.

"Now try lifting your dress up your thighs and sort of fan it at him," he says.... This drives the gorilla absolutely crazy and now he's doing flips.

Then the husband grabs his wife by the hair, rips open the door to the cage, flings her in with the gorilla and slams the cage door shut.

"Now, tell HIM you have a headache!"

Visitor to hospital patient: "I heard they're bringing in a case of diarrhoea."

Patient: "Well, anything's better than the coffee they keep giving us."

Father O'Leary invites Rabbi Levy round for tea and offers him a ham sandwich.

"It looks very tempting," says the rabbi. "But you know I can't eat ham."

"Oh, go on," says the priest. "Just a little bit. To be sure, it won't do you any harm."

"No, I'd better not," says the rabbi.

"Oh, go on," insists the priest. "Don't be so old fashioned now."

"All right," says the rabbi. "I will have one – at your wedding."

A young man comes home and says, "Dad, I just got my driving license and would like to use the family car."

Father replies, "OK, son. But, first, you have to get good marks at school, keep your room clean, mow the lawn, and cut your hair. Come back in a few months and then we'll see."

Well, several months pass and the young man comes into the house with his report in his hand. "Dad, I got great marks,

I've been keeping my room as neat as a pin, and the lawn is always ship-shape. How about letting me use the car?"

Father replies, "That's all true, but, son, you didn't cut your hair."

Son says, "But, dad, Jesus had long hair."

Father replies, "Yes, son, you're perfectly right. And he walked everywhere he went."

Angry golfer to wife: "One day you'll drive me out of my mind."

Wife: "That would be a putt, dear."

Two women meet on a cruise ship. One says, "This is my first cruise. My husband saved for ages to send me on this trip."

"Oh," says the other. "Is this your first? I've been on twenty cruises. Mind you, my husband works for Cunard."

The first woman says, "Well, mine works hard too, but there's no need to swear."

Did you hear about the Conservative MP who, when drunk, revealed such terrifying views to a journalist that he was dumped by his local party organization, ostracised by his former friends and had to go and live in Australia? He is now a far off terror Tory.

❖

A husband and wife are on holiday. "Oh my God!" exclaims the wife. "I just remembered I left the oven on."

"Don't worry about it," replies her husband. "The house won't burn down. I just remembered I left the bath running."

Little Leroy came into the kitchen where his mother was making dinner. His birthday was coming up and he thought this was a good time to tell his mother what he wanted.

"Mum, I want a bike for my birthday."

Little Leroy was a bit of a troublemaker. He had gotten into trouble at school and at home. Leroy's mother asked him if he thought he deserved to get a bike for his birthday.

Little Leroy, of course, thought he did.

Leroy's mother, being a religious woman, wanted Leroy to reflect on his behaviour over the last year.

"Go to your room, Leroy, and think about how you have behaved this year. Then write a letter to God and tell him why you deserve a bike for your birthday."

Little Leroy stomped up the steps to his room and sat down to write God a letter.

Letter #1:

"Dear God,

I have been a very good boy this year and I would like a bike for my birthday. I want a red one.

Your friend, Leroy."

Leroy knew that wasn't true. He had not been a very good boy this year so he tore up the letter and started over.

Letter #2:

"Dear God,

I have been an OK boy this year. I still would really like a bike for my birthday.

Leroy."

Leroy knew he could not send this letter to God either. So he wrote a third letter.

167

Letter #3:

"God,

I know I haven't been a good boy this year. I am very sorry. I will be a good boy if you just send me a bike for my birthday. Please!

Thank you,

Leroy."

Leroy knew, even if it was true, this letter was not going to get him a bike.

By now Leroy was very upset. He went downstairs and told his mom that he wanted to go to church. Leroy's mother thought her plan had worked as Leroy looked very sad.

"Just be home in time for dinner," Leroy's mother told him.

Leroy walked down the street to the church on the corner. Little Leroy went into the church and up to the altar. He looked around to see if anyone was there.

Leroy bent down and picked up a statue of the Virgin Mary. He slipped it under his shirt and ran out of the church, down the street, into the house, and up to his room and sat down with a piece of paper and a pen.

Leroy began to write yet another letter to God.

Letter #4:

"God, I've got your mama. If you want to see her again, send the bike!

Signed,

YOU KNOW WHO."

❖

A man was proudly showing off his new apartment to friends. "What is the big brass gong and hammer for?" one of his friends asked.

"That is the talking clock," the man replied.

"How's it work?"

"Watch," the man said and proceeded to give the gong an ear shattering pound with the hammer. Suddenly, someone screamed from the other side of the wall, "Knock it off, you idiot! It's two o'clock in the morning!"

Little boy to grandfather: "Are you still growing, granddad?"

Grandfather: "I don't think so. Why do you ask?"

Boy: "It's just that the top of your head's coming out through your hair."

A man is flying in a hot air balloon and realizes he is lost. He reduces height and spots a man down below. He lowers the balloon further and shouts: "Excuse me, can you help me? I promised my friend I would meet him half an hour ago, but I don't know where I am."

The man below says: "Yes. You are in a hot air balloon, hovering approximately 30 feet above this field. You are between 40 and 42 degrees N. latitude, and between 58 and 60 degrees W. longitude."

"You must be an engineer," says the balloonist.

"I am," replies the man. "How did you know?"

"Well," says the balloonist, "everything you have told me is technically correct, but I have no idea what to make of your information, and the fact is I am still lost."

The man below says, "You must be a manager."

"I am," replies the balloonist, "but how did you know?"

"Well," says the man, "you don't know where you are, or where you are going. You have made a promise which you have no idea how to keep, and you expect me to solve your problem. The fact is you are in the exact same position you were in before we met, but now it is somehow my fault."

❖

An Indian chief has three wives living in three wigwams, and one day he offers them new bedcovers. The first asks for a buffalo hide as a cover, and this is duly delivered. The second wife asks for a bearskin hide, and, although this is more dangerous to catch, one is eventually brought to her. The third wife is the youngest and prettiest, and she asks for a hippopotamus skin as a bedcover. This proves extremely difficult to find, but eventually she has her wish. Nine months later the first wife gives birth to a boy, the second wife gives birth a girl, and the third wife has twins, a boy and a girl. Which goes to prove that the squaw on the hippopotamus is equal to the sum of the squaws on the other two hides.

❖

The young woman was visiting the male psychiatrist for the first time, and he decided to test her reactions to different pictures.

First, he held up a card on which had been drawn two circles that almost touched.

"What does this make you think of?" asked the psychiatrist.

"Two fat people about to make love," replied the young woman.

The psychiatrist showed the woman a picture of two wavy lines.

"That looks like the sand on the beach after two people have made passionate love for hours – or maybe it's a waterbed rocking in motion to some lovers in action."

"Hmm," said the psychiatrist, leaning back in his chair. "You seem to be overly preoccupied with sex."

"How dare you!" snapped the woman. "It was *you* who showed me the sexy pictures."

❖

A couple of country boys are hunting in the woods when one suddenly collapses. His friend dials the emergency services on his mobile phone and shouts to the operator, "Help me. My friend is dead! What can I do?"

The operator tries to calm him down. "Take it easy," she says. "The first thing to do is make sure he really is dead."

The next thing the operator hears is the man putting down the phone, then a rifle shot. The man picks up the phone again, "OK, so what's next … ?"

❖

A golfer is thrashing through the bushes, looking for a lost ball. An old lady watches him as she sits on a bench, knitting. After half an hour the golfer is just about to give up when the old lady says, "Excuse me, but is it against the rules if I tell you where it is?"

❖

Mick is in court for a double murder. The judge says, "You are charged with beating your wife to death with a spanner."

A man at the back of the courtroom yells out, "You bastard!"

The judge continues, "You are also charged with beating your wife's lover to death with a spanner."

The man yells out, "You absolute bastard!"

The judge looks at the man and says, "Sir, I can understand your anger at these crimes, but I will have no more outbursts. If you have anything to say, say it now."

The man gets up and says, "For fifteen years I lived next door to that bastard. And every time I asked to borrow a bloody spanner, he said he didn't have one."

❖

My youngest son thinks that a wombat is a thing you use to play wom.

❖

Three passengers are on a train discussing why the train company is losing money.

"Bad management," says one.

"Too many staff," says another.

"Not enough investment," says the third.

Then they hear the ticket inspector coming and all run to hide in the toilets.

A man phones a taxi company because his cab hasn't turned up. "I'm supposed to be at the airport for nine o'clock," says the man.

"Don't worry," says the girl. "The taxi will get you there before your plane leaves."

"I know it will," says the man. "I'm the pilot."

There was a man that owned a giant gorilla and, all its life, he'd never left it on its own.

But eventually he had to go on a business trip and had to leave his gorilla in the care of his next-door neighbour.

So he explained to his neighbour that all he had to do was feed his gorilla three bananas a day at three, six and nine o'clock.

But he was never ever, ever to touch its fur.

So the next day the man came and gave the gorilla a banana and looked at it for a while thinking, "Why can't I touch its fur?" as their didn't seem to be anything wrong with it.

Every day he came in and looked for a little while longer as he still couldn't understand until, about a week later, he'd worked himself into a frenzy and decided that he was going to touch the gorilla.

He passed it the banana and very gently brushed the back of his hand against its fur.

Suddenly the gorilla went crazy and started to jump around, then it turned and began running towards the man who, in turn, ran through the front door, over the lawn, across the street, into some one else's sports car and drove off.

In the rear-view mirror, he could see the gorilla in its own sports car, driving right behind him.

He drove for two hours until the engine began to splutter and the car just stopped. He jumped out and began to run down the street, over a brick wall, into someone's front garden and up the apple tree.

He turned around to find the gorilla right behind him beating its chest.

The man jumped down and ran back in to the street screaming, until it became dark and he thought he'd lost the gorilla.

The man ran into an alleyway then, suddenly, he saw a giant shadow coming down the street ahead.

The gorilla!

It came to the end of the alley, stood and looked straight into the bloodshot eyes of the man and came towards him slowly.

This time there was no escape. As the gorilla neared him, the man began to feel faint.

The giant beast came face to face with him, raised its mighty hand and said, "Tag! You're it!"

A woman is sitting in the park with her baby when a man comes over and says, "I'm sorry, lady, but that's the ugliest baby I've ever seen!"

The woman bursts into tears. Another man sees this and comes over to comfort her. He hands her a tissue and says, "Miss, I don't know what that guy said, but it's not worth crying over."

She smiles back at him as he reaches into his pocket.

"You cheer up now. Look, I've even got some peanuts for your monkey."

A man is playing Trivial Pursuit. He rolls the dice and lands on Science and Nature. The question is: 'If you are in a vacuum and someone calls you name, can you hear it?' The man thinks for a moment before asking, "Is the vacuum on or off?"

An artist asked the gallery owner if there had been any interest in his paintings currently on display. "I've got good news and bad news," the owner replied. "The good news is that a gentleman inquired about your work and wondered if it would appreciate in value after your death. When I told him it would, he bought all fifteen of your paintings."

"That's wonderful!" the artist exclaimed, "What's the bad news?"

With concern, the gallery owner replied, "It was your doctor."

A twelfth-century sixpence was recently uncovered at an archaeological dig in Aberdeen. Gathered around it were four skeletons on their hands and knees.

A Scotsman gets a cab to take him and his girlfriend home. She's so beautiful he can hardly keep his eyes on the meter.

A man and a boy go into a barber's shop. The man has a trim then says to the boy, "You get your hair cut while I go to the supermarket and get some shopping." The boy has his hair cut, but the man doesn't return.

"Looks like your dad's forgotten you're here," says the barber.

"That wasn't my dad," replies the boy. "That guy grabbed me on the street and said, 'How would you like a free haircut?' and dragged me in here."

I'd like to smother my mother-in-law in diamonds. Then again, there has to be a cheaper way to do it.

Once upon a time, there was a cat who died. When she got to heaven, God asked her how she liked being on earth. She told the Lord that it was awful, that she had to sleep in cold back alleys, where there was no food and life was hard. God told her that he was sorry it had turned out that way, but here, in heaven, she would be happy and He would give her the most comfortable, warm pillow to sleep on.

The cat laid down upon the pillow and was happy.

A few days later, about a dozen mice came to heaven together and God asked them how they had liked earth.

The earth was no better for them than it was for the cat.

They explained to God that it was tough and exhausting and their feet were worn out from always running from cats and dogs and people. God felt bad for the mice and decided to give them roller-skates.

One day God saw the cat again and asked her how she was liking heaven. She explained that it was absolutely wonderful. The pillow he gave her was the most comfortable place that she had ever slept on, but even better than the pillow were the meals on wheels.

One afternoon, a man was riding in the back of his Rolls when he saw two men eating grass by the road side. He ordered his driver to stop and he got out to investigate. "Why are you eating grass?" he asked one man.

"We don't have any money for food," the poor man replied.

"Oh, come along with me then."

"But, sir, I have a wife with two children!"

"Bring them along! And you, come with me too!" he said to the other man.

"But, sir, I have a wife with six children!" the second man answered.

"Bring them as well!"

They all climbed into the car, which was no easy task, even for a car as large as the Rolls. Once underway, one of the poor fellows said, "Sir, you are too kind. Thank you for taking pity on us all."

The rich man replied, "No, you don't understand, the grass at my home is about three feet tall!"

A young bride and groom-to-be had just selected their wedding rings. As the young lady admired the plain platinum and diamond band she had chosen for herself, she suddenly looked concerned. "Tell me," she asked the rather elderly salesman, "is there anything special I'll have to do to take care of this ring?"

With a fatherly smile, the salesman said, "One of the best ways to protect a wedding ring is to soak it in dishwater."

Three men are sentenced to twenty years of solitary confinement. However, they're each allowed one luxury to take to their cells. The first man asks for a stack of law books. The second man asks for a pile of medical books. And the third man asks for two hundred cartons of cigarettes. At the end of the twenty years they open up the first man's cell. He comes out and says, "I studied so hard that I can now qualify as a lawyer."

They open up the second man's door. He says, "After all that learning I can now become a doctor."

They open up the third man's door. He comes out and says, "Anybody got a match?"

President Calvin Coolidge once invited friends from is home town to dine at the White House. Worried about their table manners, the guests decided to do everything that Coolidge did. This strategy succeeded until coffee was served. The president poured his coffee into the saucer. The guests did the same. The president added sugar and cream. The guests did the same.

Then Coolidge bent down and put his saucer on the floor for the cat.

A man enters a barber's shop for a shave. While the barber is foaming him up, the man mentions the problem he has getting a close shave around his cheeks.

"I have just what you need," says the barber, giving him a small wooden ball. "Just place this between your cheek and gum."

The man does so and the barber starts to give him the closest shave the man has ever experienced. After a few moments the client says, "Hey, what if I swallow this thing?"

"No problem," replies the barber. "Just bring it back tomorrow like everyone else."

The shop steward announces the results of negotiations with the employers. "From now on," he tells his members, "all wages are going to be doubled, holidays will be six months a year, and we are only going to have to work on Friday."

"What!" comes a cry from the back of the hall. "Every bloody Friday?"

A man goes into a barber's shop and notices that a little dog is watching the barber intently.

"That dog seems very interested in what you're up to," says the man.

"He's hoping for a treat," replies the barber, sharpening his razor. "If I sneeze he sometimes gets a bit of ear."

President Clinton and Hillary are in the front row at the Yankee Stadium. The row behind them is taken up with secret service agents. One of them leans over and whispers in the president's ear. Clinton nods, then grabs Hillary by the scruff of the neck and heaves her over the railing. The secret service agent leans over again and says, "Mr President, I said, 'It's time to throw out the first pitch.'"

Two old soldiers are sitting in their club. One turns to the other and says, "When was the last time you made love to a woman?"

He thinks for a moment, then says, "1947."

"Good heavens," says his pal. "That's a very long time ago."

"Not really," he says. "It's only five past eight now."

A defence lawyer meets with his client. "The blood tests have come back, and we have good news and bad news."

"So what's the bad news?" asks the client.

"Your DNA matches the blood found on the victim, the murder weapon and the getaway car."

"Oh!" says the defendant. "So what's the good news?"

The lawyer replies, "Your cholesterol is down to 120."

The George W. Bush Presidential Library has just been destroyed by fire. Tragically, both books were lost, and he hadn't even finished colouring in the second one.

A woman was trying hard to get the ketchup to come out of the bottle. During her struggle the phone rang so she asked her four-year-old daughter to answer the phone.

"It's the vicar, mummy," the child said to her mother. Then she added, "Mummy can't come to the phone right now. She's hitting the bottle."

A policeman has just pulled a car over. The man rolls down the window and says, "What's the problem, officer?"

"I stopped you for running that red light behind you."

Just then the man's wife leans forward from the driver's seat and says with a very loud voice, "I told him to stop at that light. But did he listen? No. He just kept right on going."

The man turns to his wife and yells, "Shut up, stupid!"

The policeman continues, "And just before the light I clocked you doing 50 m.p.h. and the speed limit is only 30."

His wife leans forward again and squawks, "I told him to slow down. But did he listen to me. No! He never listens to me."

And again the man shouts at his wife, "Listen, stupid, I told you to SHUT UP!"

The policeman looks at the woman and says, "Does he always talk to you this way?"

"Only when he has been drinking."

When the train comes out of the tunnel Claudia Schiffer and the Scotsman are sitting as if nothing has happened, and the Englishman is nursing a sore face.

The Englishman is thinking, "The Scottish fella must have kissed Claudia Schiffer, she slapped him but missed and got me instead."

Claudia Schiffer is thinking, "My God, that English fella

181

must have tried to kiss me, kissed the Scotsman instead and got slapped for it."

The Scotsman is thinking, "This is great. The next time the train goes through a tunnel I'll make that kissing noise and slap the Englishman again."

The Mafia in New York was looking for a new man to make weekly collections from all the private businesses that they were 'protecting.'

Feeling the heat from the police force, they decide to use a deaf person for this job.

If he were to get caught, he wouldn't be able to communicate to the police what he was doing.

Well, on his first week, the deaf collector picks up over $40,000.

He gets greedy, decides to keep the money and stashes it in a safe place.

The Mafia soon realizes that their collection is late, and sends some of their hoods after the deaf collector.

The hoods find the deaf collector and ask him where the money is.

The deaf collector can't communicate with them, so the Mafia drags the guy to an interpreter.

The Mafia hood says to the interpreter, "Ask him where the money is."

The interpreter signs, "Where's the money?"

The deaf man replies, "I don't know what you're talking about."

The interpreter tells the hood, "He says he doesn't know what you're talking about."

The hood pulls out a .38 and places it in the ear of the deaf collector. "Now ask him where the money is!"

The interpreter signs, "Where is the money?"

The deaf man replies, "The $40,000 is in a tree stump in Central Park."

The interpreter says to the hood, "He says he still doesn't know what you're talking about, and doesn't think you have the nerve to pull the trigger."

A neutron walks into a bar. "I'd like a beer," he says. The bartender promptly serves up a beer. "How much will that be?" asks the neutron.

"For you?" replies the bartender. "No charge."

A mathematician, a physicist and an engineer were all given a red rubber ball and told to find the volume. The mathematician carefully measured the diameter and evaluated a triple integral. The physicist filled a beaker, put the ball in the water and measured the total displacement. The engineer looked up the model and serial numbers in his red-rubber-ball table.

Driving to work, a man had to swerve to avoid a box that fell out of a truck in front of him. Seconds later, a policeman pulled him over for reckless driving. Fortunately, another officer had seen the carton in the road. The policemen stopped traffic and recovered the box. It was found to contain large upholstery tacks.

"I'm sorry, sir," the first policeman told the driver, "but I am still going to have to book you."

Amazed, the driver asked for what.

The trooper replied, "Tacks evasion."

An Englishman, an Irishman and a Scotsman walk into a pub and buy beers. Just as they raise their drinks to their lips, a fly lands in each of the pints. The Englishman pushes his beer away in disgust. The Irishman fishes the fly out of his beer and carries on drinking. The Scotsman picks the fly out of his drink and starts shaking it, "Spit it oot, ye thieving wee bastard! Spit it oot … !"

❖

A policeman was patrolling a local parking spot overlooking a golf course. He drove by a car and saw a couple inside with the interior light on. There was a young man in the driver's seat reading a computer magazine and a young lady in the back seat knitting. He stopped to investigate. He walked up to the driver's window and knocked. The young man looked up, cranked the window down, and said, "Yes, officer?"

"What are you doing?" the policeman asked.

"What does it look like?" answered the young man. "I'm reading this magazine."

Pointing towards the young lady in the back seat, the officer then asked, "And what is she doing?"

The young man looked over his shoulder and replied, "What does it look like? She's knitting."

"And how old are you?" the officer then asked the young man.

"I'm nineteen," he replied.

"And how old is she?" asked the officer.

The young man looked at his watch and said, "Well, in about twelve minutes she'll be sixteen."

A man on a business trip in Mexico decides to take in a bull fight. After the event, he stops in the little dive next to the venue called 'The Matador'.

As he checks out the menu trying to decide what he wants he sees a waiter bring a dish to another customer. The dish is spaghetti with these two huge meat balls. When the waiter comes to his table, he inquires.

"That is the Matador Special," replies the waiter. "Spaghetti and Bull testicles. We get them after the bull fight. It is exquisite!"

"That's what I'll have!" says the businessman.

"I'm very sorry, senor, but that dish is only available once per day."

Disappointed, the man orders another dish and plans to try again the next day.

So again, the next day he goes to the bull fights, and afterwards stops in the dive. Just as the waiter is coming to his table, he sees another waiter bringing the Matador Special to another customer who was there before him.

"Damn!" he says to himself. "And tomorrow's my last day here."

So the next day, he skips the bull fight, and stands in line at the cafe. He is the first one seated, and proudly

proclaims, "I'll have the Matador Special!"

"Very well, senor!" responds the waiter. Soon afterwards, the waiter brings out his dish, but the meat balls are disappointingly small. Very small, as a matter of fact.

"What's with this!" the now angry man shouts.

"I'm very sorry, senor," says the waiter, "but the bull does not always lose!"

A large two-engined train was crossing America. After they had gone some distance one of the engines broke down. *No problem*, the engineer thought, and carried on at half power.

Farther on down the line, the other engine broke down, and the train came to a standstill.

The engineer decided he should inform the passengers about why the train had stopped, and made the following announcement:

"Ladies and gentlemen, I have some good news and some bad news. The bad news is that both engines have failed, and we will be stuck here for some time. The good news is that you decided to take the train and not fly."

Where can you catch a ghost train? At a manifestation.

One night, Tim was walking home when, all of a sudden, a thief jumped on him. Tim and the thief began to wrestle. They rolled about on the ground and Tim put up a tremendous fight. However, the thief managed to get the better of him and pinned him to the ground. The thief then went through Tim's pockets and searched him. All the thief could find on Tim was 25p. The thief was so surprised at this that he asked Tim why he had bothered to fight so hard for 25p.

"Was that all you wanted?" Tim replied. "I thought you were after the five hundred quid I've got in my shoe!"

A man goes into a barber's shop and asks for a haircut that leaves his fringe at different lengths round his head, creates two bald spots near the back, a spiky bit at the side and leaves a large nick on his ear.

"I'm not sure we could manage that," says the barber. "It sounds pretty tricky."

"I don't see why," says the man. "It's the same haircut you gave me the last time I was here."

When I went on a diet of baked beans and garlic all I lost was ten friends.

How do you spot a Scottish ship? It's the one not being followed by seagulls.

A Russian, an American and a blonde get talking.

The Russian says, "We were first in space!"

The American says, "We were first on the moon!"

The blonde says, "So what? We're going to be the first on the sun!"

"You can't land on the sun, you idiot!" says the Russian. "You'll burn up!"

The blonde replies, "Duhhh. We're going at night!"

A man walks up to the bar with an ostrich behind him and, as he sits, the bartender asks for their order.

The man says, "I'll have a beer," and turns to the ostrich. "What's yours?"

"I'll have a beer too," says the ostrich.

The bartender pours the beer and says, "That will be $3.40 please," and the man reaches into his pocket and pays with the exact change for payment.

The next day, the man and the ostrich come again, and the man says, "I'll have a beer."

The ostrich says, "I'll have the same."

Once again the man reaches into his pocket and pays with exact change.

This became a routine until late one evening, the two enter again. "The usual?" asks the bartender.

"Well, it's close to last call, so I'll have a large Scotch," says the man.

"Same for me," says the ostrich.

"That will be $7.20," says the bartender.

Once again the man pulls exact change out of his pocket and places it on the bar.

The bartender can't hold back his curiosity any longer. "Excuse me, sir. How do you manage to always come up with the exact change out of your pocket every time?"

"Well," says the man, "several years ago I was cleaning the attic and I found this old lamp. When I rubbed it a Genie appeared and offered me two wishes. My first wish was that if I ever needed to pay for anything, I just put my hand in my pocket and the right amount of money would be there."

"That's brilliant!" says the bartender. "Most people would wish for a million dollars or something, but you'll always be as rich as you want for as long as you live!"

"That's right! Whether it's a gallon of milk, or a Rolls Royce, the exact money is always there," says the man.

"That's fantastic!" says the bartender. "You are a genius! ... Oh, one other thing, sir, what's with the ostrich?"

The man replies, "Oh, my second wish was for a chick with long legs."

Sign outside a Scottish cinema: "Free admission for old age pensioners if accompanied by both parents."

A man was in the doctor's waiting room and a young man came in with an expensive watch for the doctor.

"Thank you, thank you, thank you!" said the man, giving the doctor the expensive watch. "This is a small token of my thanks for all your excellent treatment of my uncle."

"But he died last week," said the doctor.

"I know," replied the young man. "Thanks to your treatment I've just inherited five million pounds."

A couple go on holiday to a fishing resort in northern Minnesota.

The husband likes to fish at the crack of dawn. The wife likes to read.

One morning the husband returns after several hours of fishing and decides to take a nap.

Although not familiar with the lake, the wife decides to take the boat out. She motors out a short distance, anchors, and continues to read her book.

Along comes a game warden in his boat. He pulls up alongside the woman and says, "Good morning, Ma'am. What are you doing?"

"Reading a book," she replies (thinking it was obvious).

"You're in a restricted fishing area," he informs her.

"I'm sorry, officer, but I'm not fishing, I am reading," she replies.

"Yes, but you have all the equipment. I'll have to take you in and write you up," the warden says.

"If you do that, I'll have to charge you with sexual assault," says the woman.

"But I haven't even touched you!" says the game warden.

"That's true, but you have all the equipment."

"Doctor, Doctor! Every time I eat fruit I get this strange urge to give people all my money."

"Would you like an apple or a banana?"

A school class goes on a field trip to the local police station where they see pictures of the country's ten most wanted criminals. A little boy points to a picture and asks if it really is the photo of a wanted person.

"Yes," says the policeman. "The detectives want to capture him very badly."

The boy replies, "So why didn't you keep him when you took his picture?"

A man is driving home late one afternoon above the speed limit. He notices a police car with its lights on in his rear view mirror. He thinks, *I can outrun him*, so he floors it and the race is on. The cars are racing down the road: 60, 70, 80, 90 miles an hour.

Finally, as his speedometer passes 100, the man thinks, *what the heck*, and gives up. He pulls over to the kerb.

The police officer gets out of his car and approaches the man. He leans down and says, "Listen, mister, I've had a really lousy day, and I just want to go home. Give me a good excuse and I'll let you go."

The man thought for a moment and says, "Three weeks ago, my wife ran off with a police officer. When I saw your car in my rear view mirror, I thought that you were the officer and that you were trying to give her back to me!"

An old lady is at her husband's funeral. She tells her granddaughter that throughout their married life they had enjoyed physical relations each and every Sunday morning in time to the church bells.

"Maybe he was getting a bit old for that sort of thing,"

says the granddaughter.

"Nonsense," replies the old lady. "If it hadn't been for that ice cream van he'd be alive today."

Bernie was invited to his friend's home for dinner. Morris, the host, preceded every request to his wife by endearing terms, calling her Honey, My Love, Darling, Sweetheart, Pumpkin, etc. Bernie looked at Morris and remarked, "It's really nice that after all the years you have been married, you keep calling your wife those pet names."

Morris hung his head and whispered, "To tell the truth, I forgot her name about three years ago."

A philosophy teacher stood before her class and had some items in front of her. When the class began, silently she picked up a large empty mayonnaise jar and proceeded to fill it with stones. She then asked the students if the jar was full? They agreed that it was. So the professor then picked up a box of pebbles and poured them into the jar. She shook the jar lightly. The pebbles, of course, rolled into the open areas between the stones. She then asked the students again if the jar was full. They again agreed it was.

The teacher picked up a box of sand and poured it into the jar. Of course, the sand filled up everything else.

"Now," said the professor, "I want you to recognize that this is your life. The stones are the important things - your family, your partner, your health, your children - things that if everything else was lost and only they remained, your life would still be full. The pebbles are the other things that matter like your job, your house, your car. The sand is everything else. The small stuff. If you put the sand into the jar first, there is no room for the pebbles or the stones. The same goes for your life. If you spend all your time and energy on the small stuff, you will never have room for the things that are important to you.

Pay attention to the things that are critical to your happiness. Play with your children. Take time to get medical check-ups. Take your partner out dancing. There will always be time to go to work, clean the house, give a dinner party and fix the disposal. Take care of the stones first - the things that really matter. Set your priorities. The rest is just sand."

A student then took the jar which the other students and the professor agreed was full, and proceeded to pour in a glass of beer. Of course the beer filled the remaining spaces within the jar making the jar truly full.

The moral of this tale is that no matter how full your life is, there is always room for BEER.

Why don't Scotsmen buy fridges? They don't believe the light goes out when you close the door.

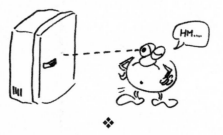

A man and a priest are playing golf. The man takes his first shot, misses and says, "Jesus, damnit, I missed."

The priest is shocked. "Don't use that kind of language or God will punish you."

The man takes his second shot but misses again. Under his breath he says, "Jesus effing Christ …"

The priest overhears him and says, "My son, please refrain from blasphemy or God will surely punish you."

The man takes his shot and misses again. He can't help himself and mutters, "Jesus H Christ, I missed again …"

Suddenly a bolt of lightning strikes down and kills the priest. From the clouds a booming voice mutters, "Oh, Jesus, missed again ..."

A Texan bought a round of drinks for all in the bar and said that his wife had just produced a typical Texas baby weighing twenty pounds.

Two weeks later he returned to the bar. The bartender recognized him and asked, "Aren't you the father of the typical Texas baby that weighed twenty pounds at birth?"

"Yup, sure am!"

"How much does he weigh now?"

The proud father answered, "Ten pounds."

The bartender said, "Why, what happened? He did weigh twenty pounds."

The proud Texas father said, "Just had him circumcised!"

What's the difference between a Yorkshire man and a coconut?

You can get a drink out of a coconut.

An eight-year-old boy went into a shop and picked out a large box of detergent. The grocer walked over and asked the boy if he had a lot of laundry to do. "Oh, no laundry," the boy said, "I'm going to wash my dog."

"But you shouldn't use this to wash your dog," said the grocer. "It's very powerful and if you wash your dog in this, he'll get sick. In fact, it might even kill him." But the boy was not to be stopped and carried the detergent to the counter and paid for it.

A week later, the boy was back in the store to buy some candy. The grocer asked the boy how his dog was doing. "Oh, he died," the boy said.

The grocer said he was sorry, but added, "I tried to tell you not to use that detergent on your dog."

"Well," the boy replied, "I don't think it was the detergent that killed him."

"Oh? What was it then?"

"I think it was the spin cycle!"

❖

While I was in the doctor's waiting room there was this tiny man only about six inches tall. Although he was there before me, he let me see the doctor first. I suppose he just had to be a little patient.

❖

What do you call a Scouser in a suit?
The accused.

❖

Mr and Mrs Smith and Mr and Mrs Brown had known each other for many years and frequently went on holiday together. This year Mr Smith suggested to Mr Brown that to add spice to their holiday, perhaps they should exchange partners. Mr Brown considered this for a moment, then agreed that it was a good idea. Both men got their wives to agree, too. Thus it was that after their first night in Malta, Mr Brown turned to his holiday partner in bed and said, "That was certainly exciting and different."

"Yes," said Mr Smith.

A mathematician, an accountant and an economist apply for the same job. The interviewer calls in the mathematician and asks, "What does two plus two equal?"

The mathematician replies, "Four."

The interviewer asks, "Four exactly?"

The mathematician looks at the interviewer incredulously and says, "Yes, four exactly."

Then the interviewer calls in the accountant and asks the same question, "What does two plus two equal?"

The accountant says, "On average, four - give or take ten percent - but on average, four."

Then the interviewer calls in the economist and poses the same question, "What does two plus two equal?"

The economist gets up, locks the door, closes the shade, sits down next to the interviewer and says, "What do you want it to equal?"

Two hunters in America are dragging a dead deer back to their truck when a man approaches them and says, "Y'know it's much easier if you drag it the other way round – then the antlers won't dig into the ground and slow you up." The hunters try this method and make good progress.

The first hunter says the other, "That guy really knew what he was talking about, didn't he?"

"Yes," replies the second hunter, "but on the other hand we are getting further away from the truck."

"Darling, just imagine – we've now been married for twenty-four hours."

"Yes, dear, it's incredible. And it seems as if it was only yesterday."

A driver tucked this note under the windshield wiper of his car. "I've circled the block for 20 minutes. I'm late for an appointment and if I don't park here I'll lose my job. Forgive us our trespasses."

When he came back he found a parking ticket and this note: "I've circled the block for 20 years, and if I don't give you a ticket, I'll lose my job. Lead us not into temptation."

A man has been drinking at the golf club. On his way home his car is pulled over by the police, who tell him he's too drunk to drive. "Too drunk to drive?" responds the drunk. "I can barely putt."

An old farmer and his wife were leaning against the edge of their pig-sty when the old woman wistfully recalled that the next week would mark their golden wedding anniversary.

"Let's have a party," she suggested. "Let's kill a pig."

The farmer scratched his grizzled head. "Well, Ethel," he finally answered, "I don't see why the pig should take the blame for something that happened fifty years ago."

❖

A reporter goes to Israel to cover the fighting. She is looking for something emotional and positive and of human interest. Something like that guy in Sarajevo who risked his life to play the cello everyday in the town square.

In Jerusalem, she heard about an old Jew who had been

going to the Wailing Wall to pray, twice a day, every day, for a long, long time. So she went to check it out. She goes to the Wailing Wall and there he is! She watches him pray and after about 45 minutes, when he turns to leave, she approaches him for an interview.

"Rebecca Smith, CNN News. Sir, how long have you been coming to the Wailing Wall and praying?"

"For about 50 years."

"What do you pray for?"

"For peace between the Jews and the Arabs. For all the hatred to stop. For all of our children to grow up in safety and friendship."

"How do you feel after doing this for 50 years?"

"Like I'm talking to a bloody wall!"

An old man goes to his doctor and says, "Can you give me something to lower my sex drive."

The doctor replies, "I would have thought at your age it's all in the mind."

"It is," agrees the old man. "That's why I want it lower."

❖

A man is driving down a country road, when he spots a farmer standing in the middle of a huge field of grass. He pulls the car over to the side of the road and notices that the farmer is just standing there, doing nothing, looking at nothing.

The man gets out of the car, walks all the way out to the farmer and asks him, "Ah, excuse me, mister, but what are you doing?"

The farmer replies, "I'm trying to win a Nobel Prize."

"How?" asks the man, puzzled.

"Well, I heard they give the Nobel Prize . . . to people who are out standing in their field."

❖

Signs That You are Too Drunk

You lose arguments with inanimate objects.

You have to hold onto the lawn to keep from falling off the earth.

Your job is interfering with your drinking.

Your doctor finds traces of blood in your alcohol stream.

The back of your head keeps getting hit by the toilet seat.

You sincerely believe alcohol is the elusive 5th food group.

24 hours in a day, 24 beers in a case - coincidence? I think not!

Two hands and just one mouth - now THAT'S a drinking problem!

You can focus better with one eye closed.

The car park seems to have moved while you were in the pub.

You fall off the floor.

Hey, 5 beers has just as many calories as a hamburger, screw dinner!

Mosquitoes catch a buzz after attacking you.

At AA meetings you begin: 'My name is.. uh..'

Your idea of cutting back is to cut out the peanuts.

You wake up in the bedroom, your underwear is in the bathroom, you fell asleep clothed.

The whole pub says 'Hi' when you come in.

You think the four basic food groups are caffeine, nicotine, alcohol, and women.

Every night you're beginning to find your cat more and more attractive.

You don't recognize the wife unless you see her through the bottom of a glass.

That damned pink elephant followed you home again.

You're as sober as a judge.

The shrubbery's drunk from too frequent watering.

Stages of Drunkenness

0 - Stone cold sober. Brain as sharp as an army bayonet.

1 - Still sober. Pleasure senses activated. Feeling of well-being.

2 - Lager warming up head. Barmaid complimented on choice of blouse.

3 - Crossword in newspaper is filled in. After a while blanks are filled with random letters and numbers.

4 - Barmaid complimented on choice of bra, partially visible when bending to get packets of crisps. Try to instigate conversation about bras. Order half a dozen packets of crisps one by one.

5 - Have brilliant discussion with guy on the next bar stool. Devise fool-proof scheme for wining lottery, sort out Manchester United's problems.

6 - Feel like a Demi-God. Map out rest of life on cigarette packet. Realize that everybody loves you. Call parents and tell them you love them. Call girlfriend to tell her you love her and she still has an amazing figure.

7 - Send drinks over to woman sitting at table with

boyfriend. No reaction. Scribble out message of love on five cocktail napkins and Frisbee them to her across the room. Boyfriend asks you outside. You buy him a Slim Panatela.

8 - Some slurring. Offer to buy drinks for everyone in room. Lots of people say yes. Go round the bar hugging them one by one. Fall over. Get up.

9 - Head-ache kicks in. Beer tastes off. Send it back. Next bottle comes back tasting same. Say, "That's much better." Fight nausea by trying to play old Space Invaders game for ten minutes before seeing out of order sign.

10 - Some doubling of vision. Stand on table shouting abuse at all four barmen. Talked down by barmaid, who you offer to give a baby to. Fall over. Get up. Fall over. Impale head on corner of table. Fail to notice oozing head wound.

11 - Speech no longer possible. Eventually manage to find door. Sit and take stock. Realize you are sitting in pub cellar, having taken a wrong turning. Vomit. Pass out.

12 - Put in cab by somebody. Give home address. Taken home. Can't get key in door. Realize you've given address of your local gym. Generally pleased at way evening has gone. Pass out again.

The thing I really like about the *Oxford Dictionary of Differential Calculus* is that it doesn't try to glamorise the subject in any way.

An astronomer, a physicist and a mathematician are holidaying in Scotland. Glancing from a train window, they see a black sheep in the middle of a field.

"How interesting," observes the astronomer. "All Scottish sheep are black."

The physicist responds, "No, no! Only some Scottish sheep are black."

The mathematician tells them, "In Scotland there exists

at least one field, containing at least one sheep, of which at least one side is black."

A passenger in a taxi tapped the driver on the shoulder to ask him something. The driver screamed, lost control of the cab, nearly hit a bus, drove up over the curb and stopped just inches from a large plate glass window.

For a few moments everything was silent in the cab, then the driver said, "Please, don't ever do that again. You scared the daylights out of me."

The passenger, who was also frightened, apologized and said he didn't realize that a tap on the shoulder could frighten him so much, to which the driver replied, "I'm sorry, it's really not your fault at all. Today is my first day driving a cab. For the last 25 years I've been driving a hearse."

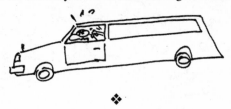

As they lay in bed on the first day of their honeymoon, John turned to his wife and sighed, "Darling, I hope you can put up with my ugly face for the rest of your life."

"That's all right, dear," she replied. "You'll be out at work all day."

"Last week my friend, Mabel, was feeling terribly ill, so her husband phoned the doctor's surgery.

"I'm afraid the doctor is busy until 10 a.m. on Thursday," said the receptionist.

"But that's three days away! My wife is terribly ill," pleaded Mabel's husband. "What if she's dead by then?"

201

"Well," replied the receptionist, "you can always phone and cancel the appointment."

The car dealer tried to sell me a car that he said was in mint condition. It had a hole in the middle.

A man comes across four golfers in a bunker. One of the golfers is lying on the sand, and the other three are arguing.

"What's the matter?" asks the man.

One of the golfers turns to him and says, "These swine will do anything to win a game. My partner's just had a stroke, and they want to add it to our score."

A man is travelling with his wife and mother-in-law in a middle-eastern country. At a sacred place his mother-in-law makes a careless remark, which the native people take as an insult to the royal family.

The man is dragged off to court with his wife and mother-in-law and they are sentenced to corporal punishment. Each of them is to receive 50 lashes on the rear end with a cane. But because the royal family doesn't wish to appear hostile to foreigners, they grant the guests in their country a wish beforehand, as long as it is capable of being fulfilled.

The wife is first.

"What do you wish for yourself?"

"I would like a pillow bound on my rear end before the lashings."

"Okay, that shall be granted to you."

She has the pillow bound to her rear end and receives her punishment. But because the pillow is too small and the executioner also hits her back a couple of times, she receives a few blows.

Next it is the mother-in-law's turn.

"What do you wish for yourself?"

"I would like a pillow bound on my rear end and a pillow bound on my back before the lashings."

"Okay, that shall be granted to you."

The mother-in-law receives her fifty lashes, but hardly feels the pain through the pillows.

Then comes the man himself.

"What do you wish for yourself?"

"I have two wishes. Do you want to fulfil them for me?"

"Because you are a guest in our country, we want to fulfil your wishes for you, as long as they are reasonable."

"I would like 100 lashes instead of 50."

The executioner is surprised, but recovers again right away and replies, "Yes, that is a pious wish, it shall be granted to you. And what is your second wish?"

"I would like to have my mother-in-law bound to my back."

There was a couple who were in the iron and steel business. She did the ironing, while he went out stealing.

"How is your yearling coming along?" one gentleman asked another as they chatted in the Silver Ring at Ascot.

"It died," said the other.

"That must have lost you a fortune, with the training fees and everything," sympathised the first man.

"No, I made a profit actually," the owner chuckled. "I raffled him at £10 a ticket."

"Didn't anyone sue you for fraud?"

"No. The winner got a bit shirty, but I sent *him* his money back!"

A professor of chemistry wanted to teach his fifth grade class a lesson about the evils of liquor, so he produced an experiment that involved a glass of water, a glass of whisky, and two worms.

"Now, class. Observe the worms closely," said the professor as he put the first worm into the water. The worm in the water writhed about, happy as a worm in water could be.

The second worm, he put into the whisky. It writhed painfully, and it quickly sank to the bottom, dead as a doornail. "Now, what lesson can we derive from this experiment?" the professor asked.

Little Johnny, who naturally sits in back, raised his hand and wisely, responded, "Drink whisky and you won't get worms!"

Two hydrogen atoms are talking. One says, "I think I've lost an electron."

The other asks, "Are you sure?"

The first replies, "Yes, I'm positive."

After all of the background checks, interviews, and testing were done there were three finalists for the CIA's assassin position — two men and one woman.

For the final test, the CIA agents took one of the men to a large metal door and handed him a gun.

"We must know that you will follow your instructions, no matter what the circumstances. Inside this room you will find your wife sitting in a chair. You have to kill her."

The first man said, "You can't be serious. I could never shoot my wife."

The agent replied, "Then you're not the right man for this job."

The second man was given the same instructions. He took the gun and went into the room.

All was quiet for about five minutes. Then the agent came out with tears in his eyes. "I tried, but I can't kill my wife."

The agent replied, "You don't have what it takes. Take your wife and go home."

Finally, it was the woman's turn. Only she was told to kill her husband. She took the gun and went into the room.

Shots were heard, one shot after another. They heard screaming, crashing, banging on the walls.

After a few minutes, all was quiet. The door opened slowly and there stood the woman.

She wiped the sweat from her brow and said, "You guys didn't tell me the gun was loaded with blanks. So I had to beat him to death with the chair."

A man finishes a terrible round of golf. He turns to his caddie and says, "I've never played that badly before."

"Really, sir," replies the caddie. "So you've played before, have you?"

The new employee stood before the paper shredder looking confused. "Need some help?" a secretary, walking by, asked.

"Yes," he replied, "how does this thing work?"

"Simple," she said, taking the fat report from his hand and feeding it into the shredder.

"Thanks," he said, "but where do the copies come out?"

A woman goes into a hunting shop. "I'm here for a gun for my husband," she says.

"We've got plenty of choice," says the shopkeeper. "What gauge did he ask you to get?"

"He didn't," replies the woman. "He doesn't even know I'm going to shoot him."

❖

One day a man took the train from Paris to Frankfurt. When he got in he said to the guard:

"Sir. I really need you to do me a favour. I have to get off this train in Mannheim, but I'm very tired and it is certain that I will fall asleep. So what I want you to do is wake me up in Mannheim because I have to close a business deal there and it is very important to me. Here is 100 euros for the favour. But I warn you sometimes when people wake me up I get really violent, but no matter what I do or say you must get me off this train in Mannheim. Is that clear?"

The guard agreed and took the 100 euros. Later as the man had said he fell asleep, and when he woke up he realised that he was in Frankfurt. He was so angry at the guard that he ran over and started yelling at him.

"Are you stupid or something? I paid you 100 euros to wake me up in Mannheim. And you didn't, so I want my money back!"

While the man was yelling, two other guys who were also on the train were looking at them. One turned to the other and said:

Man 1: "Look at this guy! He is really angry!"

Man 2: "Yeah! He's almost as angry as the bloke they threw off the train in Mannheim."

A man walked into the office of the eminent psychiatrist. "I keep hallucinating that I'm a dog, a large, white, hairy Pyrenean mountain dog. It's crazy. I don't know what to do!"

"A common canine complex," said the doctor soothingly. "Come over here and lie down on the couch."

"Oh no, Doctor. I'm not allowed up on the furniture."

Why don't women blink during foreplay? They don't have time.

A drunken man was wondering around the parking lot of a pub, bumping into then rubbing the roofs of the cars.

The manager comes out of the bar and stops him.

"What the heck are you doing ?" he asks the drunk.

"I'm looking for my car, and I can't find it." he replies.

"So how does feeling the roof help you ?" asks the puzzled manager.

"Well," replies the drunk earnestly, "My car has a blue light and a siren on the roof!"

My girlfriend can never understand why her brother has five sisters and she has only four.

❖

A mathematician, a biologist and a physicist are sitting in a street café watching people going in and coming out of the house on the other side of the street. First, they see two people going into the house. Time passes. After a while they notice three people coming out of the house.

The physicist says, "The measurement was accurate."

The biologist says, "They have reproduced."

The mathematician says, "If now exactly one person enters the house, it will be empty again."

❖

A man had been driving all night and by morning was still far from his destination. He decided to stop at the next city he came to, and park somewhere quiet so he could get an hour or two of sleep. As luck would have it, the quiet place he chose happened to be on one of the city's major jogging routes. No sooner had he settled back to snooze when there came a knocking on his window. He looked out and saw a jogger running in place.

"Yes?"

"Excuse me, sir," the jogger said, "do you have the time?"

The man looked at the car clock and answered, "8:15."

The jogger said thanks and left. The man settled back again, and was just dozing off when there was another knock on the window and another jogger.

"Excuse me, sir, do you have the time?"

"8:25!"

The jogger said thanks and left. Now the man could see other joggers passing by and he knew it was only a matter of time before another one disturbed him. To avoid the problem, he got out a pen and paper and put a sign in his window saying, 'I do not know the time!' Once again he settled back to sleep. He was just dozing off when there was another knock on the window.

"Sir, sir? It's 8:45!"

A car was involved in an accident in a street. As expected a large crowd gathered. A newspaper reporter, anxious to get his story could not get near the car.

Being a clever sort, he started shouting loudly, "Let me through! Let me through! I am the son of the victim."

The crowd made way for him.

Lying in front of the car was a donkey.

A college lecturer asks Susie to stand up and tell the class what part of the human body enlarges to seven times its original size when stimulated. Susie stands up and says, "Well, I think I know, but I'm too embarrassed to tell you."

The lecturer says, "Sit down, Susie. John, tell us what part of the human body enlarges to seven times its size when stimulated."

John says, "The pupil of the eye enlarges to seven times its original size when stimulated by light."

The lecturer says, "That's right." He then turns to Susie and says, "Two things: first, you have a dirty mind, and second, as far as men are concerned you're in for a big disappointment."

A man walks into a police station and drops a dead cat in front of the duty sergeant. "Someone threw this into my front garden," says the man.

"I'll take your name, sir," says the sergeant, "and if no one claims it in three months you can keep it."

A man walked into a pub on a slow night and sat down. After a few minutes, the bartender asked him if he wanted a drink, and he said, "No thanks, I don't drink, I tried it once but I didn't like it!"

So the bartender said, "Well, would you like a cigarette?"

The man said, "No, I don't smoke, I tried it once but I didn't like it!"

The bartender asked him if he'd like to play a game of pool, and again the man said, "No I don't like pool, I tried it once but I didn't like it. As a matter of fact I wouldn't be here at all, but I'm waiting for my son!"

The bartender said, "Your only son, I presume!!"

Seen in the local paper's classified section.
FOR SALE BY OWNER
Complete set of Encyclopaedia Britannica.
45 Volumes. Excellent condition.
£1000 pounds or best offer.

Reason for sale: No longer required.
Got married last weekend.
Wife knows everything.

One night, a father passed by his son's room and heard his son praying:

"God bless mummy, daddy, and grandma. Ta ta, grandpa."

The father didn't quite know what this meant, but was glad his son was praying.

The next morning, they found grandpa dead on the floor of a heart attack.

The father reassured himself that it was just a coincidence, but was still a bit spooked.

The next night, he heard his son praying again: "God bless mummy and daddy. Ta ta, grandma."

The father was worried, but decided to wait until morning.

Sure enough, the next morning grandma was on the floor, dead of a heart attack.

Really scared now, the father decided to wait outside his son's door the next night.

And sure enough, the boy started to pray: "God bless mummy. Ta ta, daddy."

Now the father was really scared..

He stayed up all night, and went to the doctor's early the next day to make sure his health was fine. When he finally came home, his wife was waiting on the porch.

She said, "Thank God you're here; we could really use your help! We found the milkman dead on our porch this morning!"

A US army platoon is on manoeuvres in the Florida swamps. The men are running low on water so the sergeant tells a private to go down to the creek and fill up their canteens. "But, Sarge," says the private. "I saw an alligator in the creek."

"Don't be such a coward," replies the sergeant. "That alligator is four times as frightened of you as you are of it."

"He might be," replies the private. "But even if he's only twice as frightened as me that water still won't be fit to drink."

What's the best way to kill a variety act? Go for the juggler.

A man takes his friend, a trader on the stock exchange, for his first game of golf. The man tees off and shouts, "Fore!"

The trader shouts back, "Three ninety-five."

A man turns to his co-workers and says, "I feel like punching the boss in the face again."

"What d'you mean 'again'?" asks one of his colleagues.

"I felt like punching him yesterday," says the man.

A man goes into a pub and says, "I'd like something tall, icy and full of gin."

The bartender turns and shouts into the kitchen, "Oi, Doris! Someone to see you."

Two lions are walking down the aisle of a supermarket. One turns to the other and says, "Quiet in here today, isn't it?"

A psychotherapist was doing a roaring trade since he set up his own business. So much so that he could now afford to have a proper shop sign advertising his wares. So he told a kid to paint the signboard for him and put it above his entrance.

But, instead of his business building up, it began to slacken. He had especially noticed the ladies shying away after reading the sign. So he decided to check it out himself.

The boy had found a small wooden board so he had split the word into:

Psycho-
the-
rapist.

❖

When buying an old second-hand car always insist on getting one with a heated rear window. That way, in winter you can warm your hands while you're pushing it.

❖

An elderly couple had been experiencing declining memories, so they decided to take a power memory class where one is taught to remember things by association.

A few days after the class, the old man was outside talking with his neighbour about how much the class helped him.

"What was the name of the instructor?" asked the neighbour.

"Oh, ummmm, let's see," the old man pondered. "You know that flower, you know, the one that smells really nice but has those prickly thorns. What's that flower's name?"

"A rose?" asked the neighbour.

"Yes, that's it," replied the old man. He then turned toward his house and shouted, "Hey, Rose, what's the name of the instructor we took the memory class from?"

A woman picks up a jumper in a clothes shop. "This is a little overpriced, isn't it?" she says to the shop assistant.

"Not really, madam," the assistant replies. "The wool comes from a rare breed of albino sheep only found in the highest mountain of Tibet. It's a beautiful yarn."

"Yes," replies the woman. "And you tell it so well."

An admiral is standing on the deck of his battleship when the enemy is spotted on the horizon. "Fetch my red shirt," says the admiral to a nearby midshipman. "If I'm wounded fighting the enemy ship I don't want the men to see that I'm bleeding."

"Excuse me, sir," says the midshipman. "But it's not one ship, there are fifteen."

"In that case," replies the admiral, "forget the shirt and pick up my brown trousers."

214

Reasons to allow drinking at work:

1. It's an incentive to show up.

2. It reduces stress.

3. It leads to more honest communications.

4. It reduces complaints about low pay.

5. It cuts down on time off because you can work with a hangover.

6. Employees tell management what they think, not what management wants to hear.

7. It helps save on heating costs in the winter.

8. It encourages carpooling.

9. Increases job satisfaction because if you have a bad job you don't care.

10. It eliminates vacations because people would rather come to work.

11. It makes fellow employees look better.

12. It makes the cafeteria food taste better.

The famous sex therapist was on the radio taking questions when a caller asked, "Doctor, why do men always want to marry a virgin?"

To which the doctor responded, "To avoid criticism."

An attractive girl walks into a fabric shop. "I want to buy this material for a dress," she says. "How much does it cost?"

"Only one kiss per metre," replies the male sales assistant.

"Fine," replies the girl. "In that case, I'll take ten metres." The sales assistant gives her the fabric, and the girl points to a little old man standing next to her. "Thanks," she says. "Grandpa's paying the bill."

One day a lady was driving along. She frequently checked her speed to make sure she stayed within the speed limit. However, when she looked into her rear mirror, much to her dismay, she saw a police car not far behind! And, to make matters worse, the police car turned on his flashing lights. She thought to herself, *Uh-oh, what have I done now? I'm not speeding. I'm not drinking. I have my seat belt on! I have kept up my road tax and everything!*

So, she pulled over and the police car pulled over to the side right behind her car. She drove her car slowly to a stop, slowly rolled down the window, and prepared for a ticket which she knew she didn't deserve. The policeman walked up to her window, and spoke to her. The lady pointed to her ear and shook her head indicating that she was deaf. The policeman smiled slightly, and knowing sign language, signed back, "I know. I'm here to tell you that your horn is stuck."

Two women are arguing about which has the smarter dog. The first woman says, "My dog's so smart, every morning he runs to the newsagent with money in his mouth, buys a paper, runs back, lets himself into the house and brings it to me in bed."

The second woman replies, "I know."

"How could you know?" asks the first woman.

The second woman replies, "My dog told me."

A doctor of psychology was doing his rounds when he entered a patient's room. He found Patient no.1 sitting on the floor, pretending to saw a piece of wood in half. Patient no.2 was hanging from the ceiling, by his feet.

The doctor asked patient no.1 what he was doing.

The patient replied, "Can't you see I'm sawing this piece of wood in half?"

The doctor inquired of patient no.1 what patient no.2 was doing.

Patient no.1 replied, "Oh. He's my friend, but he's a little crazy. He thinks he's a light bulb."

The doctor looked up and noticed patient no.2's face was going all red.

The doctor said to patient no.1, "If he's your friend, you should get him down from there before he hurts himself."

Patient no.1 replied, "What? And work in the dark?"

❖

A film crew is on location in the Arizona desert. One day an old Indian goes up to the director and says, "Tomorrow rain." The next day it rains.

The next day the Indian goes up to the director and says, "Tomorrow storm." The next day there's a hailstorm.

The director is impressed and hires the Indian to predict the weather.

However, after several successful predictions, the old Indian doesn't show up for two weeks. Finally, the director sends for him. "I have to shoot a big scene tomorrow," he says. "What will the weather be like?"

The Indian shrugs his shoulders and says, "Don't know. Radio is broken."

A shoplifter was caught red-handed trying to steal a watch from an exclusive jewellery store. "Listen," said the shoplifter, "I know you don't want any trouble either. What do you say I just buy the watch, and we forget about this?"

The manager agreed and wrote up the sales slip. The crook looked at the slip and said, "This is a little more than I intended to spend. Can you show me something less expensive?"

What music do ghosts like? Haunting melodies.

An elderly gentleman goes into a West End furriers with his young lady and buys her a mink coat costing £15,000. "Will a cheque be OK?" asks the man.

"Certainly, sir," says the sales assistant. "But we'll have to wait a few days for the cheque to clear. Can you come back on Monday to take delivery?"

"Certainly," says the old man, and he and his girlfriend walk out arm in arm.

Next Monday the man returns. The sales assistant is furious. "You've got a nerve coming back here. It turns out there's hardly a penny in your bank account. Your cheque was worthless."

"Yes, I'm sorry about that," replies the man. "I just came in to apologise – and to thank you for the greatest weekend of my life."

Three admirals, one in the French navy, one in the American navy and one in the Royal Navy, are discussing bravery.

"I'll show you how brave a French sailor is," says the French admiral, who then orders a French seaman to climb a 25-metre flagpole and jump off the top – which he does.

The American admiral says his men are much braver. He calls over a US sailor and orders him to jump off a 50-metre flagpole – which he does.

The Royal Navy admiral says he can do better and calls over a British seaman. "See that 100-metre flagpole?" says the admiral. "Climb up to the top and jump off it."

The seaman looks at the flagpole, then looks at the admiral and says, "What? Jump off that thing? You're out of your bloody mind, sir."

The admiral turns to his colleagues and says, "Now that's bravery."

❖

A motorist is making his way down a flooded road after a night of torrential rain. Suddenly he sees a man's head sticking out of a large puddle. He stops his car and asks the man if he needs a lift.

"No thanks," says the man. "I'm on my bike."

❖

A man was sitting in a bar and noticed a group of people using sign language. He also noticed that the bartender was using sign language to speak to them.

When the bartender returned to him, the man asked how he had learned to use sign language. The bartender explained that these were regular customers and had taught him to speak in sign.

The man thought that was great.

A few minutes later the man noticed that the people in the group were waving their hands around very wildly.

The bartender looked over and signed, "Now cut that out! I warned you!" and threw the group out of the bar.

The man asked why he had done that and the bartender said, "If I told them once I told them 100 times - NO SINGING IN THE BAR!"

❖

A man goes to a psychiatrist. "Doctor, I keep having these alternating recurring dreams. First I'm a tepee; then I'm a wigwam; then I'm a tepee; then I'm a wigwam. It's driving me crazy. What's wrong with me?"

The doctor replies: "It's very simple. You're two tents."

A plague of flying ants causes a music venue in Alice Springs to be shut down. The manager rings his boss in Sydney and says, "Flying ants have stopped the show."

The manager replies, "What's your problem, mate? Book 'em for another week."

Two old ladies have played bridge together for many years, and naturally they have got to know each other pretty well. One day, during a game of cards, one lady suddenly looks up at the other and says, "I realise we've known each other for many years, but for the life of me, I just can't bring it to mind... would you please tell me your name again, dear?"

There is dead silence for a couple of minutes, then the other lady responds, "How soon do you need to know?"

A dog goes into a job centre and asks for employment.

"Wow, a talking dog," says the clerk. "With your talent I'm sure we can find you a job at the circus."

"The circus?" says the dog. "What does a circus want with a plumber?"

After the Great Britain Beer Festival, in London, all the brewery bosses decided to go out for a beer.

The guy from Corona sits down and says, "Hey, senor, I would like the world's best beer, a Corona."

The bartender dusts off a bottle from the shelf and gives it to him.

The guy from Budweiser says, "I'd like the best beer in the world. Give me 'The King Of Beers', a Budweiser."

The bartender gives him one.

The guy from Coors says, "I'd like the only beer made with Rocky Mountain spring water. Give me a Coors."

He gets it.

The guy from Guinness sits down and says, "Give me a Coke."

The bartender is a little taken aback, but gives him what he ordered.

The other brewery presidents look over at him and ask, "Why aren't you drinking a Guinness?"

The Guinness president replies, "Well, if you guys aren't drinking beer, neither will I."

At an international medical conference two African surgeons are having an argument. "I tell you it sounds like 'wooooom'," says one.

"You're wrong," says the other. "It sounds like 'woombba'."

"You're both wrong," says a passing French surgeon. "In English it is pronounced 'womb'."

"Ridiculous," replies one of the Africans. "I'll wager that you have never even seen a wild hippopotamus, let alone heard one fart underwater."

A woman is accompanying her husband on a round of golf. At the first stroke he hits the ball into the rough. She shakes her head in sympathy. On the second stroke he hits the ball into a bunker. She shakes her head and sighs. On the third stroke the man knocks the ball on the green and it rolls into the hole.

"Oh boy," says his wife. "Now you're in real trouble."

My daughter walks very quietly whenever she's near the bathroom cabinet. She says she doesn't want to wake the sleeping pills.

A scientist is surprised to see a horseshoe hanging over the desk of a colleague. He asks what it's doing there and is told it brings him luck in his experiments.

"I'm amazed you believe in superstitious rubbish like that," says the scientist.

"Oh, I don't believe it," says his colleague. "But apparently it works whether you believe in it or not."

One day two male centipedes were standing in the street when a female centipede strolled past.

One male centipede turned to the other and said, "Now, there goes a nice pair of legs, pair of legs, pair of legs, pair of legs, pair of legs …"

A humble crab falls in a love with a lobster princess. They enjoy an idyllic relationship until one day the princess tells the crab that her father, the king, will not let her see him any more.

"But why?" asks the crab.

"Daddy says that crabs are common," sobs the princess. "You're a lower class of crustacean, and you walk sideways."

The crab is shattered and scuttles away to drown his sorrows.

That night is the occasion of the Great Lobster Ball, lobsters coming from far and wide to feast and dance. The lobster princess, however, sits by her father's side, inconsolable. Suddenly, the doors crash open and in walks the crab. He

223

painstakingly makes his way to the throne, walking dead straight, one claw after another. All the lobsters' eyes are on the crab as, step by painful step, he approaches the throne. He reaches the feet of the king and looks him the eye. There's a deadly hush.

Finally the crab says, "Bloody hell, I'm pissed!"

Harry and Pete are on the beach, and Harry can't understand why Pete is getting so much female attention. "It's simple," says Pete. "Just stick a potato down your bathing trunks and walk around for a while."

Harry takes this advice, sticks a potato down his trunks and parades up and down the shoreline. However, after many hours he fails to arouse any female interest at all. Discouraged, he goes back to Pete, who immediately identifies the problem.

"You're meant to put the potato down the *front* of your trunks …"

A bartender offers his customers free drinks if they can name a cocktail he doesn't know how to make. Many people try to catch him out by naming the most obscure cocktails they can think of, but the bartender knows them all. That is until one man names a drink called a "Southampton". The bartender is stumped and has to admit he's never heard of it.

"So how do I make one?" he asks.

"It's easy," says the man. "All you need is a large port."

Tom and Dick are out playing golf, and Tom brings his Yorkshire terrier along with him. Every time Tom hits a good shot the little dog gets on its hind legs and gives him a round of applause.

"That's very impressive," says Dick. "But what does it do when you hit a bad shot?"

"He turns three or four somersaults," replies Tom. "But it depends how hard I kick him."

A woman goes to buy a fancy teas-made with all the latest gadgets. The salesman explains how everything works: how to plug it in, fill it up and set the timer so that she'll wake up to a fresh cup of tea. A few weeks later she's back in the store. The salesman asks her how she likes the teas-made.

"It's wonderful," she says. "But there's one thing I don't understand. Why do I have to go to bed every time I want a cup of tea?"

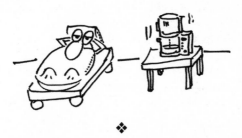

A rambler sees an old rustic character standing in a field holding a short length of rope. "What's the rope for?" asks the rambler.

"'Tis an old country way of telling the weather," says the rustic.

"And how does it work?" asks the rambler.

"Well," replies the rustic. "When it swings about, it's windy. And when it's wet, it's raining."

I wouldn't mind being the last man on earth – just to see if all those girls were telling me the truth.

A man takes early retirement and leaves the big city for a crofter's cottage in the Scottish Highlands. After a month of isolation he hears a knock on the door. He answers it and sees an enormous Scottish farmer standing outside. "I hear you're new around here," says the farmer.

"Yes, I am," says the man.

"I thought I'd introduce myself and ask you to a party I'm having," says the farmer.

"That's very nice," says the man. "I'd love to come."

"I'd better warn you there'll be lots o' drinking," says the farmer.

"I don't mind. I like a drink," says the man.

"And nee doubt there'll be a few fights breaking out," says the farmer.

"That's OK," replies the man. "I can take care of myself."

"And things get a bit frisky in the wee hours," says the farmer. "There'll be lots of sex."

"That's fine by me," says the man. "I haven't had any female company for a long time."

"Och, there'll be no lasses," says the farmer. "It's just the two of us."

What do Viagra and Disney have in common? You have to wait an hour for a two-minute ride.

One Sunday morning a vicar decides to bunk off to play golf. He leaves a note on the church door saying he's too ill to read the Sunday service then sneaks off to the golf course.

God and Saint Peter are watching this from above.

"I hope you're going to punish that man," says Saint Peter.

"Watch this," says God. The vicar tees off, and his first ball ricochets off three trees, skips across a pond, bounces off a boulder, loops the loop and drops neatly into the hole.

"I thought you were going to punish him," says Saint Peter.

"I have," says God. "Who is he going to tell?"

❖

An avid golfer is so obsessed with the game that he can't stand the idea of not playing when he's dead. To put his mind at rest he goes to a spiritualist to try to find out if there's golf in Heaven. The spiritualist communes with the spirits, then says, "I have good news and bad news."

"What's the good news?" asks the man.

"Heaven does indeed have a golf course," says the spiritualist. "It's a beautiful course with 36 holes, 24-hour access and the most magnificent clubhouse you can imagine."

"Wow," says the man. "So what's the bad news?"

The spiritualist replies, "You're booked in for a game next Tuesday."

❖

Little Johnny has a sick dog called Rex. After a visit to the vet Dad tells Johnny that Rex probably won't live for more than a month.

"But Rex wouldn't want you to be sad," says Dad. "He'd want you to have happy memories of him."

"Can we give him a funeral?" asks Johnny.

"Sure," says Dad.

"Can I invite all my friends?" asks Johnny.

"Sure you can," says Dad.

"And can we have cake and ice cream?" asks Johnny.

"You can have all the cake you want," says Dad.

"Dad," says Johnny. "Can we kill Rex today?"

A drunk goes to court. The judge says, "You've been brought here for drinking."

The drunk says, "Great. Let's get started."

Two Irishmen are out hunting duck. One shoots a flying bird, and it falls dead at his feet.

"You could've saved yourself a shot there," says the other. "From that height the fall alone would've killed it."

❖

A lady was walking down the street to work and she saw a parrot on a perch in front of a pet shop. The parrot said to her, "Hey, missus, you are really ugly."

Well, the lady is furious! She storms past the store to her work.

On the way home she sees the same parrot and it says to her, "Hey, missus, you are really ugly."

She was incredibly angry now.

The next day the same parrot again said to her, "Hey, missus, you are really ugly."

The lady was so angry that she went into the shop and said that she would sue them and kill the bird. The manager promised the bird wouldn't say it again.

When the lady walked past the store that day after work the parrot called to her, "Hey, missus..."

She paused and said, "Yes?"

The bird said, "You know."

An old gentleman goes to his doctor to complain about a problem with his sex drive. "I don't seem to have as much pep as I used to," says the old man.

"I see," says the doctor. "And how old are you and your wife?"

"I'm eighty-two," says the old man, "and my wife is seventy-eight."

"And when did you first notice the problem?" asks the doctor.

The old man replies, "Twice last night and once again this morning."

Did you hear about the transvestite who wanted a night on the town? He wanted to eat, drink and be Mary.

A man and a woman were having dinner in a fine restaurant. Their waitress, taking another order at a table a few paces away, noticed that the man was slowly sliding down his chair and under the table, with the woman acting unconcerned. The waitress watched as the man slid all the

229

way down his chair and out of sight under the table.

Still, the woman dining across from him appeared calm and unruffled, apparently unaware that her dining companion had disappeared.

After the waitress finished taking the order, she came over to the table and said to the woman, "Pardon me, ma'am, but I think your husband just slid under the table."

The woman calmly looked up at her and replied firmly, "Oh no, my husband just walked in the door."

A man walks into the office of a theatrical agent and announces that he does bird imitations. "Bird imitators are ten a penny," says the agent. "It's not worth putting you on my books."

"Oh, well," says the imitator. "I'll leave you my card just in case you change your mind." Then he drops his trousers, lays an egg and flies out of the window.

A young man who was an avid golfer found himself with a few hours to spare one afternoon. He figured if he hurried and played very fast, he could get in nine holes before he had to head home. Just as he was about to tee off an old gentleman shuffled onto the tee and asked if he could accompany the young man as he was golfing alone. Not being able to say no, he allowed the old gent to join him.

To his surprise the old man played fairly quickly. He didn't hit the ball far, but plodded along consistently and didn't waste much time. Finally, they reached the 9th fairway and the young man found himself with a tough shot. There was a large pine tree right in front of his ball - and directly between his ball and the green.

After several minutes of debating how to hit the shot the old man finally said, "You know, when I was your age I'd hit the ball right over that tree."

With that challenge placed before him, the youngster swung hard, hit the ball right smack into the top of the tree trunk and it thudded back on the ground not a foot from where it had originally lay.

The old man offered one more comment, "Of course, when I was your age that pine tree was only three feet tall."

A man goes into bookshop. He approaches a woman behind the counter and says, "Do you keep stationery?"

"No," replies the woman. "Sometimes I wriggle about a bit."

A man goes into a pub and seats himself on a stool.

The bartender looks at him and says, "What'll it be, buddy?"

The man says, "Set me up with five whiskies, and make 'em doubles."

The bartender does this and watches the man slug one down, then the next, then the next, and so on until all five are gone almost as quickly as they were served.

Staring in disbelief, the bartender asks why he's doing all this drinking.

"You'd drink 'em this fast too if you had what I have."

The bartender hastily asks, "What do you have pal?"

The man quickly replies, "I only have a quid."

A man is a person who will pay two pounds for a one-pound item that he wants. A woman will pay one pound for a two-pound item she doesn't want.

On their 40th wedding anniversary and during the banquet celebrating it, Tom was asked to give his friends a brief account of the benefits of a marriage of such long duration.

"Tell us, Tom, just what is it you have learned from all those wonderful years with your wife?"

Tom responds, "Well, I've learned that marriage is the best teacher of all. It teaches you loyalty, forbearance, meekness, self-restraint, forgiveness, and a great many other qualities you wouldn't have needed if you'd stayed single."

I think you'll find that any of my lady companions will tell you I'm a "five-times-a-night man". I really shouldn't drink so much tea before I go to bed.

A young woman with her five children get on the London train at Southampton. The children are all eating ice creams. The train is so crowded that there's nowhere to sit, so they stand in the narrow aisle, and one of the children's ice creams kept touching the expensive fur coat of one of the seated passengers.

"Oi, you!" snaps the child's mother. "Don't hold your ice cream like that. You're getting bits of fur stuck in it."

What's the difference between Niagara and Viagra? Niagara Falls.

This bloke is looking to buy a saw to cut down some trees in his back garden. He goes to a chainsaw shop and asks about various chainsaws.

The dealer tells him, "Look, I have a lot of models, but why don't you save yourself a lot of time and aggravation and get the top-of-the-line model. This chainsaw will cut a hundred cords of wood for you in one day."

So, the man takes the chainsaw home and begins working

on the trees. After cutting for several hours and only cutting two cords, he decides to quit. He thinks there is something wrong with the chainsaw. How could he cut for hours and only cut two cords? the man asks himself. Next day he would begin first thing in the morning and cut all day, he tells himself. So, the next morning the man gets up at 4 am and cuts and cuts, and cuts till nightfall, and still he only manages to cut five cords.

The man is convinced this is a bad saw, for it should cut one hundred cords of wood in a day, no problem, and he decides to take the saw back to the dealer. and explain the problem.

The dealer, baffled by the man's claim, removes the chainsaw from the case and says, "Hmm, it looks fine." The dealer starts the chainsaw, and the man says, "What's that noise?"

A ship's captain radios a lighthouse keeper. "Radio reception is very bad. Please spell out your weather report."

The keeper replies, "W-E-T-H-O-R R-E-P-O-R-T."

The captain says, "My God, that's the worst spell of weather I've had in a long time."

A mild-mannered man was tired of being bossed around by his wife so he went to a psychiatrist.

The psychiatrist said he needed to build his self-esteem, and so gave him a book on assertiveness, which he read on the way home. He had finished the book by the time he reached his house. The man stormed into the house and walked up to his wife.

Pointing a finger in her face, he said, "From now on, I want you to know that I am the man of this house, and my word is law! I want you to prepare me a gourmet meal tonight, and when I'm finished eating my meal, I expect a sumptuous dessert afterward. Then, after dinner, you're going to draw me my bath so I can relax. And when I'm finished with my bath, guess who's going to dress me and comb my hair?"

"The funeral director," said his wife.

Ever wondered about those people who pay a fortune for those little bottles of Evian water? Try spelling Evian backwards.

Harry and Tom are on the golf course when Harry slices a shot deep into a wooded ravine. He takes his eight iron and clambers down the embankment in search of his lost ball. After fifteen minutes spent hacking at the underbrush Harry spots something glistening among the leaves. He gets closer and discovers that it's an eight iron in the hands of a skeleton.

Harry calls out to Tom, "Hey! I've trouble down here!"

"What's up?" shouts back Tom.

"Bring me my wedge," replies Harry. "You can't get out of here with an eight iron."

234

A masked man runs into a bank and points a banana at the cashier. "This is a cock-up!" he shouts.

"Don't you mean a hold-up?" says the cashier.

"No," says the man. "It's a cock-up. I left the gun on the bus."

A little boy puts his shoes on by himself, but his mother notices he's got them mixed up. "Sweetie," she says. "You've put your shoes on the wrong feet."

The little boy looks at her and says, "But these are the only feet I've got."

❖

Every year Billy's father asked him what he wanted for his birthday, and every year Billy said he wanted a pink golf ball. For years and years this was the only gift he ever requested. If it was his birthday he wanted a pink golf ball. If it was Christmas he only ever wanted a pink golf ball. Nothing else would tempt him. Eventually Billy's father got tired of buying his son pink golf balls, so for his eighteenth birthday he got him a surprise present – a car. Billy liked the car and took it into town for a spin. Passing a sports goods store, he saw that they had some pink golf balls in the window, so he parked on the kerb and crossed the road to take a closer look. Halfway across the road he was hit by a truck. Billy's father came to see him in hospital. He knew that Billy wasn't going to make it, and he wanted to ask his son one question before he died. "Billy," he said. "You've never played golf, so why, for all these years, did you only ever want pink golf balls as gifts?" Billy looked up at his father, opened his mouth to speak, then died. And the moral of this story is: you should always look both ways before crossing the street.

When the Mexican fireman had twin sons he had them christened Jose and Hose B.

It was the day of the big sale. Rumours of the sale (and some advertising in the local paper) were the main reason for the long queue that formed by 8:30, the opening time.

A small man pushed his way to the front of the line, only to be pushed back, amid loud and colourful curses. On the man's second attempt, he was punched square in the face, and knocked around a bit, and then thrown to the end of the queue again. As he got up the second time, he said to the person at the end of the queue...

"That does it! If they hit me one more time, I won't open up the shop!"

Patrick and Michael go to a pub for a drink and see a sign saying: "Buy a double whisky and get a chance at free sex."

They both buy a double, then ask the bartender how to get the sex.

"It's simple," he says. "I think of a number between one and ten, and if you can guess what it is you get laid."

"OK," says Patrick. "I'll guess three."

"Sorry," says the bartender. "You're out of luck." Next day the pair return and, again, Patrick tries his luck at the free sex quiz. He guesses four.

"Sorry," says the bartender. "Better luck next time." Next day the pair come back and Patrick guesses two.

"Sorry," says the bartender. "Wrong again."

Patrick turns to Michael and says, "Y'know, I'm beginning to think this contest is rigged."

"Oh no," says Michael. "My wife tried it last week and she won three times."

Junior had just received his brand new driving licence. To celebrate, the whole family trooped out to the driveway and climbed into the car for his inaugural drive. Dad immediately headed to the back seat, directly behind the newly-minted driver. "I'll bet you're back there to get a change of scenery after all those months of sitting in the front passenger seat teaching me how to drive," said the beaming boy to his old man.

"Nope," came dad's reply, "I'm going to sit back here and kick the back of your seat while you drive, just like you have been doing to me for the past 18 years."

During the wedding rehearsal, the groom approached the vicar with an unusual offer:

"Look, I'll give you £100 if you'll change the wedding vows. When you get to the part where I'm supposed to promise to 'love, honour and obey' and 'be faithful to her forever,' I'd appreciate it if you'd just leave that out."

He passed the minister the £100 and walked away satisfied.

On the day of the wedding, when it came time for the groom's vows, the vicar looked the young man in the eye and said: "Will you promise to prostrate yourself before her, obey her every command and wish, serve her breakfast in bed every morning of your life, and swear eternally before God and your lovely wife that you will not ever even look at another woman, as long as you both shall live?"

The groom gulped and looked around, and said in a tiny voice: "Yes," then leaned toward the vicar and hissed: "I thought we had a deal."

The vicar put two £50 notes into the groom's hand and whispered: "She made me a better offer."

A customer was bothering the waiter in a restaurant. First, he asked that the air conditioning be turned up because he was too hot, then he asked it be turned down cause he was too cold, and so on for about half an hour.

Surprisingly, the waiter was very patient, he walked back and forth and never once got angry. So finally, a second customer asked him why he didn't throw out the pest.

"Oh, I really don't care," said the waiter with a smile. "We don't even have an air conditioner."

Two drunks get talking in a bar. The first man says, "Where are you from?"

"I'm from Ireland," replies the second man.

"You don't say," says the first man. "I'm from Ireland too! Let's have a drink." They both knock back their drinks, and the first man asks, "Where abouts in Ireland are you from?"

"Dublin," comes the reply.

"I can't believe it," says the first man. "I'm from Dublin too! Let's have another drink!" Then the first man asks, "So what school did you go to?"

"Saint Mary's," replies the second man.

"This is unbelievable," replies the first man. "I went to Saint Mary's as well. Let's have another drink!"

One of the other customers says to the bartender, "What are those two celebrating?"

"Nothing," replies the bartender. "It's just the O'Malley twins getting drunk again."

The rugby team is being driven through Dublin. The driver shouts out, "And if you look to your left you'll see that we're going past the biggest pub in the city."

A voice from the back shouts, "Why?"

A bank had been robbed three times by the same bandit. An FBI agent looking for clues interviews one of the bank tellers. "Have you noticed anything distinctive about the man?" he asks.

"Not really," replies the teller, "but each time he turns up he's better dressed."

Two old men were fishing off a bridge as they had done daily for many years. Suddenly a funeral procession came down the road.

The one old man reeled in his line, laid down his pole, faced the street and bowed his head until the procession had passed. He then picked up his pole and started fishing again.

The other fisherman was amazed and stated, "I didn't know you were that religious."

The other looked at him and said, "Least I could do; we'd been married 42 years!"

When the waitress in a New York City restaurant brought him the soup du jour, the Englishman was a bit dismayed. "Good heavens," he said, "what is this?"

"Why, it's bean soup," she replied.

"I don't care what it has been," he sputtered. "What is it now?"

A small boy was peering through a hole in the fence of a nudist colony. His friend, Paul, came up to him and asked, "Tim, what can you see? Are they men or women or women in there?"

"I don't really know," replied Tim. "None of them has got any clothes on."

A man left work one Friday afternoon. But, being payday, instead of going home, he stayed out the entire weekend partying with the boys and spending his entire pay check.

When he finally appeared at home, Sunday night, he was confronted by a very angry wife and was barraged for nearly two hours with a tirade befitting his actions.

Finally his wife stopped the nagging and simply said to him, "How would you like it if you didn't see me for two or three days?"

To which he replied. "That would be fine with me."

Monday went by and he didn't see his wife. Tuesday and Wednesday came and went with the same results.

240

Come Thursday, the swelling went down just enough that he could see her a little out of the corner of his left eye.

Man to woman: "Am I the first man you ever made love to?"

Woman: "You might be. Now you come to mention it, your face does look familiar."

The patient says, "Give me the bad news first!"

Doctor replies, "You've got AIDS."

"Oh, no! What could be worse than that?" asks the patient.

"You've also got Alzheimer's Disease."

Looking relieved the patient says, "Oh...Well, that's not so bad. At least I don't have AIDS."

Two cannibals, a father and son, were elected by the tribe to go out and get something to eat. They walked deep into the jungle and waited by a path.

Before long, along came this little old man. The son said, "Ooh, dad, there's one."

"No," said the father. "There's not even enough meat on that one to feed the dogs. We'll just wait."

Well, a little while later, along came this really fat man. The son said, "Hey, dad, he's plenty big enough."

"No," the father said. "We'd all die of a heart attack from the fat in that one. We'll just wait."

241

About an hour later, here comes this absolutely gorgeous woman.

The son said, "Now there's nothing wrong with that one, dad. Let's eat her."

"No," said the father. "We'll not eat her either."

"Why not?" asked the son.

"Because we're going to take her back alive and eat your mother."

A boy had been warned that he must be on his best behaviour when his wealthy aunt arrived for a brief holiday visit. It was at tea during the first day of her stay that the boy kept looking at his aunt. When the meal was almost finished, he asked, "Auntie, when are you going to do your trick?"

"What trick is that, dear?" she inquired.

"Well, daddy says you can drink like a fish."

A man gets a job as a weatherman in the Far East. Try as he might, however, he can never get a forecast right. Eventually he's sacked and has to fly home. A friend asks why he's back so soon.

"The climate didn't agree with me."

A married couple were in a terrible accident where the woman's face was severely burned. The doctor told the husband that they couldn't graft any skin from her body because she was too skinny. So the husband offered to donate some of his own skin.

However, the only skin on his body that the doctor felt was suitable would have to come from his buttocks.

The husband and wife agreed that they would tell no one about where the skin came from, and requested that the doctor also honour their secret. After all, this was a very delicate matter.

After the surgery was completed, everyone was astounded at the woman's new beauty. She looked more beautiful than she ever had before! All her friends and relatives just went on and on about her youthful beauty!

One day, she was alone with her husband, and she was overcome with emotion at his sacrifice. She said, "Dear, I just want to thank you for everything you did for me. How can I possibly repay you?"

"My darling," he replied, "I get all the thanks I need every time I see your mother kiss you on the cheek."

It was Christmas morning and the family were plodding home from church through the snow, discussing the service. They all seemed to have a bad word to say.

Dad thought the bells had been rung dreadfully; Mum thought that the hymns were badly chosen; the eldest son fell asleep during the sermon, and his twin sister could not agree with the prayers. Only the youngest boy disagreed, opining, "I don't know what you are all complaining about. I thought it was a damn good show for a penny!"

Two men are having a drink together. One says, "I had sex with my wife before we were married. What about you?"

"I don't know," says the other. "What was her maiden name?"

A little girl asks her mother about her origin. "How did I get here, Mummy?" she asks.

Her mother replies, "Why, God sent you, honey."

"And did God send you too, Mummy?" she continues.

"Yes, sweetheart, he did."

"And Daddy and Grandma and Grandpa and their mums and dads, too?"

"Yes, honey, all of them, too."

The child shakes her head. "So you're telling me there's been no sex in this family for about 200 years? Heck, no wonder everyone's so grouchy!"

How husbands irritate wives:

Start asking her questions (don't mistakenly do anything) about cooking, cleaning, and laundry. Say, "I think it's time I learn to take care of myself. You know, just in case."

Volunteer to cook for her. Make sure it's really greasy. Use every pot and pan in the house and be sure you spill and/or drop some of everything everywhere.

While brushing your teeth, flick the toothbrush first at the sink and then at the mirror.

Never ask her to get you something from the kitchen when she's in the kitchen. Let her spend a good 30 minutes in there and when she reaches the sofa with a sigh of relief say, "Will you PLEASE do me a big favour and get me a cup of tea; my back is just killing me today."

Be sure to load up all your pockets with tissues before you drop them in the clothes hamper.

Leave yourself a trail of clothing, towels, dishes, and everything else you put your hands on. This will ensure you never lose your way.

Wait until she's overwhelmed with work, lean in close and say, "Did you see how dusty the leaves on your house plants are?"

Put on a TV programme and then pretend to keep falling asleep. Wake up each time she tries to change the channel and say, "Cut it out; you know how much I've been looking forward to watching this. Don't be so selfish."

Wait until she is totally engrossed in a movie then tell her something is bugging you and you really need to talk about it. Be sure it's as stupid, boring, and long winded as you can make it.

Keep calling her at work to find out what time she plans to get home and what she plans to make for dinner. Make sure you're just not in the mood for whatever she's making.

When the opportunity arises be sure to cut the grass in your brand new white sneakers.

When you retrieve your clothes from the wardrobe leave the hanger in place and pull on the clothing until the hanger is mangled enough to allow the article to slip off.

Tell her something for the first time and act shocked that she didn't know about it. Pout and exclaim, "And you have the nerve to say I never listen to YOU."

When you know she's grocery shopping, disappear! Come home just in time to watch her carry the last bag in. Grab the receipt and say, "I'll get the rest of it for you dear." Feign surprise when she says that's it. End with, "This is all you got. For how much?"

On the odd occasion you actually clean up a disgusting mess you made, use the best towels in the house.

As your stomach grows just wear your pants lower and flop it over the waistband; then brag that unlike your wife, you still wear the same size you did when you got married.

Wait until the night before you go on holiday and say, "Hon, you know the underwear and socks you packed for me? Well the elastic is gone and I need new ones."

Always leave the shower head at just the right angle to hit her in the face with that jet of cold water when she turns it on.

When doing filthy jobs around the house be sure to wear your good clothes.

Harass her into telling people a story and proceed to interrupt every other sentence with: "No that's not what..."

Whenever something is ready to break make sure your wife is the next to use it. When it breaks, look at her and say, "What the hell did you do. I never had a problem with it."

Whenever the dog, cat, or the kids are being cute, they're yours. When they need something, they're hers.

A tourist is travelling with a guide through one of the thickest jungles in South America, when he comes across an ancient Mayan temple. The tourist is entranced by the temple, and asks the guide for details. To this, the guide states that archaeologists are carrying out excavations, and still finding great treasures. The tourist then asks how old the temple is.

"This temple is 1503 years old," replies the guide.

Impressed at this accurate dating, he inquires as to how he gave this precise figure.

"Easy," replies the guide, "the archaeologists said the temple was 1500 years old, and that was three years ago."

An elderly Italian man goes to confession. "Father," he says, "I'd like to ask you a moral question."

"Certainly, my son," says the priest.

"During the war a beautiful Jewish woman knocked on my door," says the old man. "She asked me to hide her in return for sexual favours."

"That was wrong of you," replies the priest. "You shouldn't have taken advantage of the woman. But you did a good

246

deed in saving her life. Say fifty Hail Marys."

"No, Father," says the old man. "That wasn't the question."

"Then what is your question?" asks the priest.

The old man says, "Do I have to tell her the war is over?"

Grandmother is so stupid she's gone on the pill because she doesn't want any more grandchildren.

Mother: "If you smartened yourself up you could get a job."

Son: "Why?"

Mother: "Because in a job you get paid."

Son: "So?"

Mother: "So then you can save some money."

Son: "What for?"

Mother: "If you save enough you can eventually retire and not work any more."

Son: "But I'm not working now."

"Mum, did you know that Marconi was a famous inventor?"

"Yes, dear. But it's not polite to say Ma Coni – you should say Mrs Coni."

A woman accompanied her husband to the doctor's office. After his check-up, the doctor called the wife into his office alone.

He said, "Your husband is suffering from a very severe disease, combined with horrible stress. If you don't do the following, your husband will surely die. Each morning, fix him a healthy breakfast. Be pleasant, and make sure he is in a good mood. For lunch make him a nutritious meal he can take to work. And for dinner, prepare an especially nice meal for him. Don't burden him with chores, as this could further his stress. Don't discuss your problems with him; it will only make his stress worse. Try to relax your husband in the evening by wearing lingerie and giving him plenty of backrubs. Encourage him to watch some type of team sporting event on television. And most importantly, make love with your husband several times a week and satisfy his every whim. If you can do this for the next 10 months to a year, I think your husband will regain his health."

On the way home, the husband asked his wife, "What did the doctor say?"

"You're going to die," she replied.

A boy walks into his classroom wearing a single glove. His teacher asks him what he's doing.

"Well, ma'am," he says. "I was watching the weather forecast on TV, and it said it was going to be sunny, but on the other hand it could get quite cold."

Jack and Betty are celebrating their 50th wedding anniversary.

"Betty, I was wondering if you have ever cheated on me?"

"Oh, Jack, why would you ask such a question now? You don't want to ask that question..."

"Yes, Betty, I really want to know. Please."

"Well, all right. Yes, three times."

"Three? When were they?"

"Well, Jack, remember when you were 35 years old and you really wanted to start the business on your own and no bank would give you a loan? Remember how one day the

248

bank manager himself came over to the house and signed the loan papers, no questions asked?"

"Oh, Betty, you did that for me! I respect you even more than ever, that you would do such a thing for me! So, when was number two?"

"Well, Jack, remember when you had that last heart attack and you were needing that very tricky operation, and no surgeon would touch you? Remember how Dr. Baker came all the way up here, to do the surgery himself, and then you were in good shape again?"

"I can't believe it! Betty, I love that you should do such a thing for me, to save my life! I couldn't have a more wonderful wife. To do such a thing, you must really love me darling. I couldn't be more moved. When was number three?"

"Well, Jack, remember a few years ago, when you really wanted to be president of the golf club and you were 17 votes short?"

A little girl found an old, abandoned family Bible in the attic and opened it to find a large leaf pressed between its heavy pages.

"Oh, look," she said. "Adam left his clothes here."

Two men, Jack and John, go on a skiing trip and get caught in a blizzard. They pull into a farm and ask the lady of the house, a good-looking widow, if they can sleep on her couch.

She agrees, and they turn in for the night. Next morning they go on their way and enjoy a weekend of skiing. A few months later Jack gets a letter from the widow's lawyer. He says to John, "You remember that good-looking widow we met on our skiing holiday?"

"Yes," says John.

"Did you get up in the middle of the night, go up to her room and have sex with her?" asks Jack.

"Yes," admits John, a little embarrassed.

"I see," says Jack. "And when you had sex did you happen to use my name instead of yours?"

John's face turns red. "Yeah, sorry," he says. "I'm afraid I did."

"Well," says Jack. "You must have been damn good. She's just died and left everything to me."

A woman wakes up one morning and says to her husband, "I dreamed you gave me a pearl necklace for Valentine's day. What do you think it means?"

"You'll know tonight, darling," he says. That evening the husband comes home with a small package and gives it to his wife. Delighted, she opens it – and finds a book entitled *The Meaning of Dreams*.

What's a bigamist?
Fog in Italy.

A man walks into a bar and says, "Who's the owner of that Great Dane tied up outside?"

A man replies, "It's mine. Why do you ask?"

The first man says, "I'm sorry, but my dog just killed your dog."

The owner of the Great Dane is shocked. "Are you kidding? That dog was huge!"

"I know," says the first man, "but he just choked on my Chihuahua."

Harry is in the middle of a speech when someone at the back calls out, "I can't hear you."

Someone at the front calls back, "Could we swap places?"

Man: "Have you been to bed with anyone?"

Girl (angrily): "That's my business."

Man: "Oh! I didn't know you were a professional."

❖

There was a perfect man who met a perfect woman. After a perfect courtship, they had a perfect wedding. Their life together was, of course, perfect.

One snowy, stormy Christmas Eve this perfect couple was driving along a winding road when they noticed someone at the roadside in distress. Being the perfect couple, they stopped to help.

There stood Santa Claus with a huge bundle of toys. Not wanting to disappoint any children on the eve of Christmas, the perfect couple loaded Santa and his toys into their vehicle.

Soon they were driving along delivering the toys. Unfortunately, the driving conditions deteriorated and the perfect couple and Santa Claus had an accident.

Only one of them survived the accident. Who was the survivor?

The perfect woman.

She's the only one that really existed in the first place.

Everyone knows there is no Santa Claus and there is no such thing as a perfect man.

* A Male's Response *

So, if there is no perfect man and no Santa Claus, the perfect woman must have been driving. This explains why there was a car accident.

The rabbi and the priest lived next door to each other and bought new cars at almost exactly the same time.

Looking out of his window, the rabbi saw the priest with a small bowl of water, sprinkling the contents over the car and blessing it.

Not to be outdone, the rabbi got a hacksaw and cut half an inch off the exhaust pipe of his own car.

For sale: Parachute. Only used once, never opened, small stain.

A man spots an old school friend getting out of a new Rolls Royce. "How did you do so well?" asks the man.

"Oh," says his stuttering friend. "J-j-j-j-j-j-j-just by selling c-c-c-c-c-c-copies of the B-b-b-b-b-bible d-d-d-d-door to d-d-d-d-door."

"That's amazing," says the man. "How do you manage to sell so many."

"W-w-w-well," says his friend. "I j-j-just kno-o-ock on p-p-p-p-p-people's d-d-d-doors, show them a c-c-c-c-c-c-copy of the B-b-b-b-b-bible and ask them if they w-w-w-w-would rather b-b-b-b-buy it or h-h-have me r-r-read it to them."

A man spends all night drinking in a pub. When it's time to go he stands up and falls flat on his face, so he decides to crawl outside in the hope that the fresh air will sober him up. Once outside he stands up and falls over, so he has to crawl the half mile to his house. When he gets home he manages to prop himself upright so he can unlock the front door, then he falls on his face again and crawls up the stairs. When he reaches his bed he tries to stand one last time but collapses and falls fast asleep. The next morning he's woken by his wife's shouting. "You've been out on the booze again, haven't you?"

"What makes you say that?" asks the man.

"Don't bother to lie about it!" shouts his wife. "The pub rang. You left your wheelchair behind again."

It's winter and a garage-owner hears a knock at the door. He opens it and see a little metal monkey shivering outside. "Excuse me," says the monkey. "But do you do welding?"

The beautiful young girl was walking along the street when a young man walked up beside her and said, "Hello, beautiful! Haven't we met somewhere before?"

The girl gave him a frosty stare and continued walking.

"Huh!" snorted the young man. "Now I realise my mistake – I thought you were my mother."

"That's impossible," retorted the girl. "I'm married."

People laughed at me when I told them I intended to become a comedian. Well, they're not laughing now.

A student had spent all his money, so he called his mother from college and asked if she could send him some.

"Of course, I'll send you some money, dear," mum said. "By the way, you left your calculus book here when you visited last month. Would you like me to send that to you too?"

"Ummmmm, oh yeah. OK, mum," the boy replied.

So she wrapped the book, together with the money, kissed dad goodbye and went to the post office to send the parcel.

When she returned, dad asked, "So, how much did you send him this time?"

"I wrote two cheques, one for £20, and the other for £500," mum replied.

"Have you lost your mind?" dad exclaimed. "That's £520!"

"Not to worry," mum said calmly, as she kissed the top of dad's head. "I taped the £20 cheque to the cover of his book, but I put the £500 cheque somewhere between the pages in Chapter 19!"

A priest, a rabbi and a vicar walk into a pub. The bartender says, "Is this some kind of joke?"

A young man was walking through a supermarket to pick up a few things when he noticed an old lady following him around. Thinking nothing of it, he ignored her and continued on. Finally he went to the checkout, but she got in front of him.

"Pardon me," she said, "I'm sorry if my staring at you has made you feel uncomfortable. It's just that you look just like my son, who just died recently."

"I'm very sorry," replied the young man. "Is there anything I can do for you?"

"Yes," she said, "As I'm leaving, can you say 'Good bye, mother!'? It would make me feel so much better."

"Of course," answered the young man.

As the old woman was leaving, he called out, "Good bye, mother!"

As he stepped up to the checkout counter, he saw that his total was £127.50.

"How can that be?" he asked, "I only bought a few things!"

"Your mother said that you would pay for her stuff," said the assistant.

Policeman: "Madam, I have just recorded you at about 50."

Female speeding motorist: "Don't be ridiculous, officer! These clothes always make me look a lot older."

A man has six children and is very proud of his achievement. He is so proud of himself, that he starts calling his wife, 'Mother of Six' in spite of her objections.

One night, they go to a party. The man decides that it's time to go home and wants to find out if his wife is ready to leave as well. He shouts across the room at the top of his voice, "Shall we go home, Mother of Six?'"

His wife, irritated by her husband's lack of discretion shouts right back, "Anytime you're ready, Father of Four."

Two doctors in the USA were talking.

First doctor: "Why did you perform that operation on Mrs Weitzman?"

Second doctor: "Twenty thousand dollars."

First doctor: "No. Perhaps you didn't hear me correctly. What did Mrs Weitzman have?"

Second doctor: "Twenty thousand dollars."

A small boy is woken by a huge crash of thunder. He runs into his parents' room, where his father comforts him. "Don't be afraid of the thunder," he says. "It's just a noise that God makes when someone tells a lie."

"But why is it thundering now?" asks the boy. "It's the middle of the night and everyone's asleep."

"I know," replies father. "But it's around this time that they start to print the newspapers."

Sean gets home in the early hours of the morning after a night in the pub. He makes such a racket that he wakes up his missus.

"What on earth are you doing down there?" she yells down from the bedroom. "Get yourself to bed and don't wake the neighbours."

"I'm trying to get a barrel of Guinness up the stairs," shouts Sean.

"Leave it till the morning," she yells back.

"I can't," he shouts. "I've drunk it."

Farmer Jim was very worried about the poor performance of his prize bull for which he had paid an astronomical sum. He talked to all his friends every time he went to the market and one day learned from a cousin that there was an amazing vet way down in the West Country.

He was so depressed about the bull that he decided this last resort was the answer, and he took himself off to Cornwall to find the vet. At last he found the chap, who urged him to give his bull a great big pill once a day.

A few months later he met his cousin, who asked him how he had got on.

"Oh, it was marvellous," he said. "The vet gave me these pills for the bull, and I had no sooner started him off on them than he hit the jackpot. In fact I'm making a fortune out of the local farmers – they can't get their cows round here fast enough!"

"What are these pills, then?" asked his cousin.

"Oh," said Farmer Jim, "huge great green jobs like bombs and with a peppermint taste!"

Lawyer: "Now that you have been acquitted, will you tell me truly? Did you steal the car?"

Client: "After hearing your amazing argument in court this morning, I'm beginning to think I didn't."

A man woke up in a private hospital bed and called for his doctor. He asked, "Give it to me straight. How long have I got?"

The physician replied that he doubted that the man would survive the night.

The man then said, "Call for my lawyer."

When the lawyer arrived, the man asked for his physician to stand on one side of the bed, while the lawyer stood on the other. The man then laid back and closed his eyes. When he remained silent for several minutes, the physician asked what he had in mind.

The man replied, "Jesus died with a thief on either side. I just thought I'd check out the same way."

There is this bloke in a pub, just looking at his drink. He stays like that for half an hour. In walks a big, trouble-making truck driver who takes the drink from him and just drinks it all down. The poor man starts crying.

The truck driver says, "Come on, mate, I was just joking. Here, I'll buy you another drink. I can't stand to see a man cry."

"No, it's not that. This day is the worst of my life. First, I fall asleep, and get to my office late and get fired. When I leave the building I find my car has been stolen and the police say that they can do nothing. I get a cab home and leave my wallet and credit cards inside. I go into my house and find my wife in bed with the gardener. I leave home, and come to this pub. And just when I'm ready to put an end to my life, you come in and drink my poison."

A man was walking in the city, when he was accosted by a particularly dirty and shabby-looking beggar who asked him for a couple of pounds for dinner.

The man took out his wallet, extracted a fiver and asked, "If I give you this money, will you take it and buy whisky?"

"No, I stopped drinking years ago," the bum said.

"Will you use it to gamble?"

"I don't gamble. I need everything I can get just to stay alive."

"Will you spend the money on greens fees at a golf course?"

"Are you mad?! I haven't played golf in 20 years!"

The man said, "Well, I'm not going to give you any money. Instead, I'm going to take you to my home for a terrific dinner cooked by my wife."

The beggar was astounded.

"Won't your wife be furious with you for doing that? I know I'm dirty, and I probably smell pretty bad."

The man replied, "That's OK. I just want her to see what a man looks like after giving up drinking, gambling and golf."

A word to the wise isn't necessary. It's the stupid ones who need the advice.

Wisdom is the comb that life gives you after you lose your hair.

Knowledge is knowing a tomato is a fruit. Wisdom is not putting it in a fruit salad.

By the time you can make ends meet, they move the ends.

By the time a man is wise enough to watch his step, he's too old to go anywhere.

Age doesn't always bring wisdom; sometimes it arrives alone.

A verbal contract isn't worth the paper it's written on.

Experience is that marvellous thing that enables you to recognise a mistake when you make it again.

A thing not worth doing isn't worth doing well.

Don't become superstitious. It's bad luck.

Everybody lies, but it doesn't matter since nobody listens.

Good judgement comes from bad experience, and a lot of that comes from bad judgement.

Good news is just life's way of keeping you off balance.

If you can tell the difference between good advice and bad advice, you don't really need advice.

If a thing's worth doing, it would have been done already.

Intelligence has much less practical application than you'd think.

It's so simple to be wise. Just think of something stupid to say and then don't say it.

Everywhere is walking distance if you have the time.

All generalisations are false.

There once was a nonconformist bird that decided not to fly south for the winter. He said, "I've had enough of this flying south every winter. I'll just stay right here on this farm. What's the big deal, anyway?"

So he stayed. Winter came and was very cold. The nonconformist bird had never felt such cold weather and was afraid that he might freeze to death. Realizing he had made a big mistake by staying, he headed to a nearby barn for shelter. On his way to the barn it began to snow. The poor bird was cold, tired and hungry. *Why did I stay?* he asked himself as he collapsed on the ground. As he lay there covered by the snow, a cow happened by. The cow, feeling the need to relieve himself, crapped right on the bird. At first being angry the bird said, "Who did this horrible thing to me? How dare someone crap on me. I'll get him for this!"

260

The crap was too heavy for him to free himself. But, after a while the crap began to warm him and he forgot all about his anger. In fact he was so warm that he began to sing. A buzzard passing overheard the singing and went down to investigate. As he cleared away the crap to his delight he found the bird. The bird was so happy to be free from the crap that he thanked the buzzard, who then decided to eat the little bird.

The moral of this story: Just because someone craps on you, it does not make them your enemy, and just because someone gets you out of the crap, it does not make them your friend.

Condoms are not completely safe. A friend of mine was wearing one and he got hit by a bus.

Man on phone: "Help! Come quickly! My house is on fire!"

Fire brigade officer: "How do we get to your house?"

Man on phone: "What? Don't you still have those big red trucks?"

Two yokels bought themselves a horse each and decided to keep them in the same field.

"How shall we tell which horse is which?" asked one.

"I'll tie a blue ribbon to the tail of my horse," replied the other.

Unfortunately, the ribbon on the first ones horse fell off one day so the two were again faced with the problem of deciding which horse was which.

"I know," suggested one. "You have the brown horse, and I'll have the white one."

A drunk staggers to the men's room of a large restaurant. On his way back to his seat he stops and asks a young woman if he had stepped on her foot a few minutes ago.

"Yes," she replies testily. "Yes, you did."

"Great," he replies. "I knew my table was around here somewhere."

A Sunday school teacher was giving her class their homework for the next week.

"Next Sunday," she said, "we are going to talk about liars, and in preparation for our lesson I want you all to read the seventeenth chapter of Mark."

The following week, at the beginning of the class meeting, the teacher said, "Now then, all of you who have prepared for the lesson by reading the seventeenth chapter of Mark, please step to the front of the room."

About half the class rose and came forward.

"The rest of you may leave," said the teacher. "These students are the ones I want to talk to. There is no seventeenth chapter in the Book of Mark."

A sex researcher phones one of the participants in a survey to check on a discrepancy. He asks the man, "In response to the question on frequency of intercourse you answered 'twice weekly'. You wife, on the other hand, answered 'several times a night'."

"That's right," replies the man. "And that's how it's going to be until the mortgage is paid off."

A drunk falls into one of the fountains in Trafalgar Square. Floundering around, he looks up and sees Nelson standing on his column. "Don't jump," he shouts. "This is the shallow end."

Harold's wife bought a new line of expensive cosmetics guaranteed to make her look years younger. After a lengthy sitting before the mirror applying the 'miracle' products, she asked,

"Darling, honestly, what age would you say I am?"

Looking over her carefully, Harold replied, "Judging from your skin, twenty; your hair, eighteen; and your figure, twenty-five."

"Oh, you flatterer!" she gushed.

"Hey, wait a minute!" Harold interrupted. "I haven't added them up yet."

A Chinese couple had a new baby. The nurse brings over a lovely, healthy, bouncy, black baby boy.

"Congratulations," says the nurse to the new parents. "What will you name the baby?"

The puzzled father looks at his new baby boy and says, "I think we will name him Sum Ting Wong."

Stockbroker patient: "Tell me, nurse, what is my temperature?"

Nurse: "A hundred and one."

Stockbroker patient: "When it gets to a hundred and two, sell."

"Sir, I understand you admit to having broken into the dress shop four times," the judge said.

"Yes, Your Honour," the suspect replied.

"What did you steal?" the judge asked.

"I stole a dress, Your Honour," replied the suspect.

"One dress?" the judge bellowed. "But you have admitted to breaking in four times!"

"Yes, Your Honour," sighed the suspect, "but the first three times my wife didn't like the colour!"

A woman from New York is driving through a remote part of Texas when her car breaks down. An Indian on horseback comes along and offers her a ride. She climbs up behind him, and they ride off. The trip is uneventful except that every few minutes the Indian lets out a loud whoop. When they arrive in town, he lets her off at the gas station, yells one final "Yahoo!" and rides off.

"What did you do to get that Indian so excited?" asks the gas station attendant.

"Nothing," shrugs the woman. "I just sat behind him, put my arms around his waist and held on to his saddle horn to keep me steady."

"That'll explain it," says the attendant. "The Indian was riding bareback."

When I was young I used to pray for a bicycle.
Then I realized that God doesn't work that way.
So I stole a bicycle and prayed for forgiveness.

It was many years since the embarrassing day when a young woman, with a baby in her arms, had entered the butcher's shop and confronted the owner with the news that her baby was his, and then asked what was he going to do about it? Finally he had offered to provide her with free meat until the boy was sixteen. She agreed.

He had been counting the years off on his calendar, and one day the teenager, who had been collecting the meat each week, came into the shop and said, "I'll be sixteen tomorrow."

"I know," said the butcher with a smile. "I've been counting too. Tell your mother, when you take this meat home, that it is the last free meat she'll get, and watch the expression on her face."

When the boy arrived home he told his mother.

The woman nodded and said, "Son, go back to the butcher and tell him I have also had free bread, free milk, and free groceries for the last sixteen years and watch the expression on his face!"

Tom is driving around town in a Rolls Royce when he sees his friend Harry. He pulls over to say hello.

"How did you get the car?" asks Harry.

"Well," says Tom. "I was walking down the street when a gorgeous woman pulled up in this car and offered me a ride. I got in and she asked me to kiss her, so I did. Then she parked up in a lane and took off all her clothes except her silk knickers. Then she lay back in her seat and said, 'Take anything you want from me …'"

"Wow," says Harry. "What did you do then?"

"Well," says Tom. "I could see that her underwear would never fit me, so I took the car."

Bob's wife was a surgeon, and so when he had to go into hospital for an operation she insisted on doing the surgery. She said she didn't want anyone else opening her male.

A new monk arrives at the monastery. He is assigned to help the other monks in copying the old texts by hand. He notices, however, that they are copying copies, not the original books. So, the new monk goes to the head monk to ask him about this. He points out that if there was an error in the first copy, that error would be continued in all of the other copies.

The head monk says, "We have been copying from the copies for centuries, but you make a good point, my son." So, he goes down into the cellar with one of the copies to check it against the original.

Hours later, nobody has seen him. So, one of the monks goes downstairs to look for him. He hears a sobbing coming from the back of the cellar, and finds the old monk leaning over one of the original books crying. He asks what's wrong.

The old monk sobs, "The word is *celebrate*."

Paddy was driving down the street in a sweat because he had an important meeting and couldn't find a parking place. Looking up to heaven he said, "Lord, take pity on me. If you find me a parking place I will go to Mass every Sunday for the rest of my life and give up my whiskey." Miraculously, a parking place appeared. Paddy looked up again and said, "Never mind, I found one."

Woman A: "That man's annoying me."
Woman B: "Why? He's not even looking at you."
Woman A: "I know. *That's* what's annoying me!"

A priest and a taxi driver both died and went to heaven. St. Peter was at the Pearly Gates waiting for them.

"Come with me," said St. Peter to the taxi driver.

The taxi driver did as he was told and followed St. Peter to a mansion. It had anything you could imagine from a bowling alley to an Olympic size pool.

"Wow, thank you," said the taxi driver.

Next, St. Peter led the priest to a rugged old shack with a bunk bed and a little old television set.

"Wait, I think you are a little mixed up," said the priest. "Shouldn't I be the one who gets the mansion? After all I was a priest, went to church every day, and preached God's word."

"Yes, that's true. But during your sermons people slept. When the taxi driver drove, everyone prayed!"

A mohel (a person who carries out the Jewish circumcision operation) opened a shop and displayed some plastic dustbins in the window.

A man went into the shop and said, "I'd like a plastic dustbin, please."

The mohel replied, "I'm afraid I don't sell them."

"But you've got plastic dustbins in the window!" exclaimed the man.

"So?" shrugged the mohel. "What would *you* have put in the window?"

Harry gets a job painting white dotted lines down the middle of roads. On his first day he does very well and paints six miles of road. On the second day he does four miles, but on the third day he's down to only two.

"I don't understand it," says his foreman. "You were doing so well. What happened?"

"Well, it's obvious," says Harry. "Every day I'm getting further and further away from the tin of paint."

"I went to the dentist this morning."
"Does your tooth still hurt?"
"I don't know – the dentist kept it."

❖

Facts of Life

Women love to talk on the phone. A woman can visit her girlfriend for two weeks, and upon returning home, she will call the same friend and they will talk for three hours.

Women will drive miles out of their way to avoid the possibility of getting lost using a short cut.

Women do NOT want an honest answer to the question, 'How do I look?'

PMS stands for: Permissible Man-Slaughter (or at least men think it means that). PMS also stands for Preposterous Mood Swings and Punish My Spouse.

Women will make three left turns to avoid making one right turn.

'Oh, nothing,' has an entirely different meaning in woman-language than it does in man-language.

Women cannot use a map without turning the map to correspond to the direction that they are heading.

All women are overweight by definition; don't agree with them about it. Women always have 5 pounds to lose, but don't bring this up unless they really have 5 pounds to gain.

If it is not Valentine's Day and you see a man in a flower shop, you can probably start up a conversation by asking, 'What did you do?'

Only women understand the reason for 'guest towels' and the 'good china'.

Women buy fuzzy toilet covers which makes it impossible for the lid to stay up. Thus it gets peed on by the guys (which gets them in trouble).

Women never check to see if the lid is up. They seem to plonk themselves down on the bowl and then complain that the man left the seat up, instead of taking two seconds and lowering it themselves.

Women can get out of speeding tickets by pouting. This will get men arrested.

Women don't really care about a sense of humour in a man despite claims to the contrary. You don't see women trampling over Tom Cruise to get to Ken Dodd, do you?

Men can never catch women checking out other men; women will always catch men checking out other women.

Why did the bad comedian tell the same jokes three nights running? His audience could have caught him if he'd been standing still.

One day a travelling salesman was driving down a country road at about 30 mph when he noticed that there was a three-legged chicken running alongside his car. He stepped on it but at 50 miles per hour the chicken was still keeping up. After about a mile of running the chicken ran up a farm lane and into a barn behind an old farm house.

The salesman had some time to kill so he turned around and drove up the farm lane. He knocked at the door and when the farmer answered he told him what he had just seen.

The farmer said that his son was a geneticist and he had developed this breed of chicken because he, his wife and his son each liked a drumstick and this way they only had to kill one chicken.

"That's the most fantastic thing I've ever heard," said the salesman. "How do they taste?"

"I don't know," said the farmer. "We've never caught one."

Bob was walking along the street one day when a young man rushed up to him and said, "Can you show me the quickest way to get to the hospital?"

Bob pushed him under a bus.

After seeing footage of a young Bosnian soldier throwing grenades, the coach of an American football team decides to take him on as a quarterback. This proves to be a great move, and the team soon wins the Superbowl. The young man excitedly rings home to tell his mother. "Mother, I just helped my team win the Superbowl. Aren't you happy?"

"No, I'm not!" she snaps back. "Here we have the sound of gunshots all day, we are living in a slum, your sister has been molested three times, and gangsters have broken your brother's legs. Why the hell did you make us move to Detroit?"

A TV station in the USA rings up the British ambassador and asks him what he'd like for Christmas.

"I couldn't possibly accept gifts in my position," says the ambassador.

The TV station insists and says he can anything he wants, no matter how big or small.

"Well," says the ambassador. "If you insist, I suppose I could accept a small box of chocolates."

A month later the ambassador is watching TV when the news presenter says, "A while back we asked a number of ambassadors what they would like for Christmas. The French ambassador said he'd like world peace. The German ambassador said he would like prosperity for the world's poor. And the British ambassador said he'd like a small box of candy."

Q: What do you call any elephant who is an expert on skin disorders?

A: A pachydermatologist.

271

Q: How do you stop an elephant from charging?
A: Take away his credit card.

Q: What do you get when you cross an elephant with a hooker?
A: A two-ton pickup.

Q: What did the female elephant say during sex?
A: "Can I be on top this time?"

Q: What did the elephant say to the nude man?
A: Cute, but can you breathe through it?

Q: What do you know when you see three elephants walking down the street wearing pink sweatshirts?
A: They're all in the same team.

Q: How do you know if there's an elephant in bed with you?
A: She has a big 'E' on her pyjama jacket pocket.

Q: Why won't they allow elephants in public swimming pools?
A: Because they might let down their trunks.

Eleven people were hanging on a rope under a helicopter, ten men and one woman. The rope was not strong enough to carry them all, so they decided that one had to leave, because otherwise they were all going to fall. They weren't able to name that person, until the woman gave a very touching speech. She said that she would voluntarily let go of the rope, because, as a woman, she was used to giving up everything for her husband and kids, or for men in general, and was used to always making sacrifices, with little in return.

As soon as she finished her speech, all the men started clapping their hands.

An elderly couple are attending a church service; about halfway through the service, the woman leans over and says, " I just did a silent fart. What do you think I should do?" Her husband replies, "Put a new battery in your hearing aid."

A tramp walks into a country pub and orders a pint of beer. The landlord pours him one, but the tramp changes his mind and asks for a ploughman's lunch instead. The landlord gives him a ploughman's, but, when the time comes to the pay, the tramp says he doesn't owe anything – the ploughman's had been given in exchange for a pint of beer that he had never received. The landlord is cross at being had but decides to make the best of it. "Here," he says, taking a £10 note out of his pocket. "Take this tenner and play the same trick in the Red Lion down the road."

"Well, I would," says the tramp, "but the landlord of the Red Lion paid me a tenner to play the trick on you."

A woman named Shirley had a heart attack and was taken to hospital. While on the operating table, she had a near-death experience. She saw God and asked, "Is this it?"

God said, "No, you have another 30 to 40 years to live."

Upon her recovery, she decided to stay in the hospital and have collagen shots, cheek implants, a face lift, liposuction and breast augmentation. She even had someone dye her hair. She figured since she had another 30 to 40 years, she might as well make the most of it.

She walked out after the last operation and was killed by an ambulance speeding up to the hospital. She arrived in front of God and said, "I thought you said I had another 30 to 40 years?"

God replied, "Shirley! I'm sorry but I didn't recognize you!"

Paddy was in New York. He was patiently waiting and watching the traffic cop on a busy street crossing. The cop would stop the flow of traffic and shout, "Okay, pedestrians!"

Then he'd allow the traffic to pass. He'd done this several times, and Paddy still stood on the sidewalk.

After the cop had shouted 'Pedestrians' for the tenth time, Paddy went over to him and said, "Is it not about time ye let the Catholics across?"

❖

It was half an hour before curfew in a Mexican town, and a tourist sees a soldier gun down a man in the street.

"Why did you do that?" asks the tourist.

"Breaking the curfew," replies the soldier.

"But it's half an hour before curfew," says the tourist.

"I know," says the soldier. "But I know where he lives, and he was never going to get home in thirty minutes."

"My girlfriend says I'm handsome."
"That's only because you feed her guide dog."

Two blokes are comparing notes on their summer holiday. "I was staying in a hotel in Poole," says one.
"In Dorset?" asks the other.
"Certainly, I'd recommend it to anyone."

Tracey fell in love with her boyfriend at second sight. The first time she didn't know he had any money.

The Church of England is opening its own string of supermarkets. They're going to be called Jesus Christ Superstores.

A man books into a sleazy hotel. The receptionist tells him that it's £20 a night or £15 if he makes his own bed.
"I reckon I can do that," says the man. "Give me a £15 room."
"Here's the key," replies the receptionist. "Pick up your timber and nails at the top of the stairs."

❖

The phone at the reception desk of a hotel starts ringing at three o'clock in the morning. The desk clerk answers it. It's a call from a drunk asking what time the bar opens.

"The bar opens at noon," answers the clerk. An hour later the same man calls again. He sounds even drunker but still wants to know when the bar opens.

"Same time as before," replies the clerk. Another hour passes, and the drunk calls again.

"What time joo shay the bar opens at?" he slurs.

The clerk replies, "It opens at noon, but if you really can't wait, I'll have room service send you up a drink."

"I don't wanna get in!" shouts the man. "Ah wanna get out!"

The young man asked the beautiful girl to marry him, pointing out that his father was 103 years old and that he was heir to his father's substantial fortune.

The girl asked the young man for time to consider his offer, and, two weeks later, she became his step-mother.

❖

A man absolutely hated his wife's cat and decided to get rid of him one day by driving him half a mile from his home and leaving him at the park.

As he was getting home, the cat was walking up the driveway.

The next day he decided to drive the cat 5 miles away. He put the beast out and headed home.

Driving back up his driveway, there was the cat!

He kept taking the cat further and further and the cat would always beat him home. At last he decided to drive a hundred miles away and leave the cat there.

Hours later the man calls home to his wife: "Jen, is the cat there?"

"Yes," the wife answers. "Why do you ask?"

"Put the bugger on the phone. I need directions!"

At a remote monastery deep in the woods, the monks followed a rigid vow of silence. This vow could only be broken once a year on Christmas, by one monk, and the monk could speak only one sentence.

One Christmas, Brother Thomas had his turn to speak and said, "I love the delightful mashed potatoes we have every year with the Christmas roast!" Then he sat down. Silence ensued for 365 days.

The next Christmas, Brother Michael got his turn, and said, "I think the mashed potatoes are lumpy and I truly despise them!" Once again, silence ensued for 365 days.

The following Christmas, Brother Paul rose and said, "I am fed up with this constant bickering!"

A judge was interviewing a woman regarding her pending divorce, and asked, "What are the grounds for your divorce?"

She replied, "About four acres and a nice little home in the middle of the property with a stream running by."

"No," he said, "I mean what is the foundation of this case?"

"It is made of concrete, brick and mortar," she responded.

"I mean," he continued, "what are your relations like?"

"I have an aunt and uncle living here in town, and so do my husband's parents."

He said, "Do you have a real grudge?"

"No," she replied. "We have a two-car carport and have never really needed one."

"Please," he tried again. "Is there any infidelity in your marriage?"

"Yes, both my son and daughter have stereo sets. We don't necessarily like the music, but the answer to your question is yes."

"Madam, does your husband ever beat you up?"

"Yes," she responded, "about twice a week he gets up earlier than I do."

Finally, in frustration, the judge asked, "Lady, why do you want a divorce?"

"Oh, I don't want a divorce," she replied. "I've never wanted a divorce. My husband does. He says he can't communicate with me!"

A man goes into a DIY store and asks for some bolts. "How long do you want them?" asks the assistant.

"To tell the truth," says the man. "I was rather hoping to keep them."

It's the French Revolution, and Tom, Dick and Harry are due to be guillotined. First up on the scaffold is Tom. The revolutionaries ask him if he wants to die facing down or facing up.

"I'll die facing up at the blade," says Tom.

So they put him in the guillotine and release the blade. Luckily for Tom, the blade gets stuck halfway down, and, according to custom, he's free to go.

The revolutionaries tinker with the guillotine and finally fix it. Dick goes up next, and he, like Tom, asks to die facing the blade. Again the guillotine drops, only to stop halfway down, and Dick, too, is released. The revolutionaries attempt to fix the guillotine once more, then drag Harry up to the scaffold.

Harry says, "Like my friends, I'll die looking up at the blade." The revolutionaries put him in the guillotine and are about to release the blade when Harry shouts, "Hang on! I think I can see what's wrong with this thing … !"

I went to a bookshop and said to the saleswoman, "Where's the self-help section?"

She said, "If I told you it would defeat the purpose."

❖

If you lend someone £20 and never see that person again it was probably worth it.

Opportunities always look bigger going then coming.

Not one shred of evidence supports the notion that life is serious.

Talk is cheap because supply exceeds demand.

There is no substitute for genuine lack of preparation.

Quitters never win; winners never quit. But those who never win and never quit are idiots.

It's easier to suffer in silence if you're sure someone is watching.

The lion shall lie down the lamb, but the lamb probably won't get much sleep.

The severity of the itch is inversely proportional to the ability to reach it.

It is easier to get forgiveness than permission.

One good turn usually gets most of the blanket.

No man is really successful until his mother-in-law admits it.

When it's you against the world, I'd bet on the world.

It's hard to make a comeback when you haven't been anywhere.

Never test the depth of the water with both feet.

When you're arguing with an idiot try to make sure he isn't doing the same thing.

It is more impressive when others discover your good qualities without your help.

People are like teabags. You don't know how strong they are until you put them in hot water.

Exaggeration is a billion times worse than understatement.

If it were truly the thought that counted, more women would be pregnant.

The bigger they are the harder they hit.

You can fool some of the people some of the time, and that's sufficient.

The things that come to those who wait may be the things left by those who got there first.

If you tell the truth you don't have to remember anything.

The meek shall inherit the earth but not till the rest of us are done with it.

Always speak well of your enemies – after all, you made them.

Never confuse your career with your life.

If lawyers are disbarred and clergymen are defrocked, doesn't it follow that electricians can be delighted, musicians can be denoted, cowboys deranged, models deposed, tree surgeons debarked and dry cleaners depressed.

It's late evening, and Tom's wife catches him pouring six cans of lager down the toilet. "What on earth are you doing?" she asks.

Tom replies, "Well, it seems a waste, but I thought it'd save me getting up in the night."

I went to the shops yesterday and treated myself to a toilet brush. It's no good, though. I'm going to have to go back to paper.

A man runs into the vet's office carrying his dog, screaming for help. The vet rushes him back to an examination room and has him put his dog down on the examination table. The vet examines the still, limp body and after a few moments tells the man that his dog, regrettably, is dead. The man, clearly agitated and not willing to accept this, demands a second opinion.

The vet goes into the back room and comes out with a cat and puts the cat down next to the dog's body. The cat sniffs the body, walks from head to tail poking and sniffing the dog's body and finally looks at the vet and meows. The vet looks at the man and says, "I'm sorry, but the cat thinks that your dog is dead too."

The man is still unwilling to accept that his dog is dead.

The vet brings in a black Labrador. The lab sniffs the body, walks from head to tail, and finally looks at the vet and barks. The vet looks at the man and says, "I'm sorry, but the lab thinks your dog is dead too."

The man, finally resigned to the diagnosis, thanks the vet and asks how much he owes.

The vet answers, "£300."

"£300 to tell me my dog is dead?" exclaimed the man...

"Well," the vet replied, "I would only have charged you £50 for my initial diagnosis. The additional £250 is for the cat scan and lab tests."

281

Riding the favourite at Cheltenham, a jockey is well ahead of the field. Suddenly he's hit on the head by a salmon sandwich and a pork pie. He manages to keep control of his mount and pulls back into the lead, only to be struck by a tin of caviar and a dozen Scotch eggs. With great skill he manages to steer the horse to the front of the field once more when, on the final furlong, he's struck on the head by a bottle Chardonnay and a Bakewell tart. Thus distracted, he only manages second place. Furious, he immediately goes to the stewards to complain that he's been seriously hampered.

A sad-faced man walked into a flower shop early one morning.

The assistant was ready to take his order for a funeral wreath, based on the look on the man's face, but soon realized his assumption was wrong as he asked for a basket of flowers to be sent to his wife for their anniversary.

"And what day will that be?" the assistant asked.

Glumly he replied, "Yesterday."

❖

A married couple are travelling across country and stop off at a high-class hotel. After spending the night they check out and discover the bill is £600.

"This is ludicrous!" complains the husband. "Three hundred pounds each for one night?"

"The price also includes the use of the hotel sauna, complementary drinks at the bar and our car valet service," replies the desk clerk.

"But we didn't use the sauna," says the husband.

"You could have used it if you'd wanted to," replies the clerk.

"And we didn't have drinks at the bar," says the husband.

"You could have if you'd wanted to," replies the clerk.

"And we didn't have our car valeted," says the husband.

"You could have if you'd wanted to," replies the clerk.

"I give up," says the husband and writes a cheque.

"Excuse me," says the clerk, "but this cheque is only for £100."

"I know," replies the husband, "but I'm charging you £500 for sleeping with my wife."

"I didn't sleep with your wife," says the clerk.

"No," replies the husband, "but you could have if you'd wanted to."

An old man is riding in a lift with two glamorous women. One woman takes a perfume bottle out of her bag and sprays her neck. She turns to the other woman and says, "Romance by Ralph Lauren. £150 an ounce."

The other woman takes a perfume bottle out of her bag, sprays herself and says, "Chanel No. 5. £200 an ounce."

The lift stops and the doors open. The old man steps out and lets off a huge rumbling fart. As the doors close, he looks back and says, "Broccoli. 49p a pound."

Teacher: "Now, Susan, can you tell me where God lives?"

Susan: "Miss, I think he lives in the bathroom."

Teacher: "In the bathroom! Why do you think that?"

Susan: "Because every morning I can hear my father knock on the bathroom door and say, 'God, are you still in there?'"

A husband goes out on the town on Friday night and has far too much to drink. When he eventually comes round, he discovers it's Sunday afternoon. He struggles to come up with a good explanation for his wife, then has a brainwave. He rings home and shouts down the phone, "Darling! Don't pay the ransom. I've escaped."

❖

What did the elephant say to the naked man?
"It's nice, but can it pick up peanuts?"

❖

A sadist is someone who would put a drawing-pin on an electric chair.

❖

A couple are listening to their friends' holiday experiences in the south of England. "My!" says one. "We knew you were planning to drive around Kent, but we hadn't realised you were going to take in Surrey, Hampshire and Dorset as well."

"We hadn't planned to," says the wife. "But Ted refuses to ask for directions."

❖

Bill Clinton, Al Gore and Bill Gates all die in a plane crash and go to meet their maker. God looks on Al and asks him what he thinks is the most important thing in life. Al tells him that protecting the earth's ecology is the most important thing. God says, "I like the way you think. Come and sit at my left hand."

God then asks Bill Clinton the same question. Bill says that he feels people and their personal choices are the most important thing. God says, "I like the way you think. Come and sit at my right hand."

God then turns to Bill Gates, who is staring at him indignantly. "What's your problem, Bill?" asks God.

Bill replies, "You're sitting in my damn chair."

Overheard conversation: "I don't know what to do with my hands while I'm talking."

"Why don't you hold them over your mouth?"

"My old uncle has got one foot in the grate."

"Don't you mean he's got one foot in the grave?"

"No. He wants to be cremated."

A man goes to the doctor for his test results. The doctor says, "I've got some good news and bad news."

"What's the bad news?" asks the man.

The doctor replies, "You've got a week to live."

"What!" says the man. "So what the hell is the good news?"

The doctor replies, "They're going to name the disease after you."

Man to greengrocer: "I asked for six apples. You only gave me five."

Greengrocer: "I know, but one was rotten, so I saved you the trouble of throwing it away."

One day the manager of a brokers' firm walks past a new employee who is counting call slips. The guy does it faster than anyone he has ever seen.

285

"That's amazing," says the manager. "Where did you learn to count like that?"

"Yale," answers the employee.

"Yale? I don't believe it. I went to Yale too. What's your name?"

"Yimmy Yohnson."

Two business owners are comparing working practices. One says to the other, "I make sure each of my employees takes a week off every two months."

"Why on earth would you do that?" asks the other.

The first replies, "It's the best way of finding out which ones I can do without."

A little pig walks into a bar, orders a drink and asks directions to the lavatories. The bartender tells him where the gents are, and the pig hurries off to relieve himself. A second little pig then comes in, orders a drink and asks for the lavatories. Again, the bartender tells the pig where to go, and the pig hurries away. A third little pig then appears and orders a drink.

"I suppose you'll want to know where the toilets are," says the bartender.

"No," replies the pig. "I'm the one that goes wee-wee-wee all the way home."

Just outside the church the small boy found a one pound coin and picked it up.

The vicar saw the boy and said, "Hello! I see you've found a coin. Are you going to keep it?"

"No, sir," replied the boy.

"Excellent, excellent," beamed the vicar.

"I'm going to spend it," said the boy.

The young girl was snuggling up to the young man on the sofa and said, "Would you like to see my birthmark?"

"Yes," replied the young man. "How long have you had it?"

An English tourist goes to an Irish race meet and sees a priest blessing one of the horses. To the tourist's surprise, the horse wins, as do the next two horses the priest blesses. He sees the priest bless a fourth horse and puts all his money on it. Unfortunately, the starting pistol give the horse a heart attack, and it drops dead before it can move. Later the tourist tells the priest about his disastrous bet and asks why his blessing didn't work on the fourth horse.

"Are you a Protestant?" asks the priest.

"Yes, I am," replies the tourist.

"Well, then," says the priest. "You'll not be knowing the difference between a blessing and the last rites."

If work was so good the rich would keep more of it for themselves.

A biker was riding along a California beach when suddenly the sky clouded above his head and, in a booming voice, the Lord said, "Because you have TRIED to be faithful to me in all ways, I will grant you one wish."

The biker pulled over and said, "Build a bridge to Hawaii so I can ride over anytime I want."

The Lord said, "Your request is materialistic. Think of the enormous challenges for that kind of undertaking. The supports required to reach the bottom of the Pacific! The concrete and steel it would take! It will nearly exhaust several natural resources. I can do it, but it is hard for me to justify your desire for worldly things. Take a little more time and think of something that would honour and glorify me."

The biker thought about it for a long time. Finally he said, "Lord, I wish that I could understand my wife. I want to know how she feels inside, what she's thinking when she gives me the silent treatment, why she cries, what she means when she says nothing's wrong, and how I can make a woman truly happy."

The Lord replied, "You want two lanes or four on that bridge?"

A man takes a cat and a dog to audition for a TV talent show. While the man conducts, the dog plays the piano and the cat sings.

"That's fantastic," says the TV producer. "The dog plays wonderfully, and the cat's singing is superb."

The man replies, "Look, I don't want to put you off, but I've got a confession to make: the cat can't sing a note – the dog's a ventriloquist."

Man: "Darling, if we get married do you think you will be able to live on my income?"

Woman: "Of course, darling. But what are *you* going to live on?"

Two businessmen are fishing in a rowing boat, when a storm blows up and capsizes them. One of the men can swim but the other can't.

"Can you float alone?" asks the swimmer to his sinking partner.

The partner shouts back, "This is no time to talk shop."

A man is having breakfast in a greasy spoon café when three bikers come in looking for trouble. The first biker spits in the man's food, the second pours coffee over the man's head, and the third pulls away his chair so he falls over. Without saying a word the man gets up and walks out.

"Not much of a man," says one of the bikers to the waitress.

"Nope," replies the waitress. "And he's not much of a driver, either. He just drove his lorry over three bikes."

I'm an atheist – thank God!

One day an out of work mime-artist is visiting the zoo and attempts to earn some money as a street performer.

However, as soon as he starts to draw a crowd, the zookeeper grabs him and drags him into his office.

The zookeeper explains to him that the zoo's most popular attraction, a gorilla, has died suddenly. The keeper fears that attendance at the zoo will fall off. He offers the mime-artist a job dressing up as the gorilla until they can get another one.

The next morning, before the crowd arrives, the mime-artist puts on the gorilla suit and enters the cage. He discovers that it's a great job. He can sleep all he wants, play and make fun of people and he draws bigger crowds than he ever did before.

However, eventually the crowds tire of him and he gets bored just swinging on tyres. He begins to notice that the people are paying more attention to the lion in the cage next to his.

Not wanting to lose the attention of his audience, he climbs to the top of his cage, crawls across a partition, and dangles from the top to the lion's cage. Of course, this makes the lion furious, but the crowd loves it.

At the end of the day the zookeeper comes and gives him a raise for being such a good attraction as a gorilla.

Well, this goes on for some time. He keeps taunting the lion, the crowds grow larger, and his salary keeps going up. Then one terrible day when he is dangling over the furious lion, he slips and falls. The lion gathers itself and prepares to pounce. The mime-artist is so scared that he begins to run round and round the cage with the lion close behind.

Finally, the mime-artist starts screaming and yelling, "Help, Help me!"

But the lion is quick and pounces.

The mime-artist soon finds himself flat on his back looking up at the angry lion and the lion says in a whisper, "Shut up, you idiot! Do you want to get us both fired?"

A man of thirty was talking to his girlfriend. "I've been asked to get married hundreds of times," he said.

"Oh!" replied his girlfriend, rather astonished. "Who by?"

"My parents."

"Mr Clark, I'm afraid I have bad news," says the doctor. "You only have six months to live."

"But I have no medical insurance," replies Mr Clark. "I can't possibly pay you in that time."

"All right," says the doctor. "Let's make it nine months."

Harry comes back from the hospital looking worried.

"What's the matter?" asks his wife.

"The consultant says I have to take a tablet every day for the rest of my life," groans Harry.

"Well, that's not too bad," says his wife.

"Yes, it is," says Harry. "He only gave me seven."

A firm advertises for a 'problem solver' with a salary of £100,000. Tom goes for an interview and is offered the job on the spot.

"That's great," says Tom. "But tell me, how can you afford to pay me such a high salary?"

"That," says his employer, "is your problem."

Worried young girl: "Doctor, this new diet you've put me on makes me feel so passionate and sexy that I got carried away last night and bit off my boyfriend's right ear."

Doctor: "Don't worry, it's only forty to fifty calories."

Two sailors are on shore leave. They have a few drinks and decide to go to a variety show. At the interval one of them needs the toilet and asks directions from the usherette. "Go through the exit, turn left along the corridor, turn first right, then left, then right again," she says. He follows the directions with some difficulty, relieves himself and eventually finds his way back to his seat.

"You missed the best act," says his mate. "While you were gone a sailor came on stage and pissed into the orchestra pit."

A woman went to her doctor to complain that her husband's sexual feelings for her seemed to have declined.

The doctor, being an old friend of the family, gave the woman some pills to slip into her husband's tea so that at least the man wouldn't get a complex about being a bit underpowered.

Two days later the woman was back in the doctor's surgery.

"What happened?" asked the doctor. "Did the pills work?"

"Fantastic!" replied the woman. "I was so eager to see their effects on my husband that I tipped three of them into a cup of coffee and, within seconds of drinking it, he got up, kicked over the table, pulled me down on the floor and ravished me."

"Oh!" said the doctor. "I hope you weren't too surprised."

"Surprised?" said the woman. "I'll never be able to set foot in the restaurant again...."

A union boss is telling his son a bedtime story. "Once upon a time-and-a-half..."

A man is checking into a hotel. The receptionist asks him if he would like a room with a bath or shower.

"What's the difference?" asks the man.

"You can sit down in a bath," explains the receptionist.

Why did the dinosaur cross the road?
'Cos chickens hadn't evolved yet.

Two women are talking. "You know," says one. "Eighty per cent of men think the best way to end an argument is to make love."

"Well," says the other. "That will certainly revolutionise the game of ice-hockey!"

Little Nancy was in the garden filling in a hole when her neighbour peered over the fence. Interested in what the cheeky-faced youngster was up to, he politely asked, "What are you doing there, Nancy?"

"My goldfish died," replied Nancy tearfully without looking up, "and I've just buried him."

The neighbour was very concerned. "That's an awfully big hole for a goldfish, isn't it?"

Nancy patted down the last heap of soil and replied, "That's because he's inside your cat."

The last time I sat on a committee we were presented with a plan that had two alternatives. We therefore narrowed it down to eighteen possibilities for further discussion.

"Doctor, doctor, what's the bad news?"

"We cut off the wrong leg. But the good news is that your bad leg is getting better."

"Doctor, doctor, Tell me straight. Is it bad?"

"Well, I wouldn't start watching any new soap operas."

Doctor: "You'll live to be sixty."
Patient: "I am sixty!"
Doctor: "See! What did I tell you?"

❖

A man is strolling past the mental hospital and suddenly remembers an important meeting. Unfortunately, his watch has stopped, and he cannot tell if he is late or not. Then, he notices a patient similarly strolling about within the hospital fence. Calling out to the patient, the man says, "Pardon me, sir, but do you have the time?"

The patient calls back, "One moment!" and throws himself upon the ground, pulling out a short stick as he does. He pushes the stick into the ground, and, pulling out a carpenter's level, assures himself that the stick is vertical. With a compass, the patient locates north and with a steel ruler, measures the precise length of the shadow cast by the stick. Withdrawing a slide rule from his pocket, the patient calculates rapidly, then swiftly packs up all his tools and turns back to the pedestrian, saying, "It is now precisely 3:29 pm, provided today is August 16th, which I believe it is."

The man can't help but be impressed by this demonstration, and sets his watch accordingly. Before he leaves, he says to the patient, "That was really quite remarkable, but tell me, what do you do on a cloudy day, or at night, when the stick casts no shadow?"

The patient holds up his wrist and says, "I suppose I'd just look at my watch."

A train steward calls the police after coming across a young couple having sex in a carriage. The young man is arrested for having a first-class ride with a second-class ticket.

Why did the hedgehog cross the road?
To see his flat-mate.

An Irish priest is driving down to New York and gets stopped for speeding in Connecticut. The state trooper smells alcohol on the priest's breath and then sees an empty wine bottle on the floor of the car. He says, "Sir, have you been drinking?"

"Just water," says the priest.

The trooper says, "Then why do I smell wine?"

The priest looks at the bottle and says, "Good Lord! He's done it again!"

A little girl was talking to her teacher about whales.

The teacher said it was physically impossible for a whale to swallow a human because even though they were a very large mammal their throat was very small.

The little girl stated Jonah was swallowed by a whale.

The teacher reiterated a whale could not swallow a human; it was impossible.

The little girl said, "When I get to heaven I will ask Jonah."

The teacher asked, "What if Jonah went to hell?"

The little girl replied, "Then you ask him."

A farmhand in Australia was out checking farm fences in his Landcruiser when he hit something. After viewing the damage, he radioed the farm for advice.

"There's a pig stuck in the radiator grille. He's still alive, but he's kicking and squealing so much I can't get him free," he said.

"Okay," said the boss. "In the back of the 'cruiser there's a pistol. Put it up to the pig's head and shoot it. When its body goes all limp you'll be able to get it off the grille and throw it into the bush."

About 45 minutes later the farmhand called in again.

"I did what you said, boss. I shot the pig in the head, he went all limp and I got him out of the grille, but I still can't go on."

"Why not?" asked the boss. "What's the problem?"

"Well it's his motorbike ... the flashing blue light is jammed under the wheel-arch."

"Whisper those three little words that will make me walk on air."

"Go hang yourself."

Cruise passenger to purser: "I want to complain. I just went into my cabin and found a common seaman using my shower!"

Purser: "Who did you expect in second class? The captain?"

If you love something, set it free.

If it comes back, it was, and always will be yours.

If it never returns, it was never yours to begin with.

If it just sits in your living room, messes up your stuff, eats your food, uses your telephone, takes your money, and never behaves as if you actually set it free in the first place, you probably gave birth to it!

296

Once there was a golfer whose drive landed on an anthill. Rather than move the ball, he decided to hit it where it lay. He gave a mighty swing. Clouds of sand and ants exploded from the spot. Everything but the golf ball flew. It sat in the same spot.

So he lined up and tried another shot. Clouds of sand and ants went flying again. The golf ball didn't even wiggle.

Two ants survived. One dazed ant said to the other: "What are we going to do?"

Said the other ant: "I don't know about you, but I'm going to get on the ball."

Instructor to trainee park ranger: "You see an enraged grizzly bear approaching a group of tourists. What steps do you take?"

Park ranger: "Large ones – in the opposite direction."

A guest in a country inn is appalled by the state of his bedroom. "This bed is a disgrace," he complains to the owner.

"But it's very historic," says the owner. "Dick Turpin slept in that bed."

"Yes," replies the guest. "And judging by the state of the mattress his horse slept with him."

An A-road and a motorway walk into a pub. The motorway turns white with fear and starts shaking.

"What's wrong?" asks the A-road.

"Look at the crazy guy in the corner," replies the motorway.

"How d'you know he's crazy?" says the A-road.

"It's obvious," says the motorway. "He's a cycle path."

A knight in a besieged castle offers to break out and ride for help. Unfortunately, all the horses are dead, so the knight suggests riding out on the back of a giant wolfhound.

"You can't," says the lord of the manor. "My wolfhound has a sore leg. The only other dog is this Chihuahua, and I wouldn't send a knight out on a dog like this."

Pupil to teacher: "Can you give me a cigarette?"

Teacher: "No, of course I'm not going to give you a cigarette. Do you want to get me into trouble?"

Pupil: "Well, OK … but I'd rather have a cigarette."

"Betting on horses is a funny old game," says a man to his friend. "You win one day and lose the next."

The friend replies, "So why not bet every other day?"

A guest speaker is trying to make himself heard over the racket of a boisterous rugby club dinner. He complains to the president who is sitting next to him. "It's so noisy, I can't hear myself speak."

"I wouldn't worry about it," replies the president. "You're not missing much."

A boxer goes to a doctor complaining of insomnia. "Have you tried counting sheep?" asks the doctor.

"It doesn't work," replies the boxer. "Every time I get to nine I stand up."

A man is examined by his doctor.

The doctor says, "Take this green pill with a glass of water when you get up. Take this blue pill with a glass of water after lunch. Then just before you go to bed take this red pill with another glass of water."

"Exactly what's the matter with me?" asks the man.

"You're not drinking enough water."

The gorgeous new maid had once been a gymnast in Romania. She was now trying to improve her English by working for Lord and Lady Spiffleburgson at their mansion in Dorset. The maid had been with the Spiffleburgsons for only nine days and found many English habits rather strange. But she was determined to succeed as she desperately needed her salary to help support her family in Romania.

Thus it was at a luncheon party at the mansion that she walked in carefully carrying a large bowl of salad – but the guests were rather astonished that she was completely naked. The gentlemen at the luncheon raised their eyebrows while secretly admiring her trim, lithe young body, while the ladies demurely tried to look away.

After the maid had placed the bowl of salad on the table and was leaving the room, Lady Spiffleburgson rose from her chair and accompanied her maid to the kitchen.

"My dear," said her ladyship, "why are you walking about naked?"

"I only obey your orders," said the maid. "I hear you say – you say several times – and you say it important for me to remember – I must serve salad without dressing."

The sergeant major of a Scottish regiment goes into a chemist's shop and places a tattered old condom on the counter. "How much to repair that?" asks the sergeant major.

"Oh dear," replies the chemist. "It's in a bit of a state. I can sew it up there and glue it here and here, but it'll need tape down the edges and a very thorough wash. To be honest, it might be better to buy a new one."

The sergeant major promises to think about it. Next day he returns and says, "I'll take one of your condoms, please. I had a word with the lads, and they reckon a new one would be a good investment."

The man was not very frightened when he saw the ghost, and, since it appeared to be friendly, he asked the ghost if he could try to photograph it. The ghost willingly agreed, and the man went to fetch his camera but found that the flash attachment on it was broken.

The spirit was willing – but the flash was weak.

While he is giving a physical examination, the doctor notices that his patient's shins are covered in dark, savage bruises. "Tell me," says the doctor. "Do you play hockey or football?"

"No," says the man. "But my wife and I play bridge."

One day in the Garden of Eden, Eve calls out to God, "Lord, I have a problem!"

"What's the problem, Eve?"

"Lord, I know you've created me and have provided this beautiful garden and all of these wonderful animals, and that hilarious comedy snake, but I'm just not happy."

"Why is that, Eve?" came the reply from above.

"Lord, I am lonely. And I'm sick to death of apples."

"Well, Eve, in that case, I have a solution. I shall create a man for you."

"What's a 'man', Lord?"

"This man will be a flawed creature, with aggressive tendencies, an enormous ego and an inability to empathize or listen to you properly. All in all, he'll give you a hard time. But, he'll be bigger and faster and more muscular than you. He'll be really good at fighting and kicking a ball about and hunting fleet-footed ruminants, and not altogether bad as a mate for you."

"Sounds great," says Eve, with an ironically raised eyebrow.

"Yeah, well. He's better than a poke in the eye with a burnt stick. But, you can have him on one condition."

"What's that, Lord?"

"You'll have to let him believe that I made him first."

One morning a blind bunny was hopping down the bunny trail, and he tripped over a large snake and fell right on his twitchy little nose. "Oh, please excuse me!" said the bunny. "I didn't mean to trip over you, but I'm blind and can't see."

"That's perfectly all right," replied the snake. "To be sure, it was my fault. I didn't mean to trip you, but I'm blind too, and I didn't see you coming. By the way, what kind of animal are you?"

Well, I really don't know," said the bunny. "I'm blind, and

I've never seen myself. Maybe you could examine me and find out."

So the snake felt the bunny all over, and he said, "Well, you're soft, and cuddly, and you have long silky ears, and a little fluffy tail and a dear twitchy little nose... You must be a bunny rabbit!"

Then he said, "I can't thank you enough, but by the way, what kind of animal are you?"

And the snake replied that he didn't know, and the bunny agreed to examine him, and when he was finished, the snake said, "Well, what kind of an animal am I?"

So the bunny felt the snake all over, and he replied, "You're hard, you're cold, you're slippery ... You must be a lawyer."

Mabel and Arthur had been living together for thirty-five years as man and wife.

One day Mabel was reading a romantic women's magazine when she suddenly looked up at Arthur and said, "Why don't we get married?"

"Don't be crazy," replied Arthur. "Who would want to marry us at our time of life?"

Worried that his son was spending too much money on dates, Johnny's father asked how much his last date had cost.

Little Johnny calculated a minute then replied, "Oh, about £5 or so I think."

"Well," said his father, "I'm proud of you for finally coming up with an inexpensive evening."

"To be honest, Dad," Johnny went on, "we'd have done more, but that was all the money she had."

Mrs Smith is a hypochondriac, and her doctor, fed up with her constant complaints about non-existent illnesses, starts palming her off with a mild sedative to keep her happy. One day Mrs Smith complains of chest pains and is prescribed her usual treatment. However, this time the pain is real, and Mrs Smith dies of a heart attack. The doctor hears the news and is so upset that he dies of shock. Mrs Smith and the doctor are buried in adjoining plots. Next morning the doctor hears a tapping on his coffin, and a muffled voice calls out, "Doctor, this is Mrs Smith! Do you have anything for worms?"

A passenger cruise ship passes a small desert island. Everyone watches as a tatty-looking, bearded man runs out on the beach and starts shouting and waving his hands.

"Who's that?" asks one of the passengers.

"I've no idea," replies the captain. "But every year we sail past and he goes nuts."

A woman rings the lost property office of the railway company and asks if a stray octopus has been found. They ask her what colour it is.

As the plane flew over the sea I saw something large, black and hairy in the water. It was an oil wig.

I'm a kleptomaniac, but I'm taking something for it.

Surgeon to patient: "I have good news and bad news about your operation. The bad news is that it's a risky procedure and your chances of survival are 99 to one."

"Oh my God!" says the patient. "So what's the good news"

The surgeon replies, "The good news is that my last 99 patients died."

Two drunks, Fred and Bill, were walking along the road when Fred said, "Hey! Ishn't that man over th-there the Archbishop of Canterbury?"

"No," replied Bill. "It can't be."

"It ish!" said Fred. "I'll go over and ask him."

Fred staggered over to the man and said, "Ex … excuse me. But are you the … the Archbishop of Canterbury?"

"Get lost, you pathetic drunken creep," replied the man, "or I'll smash your face in!"

Fred staggered back to Bill.

"Was it the Archbish?" asked Bill.

"I don't know," replied Fred. "The st … stupid man refushed to answer my question."

"My mother-in-law has gone to the West Indies."
"Jamaica?"
"No – she decided to go by herself."

For eleven years Duncan had put up with the fat, interfering old woman. Now he could stand it no longer.

"She's got to go," he said to his wife. "I can't stand your mother another minute!"

"*My* mother!" exclaimed Duncan's wife. "I thought she was *your* mother!"

Two country rustics are riding a train for the first time. They've brought along a bag of apples for lunch, and, just as one bites into his apple, the train enters a long tunnel. "Have you taken a bite out of your apple yet?" he asks.

"No," says the other.

"Well, don't," says the first. "I just did and I went blind."

Two avid fishermen go on a fishing trip. They rent all the equipment: the reels, the rods, the wading suits, the rowboat, the car, and even a cabin in the woods. They spend a fortune.

The first day they go fishing, but they don't catch anything. The same thing happens on the second day, and on the third day. It goes on like this until finally, on the last day of their vacation, one of the men catches a fish.

As they're driving home they're really depressed.

One guy turns to the other and says, "Do you realize that this one lousy fish we caught cost us fifteen hundred dollars?"

The other guy says, "Wow! It's a good thing we didn't catch any more!"

On a Trans-Atlantic flight, a plane passes through a severe storm. The turbulence is awful, and things go from bad to worse when one wing is struck by lightning.

One woman in particular loses it! Screaming, she stands up in the front of the plane.

"I'm too young to die. I want my last minutes on Earth to be memorable as so far no one has ever made me really feel like a woman! Well, I've had it! Is there anyone on this plane who can make me feel like a woman?"

For a moment there is silence. Everyone has forgotten their own peril, and they all stare, riveted, at the desperate woman in the front of the plane. Then, a man stands up in the rear of the plane.

"I can make you feel like a woman," he says.

He's drop-dead gorgeous. Tall, well built, with flowing black hair and jet black eyes, he starts to walk slowly up the aisle, unbuttoning his shirt one button at a time. No one moves.

The woman is breathing heavily in anticipation as the strange man approaches. He removes his shirt. Muscles ripple across his chest as he reaches her, and extends the arm holding his shirt to the trembling woman, and whispers:

"Here, iron this."

There is justice in the world. Yesterday the man stealing my tyres was run over by the man stealing my car.

A couple are walking down the street when the girl stops in a front of a jewellery store and says, "Honey, look at that necklace! It's so beautiful."

"No problem," replies the man, throwing a brick through the window and grabbing the necklace. A little later the girl points to a bracelet in the window of another shop.

"Oh, honey," she says. "I'd love that too."

"No problem," says her boyfriend and again throws a brick through the window. A little later they pass another shop, where she sees a diamond ring.

"Oh, honey," she says. "Isn't that lovely?"

"Hang on," he says. "What do you think I am? Made of bricks?"

A man takes his bride to an exclusive Moscow hotel for their honeymoon. The man is paranoid about being spied on, so he checks the room to make sure there aren't any KGB bugs still lurking around. Sure enough, he finds a suspicious round metal plate in the floor under a rug. He removes the restraining screws and throws the object out of the window. A few minutes later he hears a fleet of ambulances pulling up outside. He rings down to reception to find out what's going on.

"It's terrible," says the receptionist. "One of the chandeliers in the suite below yours has fallen on a dinner party."

A woman is complaining to her friend about the amount of housework she has to do. "I spend all day at the office then come home and wash the clothes. And every weekend I have to wash the kitchen floor and all the windows."

"But what about your husband?" asks her friend.

"I make him wash himself," says the woman.

The Emperor Nero is watching some Christians being thrown to the lions. He turns to his wife and says, "Do you know what I like most about this sport? No pitch invasions."

A statistician is walking down the corridor when he feels a twinge in his chest. Immediately, he runs to the stairwell and hurls himself down. His friend visits him in the hospital and asks why he did it.

The actuary replies, "The chances of having a heart attack while falling down the stairs are much lower than the chances of just having a heart attack."

A man goes to a travel agent to book his summer holiday.

"Last year you sold me a holiday to Bermuda, and my wife got pregnant," says the man. "The year before it was Monte Carlo, and my wife got pregnant. And the year before that it was Hong Kong, and my wife got pregnant then, as well."

"I see," says the assistant. "And what did you have in mind this year?"

"Somewhere cheaper," replies the man. "So she can come with me for a change."

Little Johnny is performing in the school play when he falls through a large crack in the floor.

Johnny's father turns to his mother and says, "Don't worry. It's only a stage he's going through."

A lovely afternoon finds one fellow and his wife golfing. They have had a wonderful time and the man has had a near perfect game. The final hole, by far the most difficult, wraps around an old barn. With a terrible slice the man puts the barn between his ball and the green. Knowing that the strokes that it will take to get around the barn will destroy his score, he begins to rant and rave. His wife hating to see him ruin such a great afternoon makes a suggestion.

"What if I were to hold open the barn doors? That way you could send it right through the barn onto the green."

He thinks this over and decides that it will work. With his wife holding open the barn door he lines up with the hole and gives the ball a terrific whack! The ball shoots through the air and right into his wife's head, killing her instantly.

Months go by, the man mourning all the while. His friends, hating to see him in such a state, convince him to go golfing with them. They end up at the same course and on the final hole, oddly enough, another terrible slice puts the old barn

308

between his ball and the green. Again he begins to rant and rave at what this dilemma will do to his score. His friend, wanting to please him, makes a suggestion.

"What if I were to hold open the barn doors? That way you could send it right through the barn onto the green."

"No," the man replies, "last time I did that I got two over par."

At the cocktail party, one woman said to another, "Aren't you wearing your wedding ring on the wrong finger?"

The other replied, "Yes, I am. I married the wrong man."

A woman, while touring a small South American country was shown a bullfight.

The guide told her, "This is our number one sport."

The horrified woman said, "Isn't that revolting?"

"No," the guide replied, "revolting is our number two sport."

A rich lawyer is grouse shooting when one of his birds falls into an adjacent field. The lawyer sees an old yokel standing in the field and asks him to pick up the grouse. "Not doing that," says the old man. "This is my field, so that be my bird."

This infuriates the lawyer. "Listen," he says, "I know the law and that bird belongs to me. If you don't hand it over I'll sue you."

The old man replies, "Round here we settle things with the Three Whack Rule. I gives you three whacks with my stick, then you give me three whacks. Whoever gives the biggest whacks wins."

The lawyer is sure he can whack harder than the old yokel, so he agrees. The old man takes his walking stick and gives the lawyer a terrific whack across the legs, then another across the nose and another across the back of his head. The lawyer has been knocked to his knees but manages to stagger to his feet. "Right. My turn," he says.

"Naahh," says the old yokel. "You win. Keep the rotten bird."

There were three men talking in the pub. Two of them are talking about the amount of control they have over their wives, while the third remains quiet.

After a while one of the first two turns to the third and says, "Well, what about you, what sort of control do you have over your wife?"

The third fellow says, "I'll tell you. Just the other night my wife came to me on her hands and knees."

The first two guys were amazed. "What happened then?" they asked.

"She said, 'get out from under the bed and fight like a man'."

John invited his mother over for dinner. During the meal, his mother couldn't help noticing how beautiful John's roommate was. She had long been suspicious of a relationship between John and his roommate, and this only made her more curious.

Over the course of the evening, while watching the two interact, she started to wonder if there was more between John and the roommate than met the eye. Reading his mom's thoughts, John volunteered, "I know what you must be thinking, but I assure you, Julie and I are just roommates."

About a week later, Julie came to John and said, "Ever since your mother came to dinner, I've been unable to find the beautiful silver gravy ladle. You don't suppose she took it, do you?"

John said, "Well, I doubt it, but I'll write her a letter just to be sure."

So he sat down and wrote: Dear Mother, I'm not saying you did take a gravy ladle from my house, and I'm not saying you did not take a gravy ladle. But the fact remains that one has been missing ever since you were here for dinner.

Several days later, John received a letter from his mother which read: Dear Son, I'm not saying that you do sleep with Julie, and I'm not saying that you do not sleep with Julie. But the fact remains that if she was sleeping in her own bed, she would have found the gravy ladle by now. Love, Mom.

Lesson of the day... Don't Lie To Your Mother.

A hunter goes into a butcher's shop and asks for a duck.

"I'm sorry," says the butcher, "we're out of duck. How about a chicken?"

"Oh yes," replies the hunter. "And how do I tell my wife that I shot a chicken?"

What's the difference between a bad golfer and a skydiver?

One goes Whack! "Awwwwwghk!"

The other goes, "Awwwwwghk!" Whack!

A cinema usher notices a man stretched cross three seats. He walks over and whispers, "Sorry, sir, but you're only allowed one seat."

The man moans but doesn't budge.

"Sir, if you don't move, I'll have to call the manager," says the usher.

Again, the man moans but stays put. The usher returns with the manager, who also asks him to move but without success. Finally, they call the police.

"All right, pal," says the policeman. "What's your name?"

"Joe," mumbles the man.

"Where you from, Joe?" asks the policeman.

The man whispers, "The balcony."

Barry and Michael are driving their truck down a country lane when they come to a bridge with a sign saying: Warning! Eleven-foot clearance.

"Damnit," says Barry. "Our truck is twelve feet high."

Michael looks out of the window and checks for onlookers. "I say we go for it," he says. "There's no one out here to report us."

There were these two blokes in a bar, which was on the top floor of a skyscraper. The first man says, "I bet you £100 I can jump out that window and come straight back in!"

The second man says, "OK, sure," and the barman holds the bet.

The first man jumps out the window and disappears for a second before jumping straight back in.

Disappointed about losing the £100, the second man says, "I'll bet you another £100 you can't do it again."

So the barman holds the bet. Sure enough, the first man jumps out the window, disappears for a second, then jumps straight back in.

Thinking he must have caught a freak gust of wind, the second man says, "OK, I bet you £300 I can jump out the window and come straight back in."

The first man says, "OK, sure."

The second man jumps out the window and falls to the footpath below. He is dead.

Back up in the bar, the barman says to the first man, "Jeez, Superman, you can be a mean sod when you've had a few drinks."

❖

A guy burned both his ears, so staff at the hospital were asking how it happened.

He said, "I was ironing my clothing and the phone rang... so instead of the phone I picked up the iron and burned my ear..."

"But how the heck did you burn the other ear?" The doctor asked.

"How do you think I called you people?"

❖

A man is being interviewed for a job as a railway signalman. "What would you do if two trains were approaching each other on the same line?" asks the interviewer.

"I'd switch the points in the signal box," he replies.

"And what would you do if the signal switch was broken?" asks the interviewer.

"I'd use the manual lever,"

"And what if that didn't work?" asks the interviewer.

"I'd use the emergency phone to call the next signal box," replies the man.

"And what if there was no answer?" asks the interviewer.

"I'd ring my uncle and tell him to come over."

"What good would that do?" asks the interviewer.

"None," replies the man. "But he's never seen a train crash."

Invited by vegetarians for dinner? Tell them about your special dietary requirements and ask for a nice steak.

Tom arrives at a hotel in a Scottish village on a cold, grey, drizzly day. The weather remains the same for two weeks. Exasperated, Tom stops a little boy in the street. "Does the weather here ever change?" he asks.

"I don't know," the boy replies. "I'm only six."

Fred owns a one-day dry-cleaning service. People give him clothes on the understanding that one day they might get them back again.

Three military men are introduced to each other. One steps forward and says, "John Collingworth. General. Married. Two sons, both doctors."

The second steps forward and says, "Marcus Hill. General. Married. Two sons, both lawyers."

The third man steps forward and says, "Bill Marsh. Lance corporal. Not married. Two sons, both generals."

What do you call it when your parachute doesn't open? Jumping to a conclusion.

What's the best way to stop a runaway horse?
Bet on it.

A man is about to be put in the electric chair, and the prison chaplain asks him if there's anything he can do for him in his dying moments.

"Yes," said the man. "Will you hold my hand?"

A husband and wife wake up one morning. The husband leans over to kiss his wife on the cheek, but she says, "Don't touch me! I'm dead!"

"What on earth are you talking about?" says the husband. "We're both lying here talking."

The wife replies, "I know. But I'm definitely dead."

"You can't be dead," replies her husband. "What in the world makes you think you're dead?"

His wife replies, "I must be dead. I woke up this morning and nothing hurts."

❖

There were three men sitting at the bar and one got up to use the gents. The other two men started talking. One man said, "So what's new in your life?"

The other responded, "Well I just found out my son got a

promotion. He used to be a janitor at the bank and now he is an executive. On top of that there's someone special in his life. He just bought his new love a Lexus."

The other man says, "My son also got a promotion and he has decided to settle down. He bought his new love a house on the beach."

The third man comes back from the gents. He looked upset so the other two men asked what was eating him. He responded, "I just found out that my son is gay. The good part is his lover has bought him a brand new Lexus and a new house on the beach."

A young man from the city goes to visit his farmer uncle. For the first few days the uncle shows him the usual things: chickens, cows, crops, etc. However, it's obvious that the nephew is getting bored, so the uncle suggests he goes on a hunt.

"Why don't you grab a gun, take the dogs and go shooting?"

This cheers up the nephew, and off he goes with the dogs in tow. After a few hours, the nephew returns.

"Did you enjoy it?" asks his uncle.

"It was great!" exclaims the nephew. "Got any more dogs?"

A man is driving along in his car when his boss calls him on his mobile.

"I'm promoting you to sales manager," he says.

The man is so surprised that he almost loses control of the car.

A few seconds later the phone rings, and it's the boss again. "Henderson has resigned. I'm promoting you to take his place as sales director."

Again, he is so surprised that the car swerves all over

the place. Seconds later the phone rings for the third time. Again, it's the boss.

"Harris has had a heart attack," he says. "You're the new managing director."

The man is so astonished that he loses control completely and careers off the road.

A man is walking through a park when he stops suddenly. A park keeper sees him and asks if everything is all right.

"I'm fine," says the man. "It's just that I could have sworn I saw one of those statues move."

"Those aren't statues," says the park keeper. "Those are council workers digging up the drains."

I'd like to praise the committee here. In other clubs half the committee does all the work and the other half is completely hopeless. But here it's quite the reverse.

There was a very high-pitched scream from the operating theatre, and then the doctor's voice could be heard: "Nurse! I said take off the patient's *spec*tacles."

A man is walking down the street with a case of beer under his arm.

His friend stops him and asks, "Hey, Bob ! What did you get the case of beer for?"

"I got it for my wife," answers Bob.

"Oh!" says his mate, "Good swap!"

Two men go to sign on for unemployment benefit after being laid off at a factory. The first man goes for an interview and tells the employment clerk that he was a panty stitcher. He's given £150 a week in benefits and goes away. The second man goes in and tells the clerk that he was a diesel fitter. He's given £200 a week and goes away. Later the two men are in the pub, and the panty stitcher finds that the diesel fitter is getting £50 more than he is. Outraged, he goes to the unemployment office to complain.

"Why should a diesel fitter get more than a panty stitcher?" he shouts.

The clerk replies, "It's a new grant given to skilled workers. Engineers like diesel fitters are eligible."

"He wasn't an engineer," says the panty stitcher. "He was in quality control. After I'd stitched a pair of panties, I'd give them to him. If he could pull them on he'd say, 'Yeah, diesel fitter'."

The police have reported the theft of a shipment of filing cabinets, document folders and labelling machines. It is believed to have been the work of organised crime.

Tom is walking down the road with a computer under one arm, a swivel chair under the other and a desk strapped to his back.

A policeman stops him and says, "I'm arresting you for impersonating an office, sir."

My dad is really annoyed. I had the TV on, and he accidentally saw the entire football match. He'd just wanted to watch the results on the news.

Once upon a time there was a female brain cell that happened to end up in a man's head by mistake.

She looked around nervously but it was all empty and quiet.

"Hello?" she cried, but no answer.

"Is there anyone here?" she cried a little louder, but still no answer.

Now the female brain cell started to feel alone and scared and again she yelled:

"HELLO, IS THERE ANYONE HERE!!?"

Then she heard a voice from far, far away:

"Hello! We're down here..."

There's this drunk standing out on the street corner, and a policeman passes by, and says, "What do you think you're doing?"

The drunk says, "I heard the world goes around every 24 hours, and I'm waiting for my house. Won't be long now, there goes my neighbour."

A golfer is in a competitive match with a friend, who is ahead by a couple of strokes. The golfer says to himself, "I'd give anything to sink this next putt."

A stranger walks up to him and whispers, "Would you give up a fourth of your sex life?"

The golfer thinks the man is crazy and that his answer will be meaningless but also that perhaps this is a good omen and will put him in the right frame of mind to make the difficult putt and says, "OK." And he sinks the putt.

Two holes later he mumbles to himself, "Boy, if I could only get an eagle on this hole."

The same stranger moves to his side and says, "Would it be worth another fourth of your sex life?"

The golfer shrugs and says, "Sure." And he makes an eagle.

Down to the final hole. The golfer needs yet another eagle to win and though he says nothing, the stranger moves to his side and says, "Would you be willing to give up the rest of your sex life to win this match?"

The golfer says, "Certainly." And he makes the eagle.

As the golfer walks to the club house, the stranger walks alongside and says, "You know, I've really not been fair with you because you don't know who I am. I'm the Devil and from now on you will have no sex life."

"Nice to meet you," says the golfer. "My name's Father O'Malley."

There were three conventions going on all at the same time, and so when I arrived all the hotels were full.

"Surely you've had a cancellation," I said to the receptionist at the biggest hotel. "Surely there's a room for me somewhere."

"I'm sorry," replied the receptionist, "but all the rooms are full."

"Isn't there perhaps another single man who is in a twin-bedded room and who might like to share the cost of the room?" I asked.

"Well," said the receptionist. "Mr Jones was forced to take a twin-bedded room three nights ago because no singles were available, and he did moan about the cost of it all. He did share the room last night with another gentleman, but that gentleman found it most uncomfortable and left."

"Why?" I inquired.

"It would appear that Mr Jones has a snore that is louder than the noise of an electric saw or an aeroplane taking off."

"That's all right," I replied. "I don't mind sharing with Mr Jones."

So I was introduced to Mr Jones, he agreed to share his room with me, and I had a peaceful and pleasant night's sleep.

The next day the receptionist asked me, "Did you sleep well?"

"Very well," I replied.

The receptionist raised her eyebrows in slight astonishment and asked, "Did you use ear-plugs?"

"No," I said. "But when it was time to go to bed I gave Mr Jones a sloppy wet kiss on his cheek and called him a gorgeous hunk of a man – and I think he spent the rest of the night sitting up, wide awake, watching me."

A man walked into the ladies department of a Macy's, and walked up to the woman behind the counter and said, "I'd like to buy a bra for my wife."

"What type of bra?" asked the clerk.

"Type?" the man inquired. "There is more than one type?"

"Look around," said the saleslady, as she showed a sea of bras in every shape, size, colour and material.

"Actually, even with all of this variety, there are really

321

only three types of bra," replied the salesclerk. Confused, the man asked what the types were.

The saleslady replied, "The Catholic type, the Salvation Army type, and the Baptist type. Which one do you need?"

Still confused the man asked, "What is the difference between them?"

The lady responded, "It is all really quite simple. The Catholic type supports the masses, the Salvation Army type lifts up the fallen, and the Baptist type makes mountains out of mole hills."

I've got nothing against watching a darts match. I just wish my IQ was low enough to enjoy it.

What's the difference between unlawful and illegal?
Unlawful means against the law; illegal is a sick bird.

A young lady I know in Hollywood has just arranged her wedding for seven o'clock in the morning – that way, if the marriage doesn't work out, she will still have most of the morning left.

Someone once asked me if I believed in clubs for promiscuous husbands. I said that poison was safer than using a club.

I read this article that said the typical symptoms of stress are eating too much, smoking too much, impulse shopping and driving too fast. That's my idea of a perfect day.

A magistrate is speaking to three men brought before him for a misdemeanour. He asks the first man why he's there.

The man replies, "For throwing peanuts in the lake."

The magistrate asks the second man why he's there.

The man replies, "For throwing peanuts in the lake."

The magistrate asks the third man why he's there.

He says, "I'm Peanuts."

Johnny is caught swearing by his teacher. "Johnny, you shouldn't use that kind of language," says the teacher. "Where on earth did you hear such talk?"

"My daddy said it," replies Johnny.

"Well that doesn't matter," explains the teacher. "You don't even know what it means."

"I do!" replies Johnny. "It means the car won't start."

A man is on trial for murder. There's strong evidence of guilt, but no corpse. In the defence's closing statement the man's lawyer says: "Ladies and gentlemen of the jury. I have a surprise for you. Within one minute, the person presumed dead in this case will walk into this courtroom."

The jury members watch the door, but after a minute has passed the lawyer says, "Ladies and gentlemen, I made up the previous statement, but you all watched the door in anticipation. I therefore put it to you that there is reasonable doubt as to whether anyone was killed and insist that you return a verdict of not guilty."

The jury retires to deliberate. A few minutes later they

return, and the foreman declares a verdict of guilty.

"What?" says the lawyer. "You must have had some doubt. You were all staring at the door."

The foreman replies, "Yes, we were all looking at the door, but your client wasn't."

Joe got a letter from his wife today. It read: "I missed you yesterday. Please come home as soon as possible and let me have another shot."

Every month Paddy would lay flowers at a lonely gravestone near his house. The name of the woman was VI Miles from Dublin.

After his motion to suppress evidence was denied by the court, the barrister addressed the judge. "Your Honour. What would you do if I called you a stupid, degenerate old fool?"

The judge replies, "I would hold you in contempt and seek to have you suspended from practising before this court again!"

"What if I only thought it?" asks the barrister.

"In that case," says the judge, "there is nothing I could do. You have the right to think whatever you like."

"I see," says the barrister. "Then, if it pleases the court, I 'think' you're a stupid, degenerate old fool."

My husband is so stupid that when I gave birth to triplets he wanted to know who the other two fathers were.

Did you hear about the idiot terrorist who tried to blow up a school bus? He burned his lips on the exhaust pipe.

A barrister is cross-examining a witness. "You strike me as an intelligent, honest man, Mr Smith. Someone who wouldn't cheat or lie."

"Thank you," replies Mr Smith. "I'd say the same about you if I wasn't under oath."

My husband isn't a hard drinker – he finds it very easy.

"Thank you for winning the case," said the grateful client to her solicitor. He had won her £35,000 from the local council when she had tripped over an uneven paving slab on the pavement and injured her leg.

"It was a pleasure," said the solicitor, handing the client his bill.

The client took the bill, then frowned. "This bill is pretty steep. Is it right?"

"Of course," replied the solicitor. "It represents good value for all our time, care, experience, expertise and legal knowledge. If it wasn't for us, you wouldn't have won the case."

"But your costs are almost half the damages," replied the client. "If it wasn't for me, you wouldn't have had a case."

"But," said the solicitor, "anyone can trip over a paving slab."

The managing director of a large company – which he had founded – received a short job application letter for the position of assistant managing director from a young man who detailed his education at a top public school, outlined his aristocratic background and intentions of marrying the daughter of a duke, yet failed to give any indication of his competency or even knowledge of the job available.

The managing director therefore felt obliged to write back to the young man: "Dear Sir, Thank you for applying for the position advertised. I am unable to employ you since we require the services of someone for managerial rather than breeding purposes."

Two magistrates are arrested for being drunk and disorderly but agree to try each other's cases the next morning. The first magistrate fines the second £2, but when it is the first magistrate's turn he gets a £50 fine.

"Why did you do that?" says the magistrate. "I only fined you £2."

"I know," says his friend, "but there's far too much of this sort of thing going on these days. Yours is the second case this morning."

A man makes a complaint at a cheap hotel. "My room is swimming in water," he says. "Does the roof always leak like that?"

"No, sir," says the receptionist. "Only when it's raining."

If at first you don't succeed, skydiving's not for you.

It was terribly embarrassing the other day. I was watching TV with my mum and dad when suddenly there was a no-holds-barred, completely explicit sex scene. I didn't know what to do. I just carried on watching the news and tried to ignore them.

A group of prisoners passes the time telling jokes to each other. Unfortunately, their repertoire is limited and they soon know all of them by heart. Indeed, they even start referring to the jokes by number.

One prisoner says, "D'you remember number thirteen?" And everyone chuckles.

Another says, "That reminds me of joke number six!" Again, everyone laughs.

"Or how about number twelve?" says another. Everyone chuckles, except for one prisoner who starts having hysterics. He laughs until tears run down his cheeks and his sides hurt. He falls to the floor, rolls about and slaps his thighs, cackling uncontrollably. Finally, he calms down and notices his friends looking at him stony-faced.

"Sorry," he says. "First time I'd heard that one."

There was a man who had worked all of his life and, being a miser, had saved all of his money.. He loved money more than just about anything. Just before he died, he said to his wife,

"Now listen. When I die, I want you to take all my money and put it in the casket with me. I want to take my money to the afterlife with me."

He made her promise with all her heart that when he died, she would put all of the money in the casket with him. Well, he died. He was stretched out in the casket, his wife was sitting there in black, and her friend was sitting next to her. When they finished the ceremony, just before the undertakers got ready to close the casket, the wife said, "Wait just a minute!"

She had a box with her, she came over with the box and put it in the casket. Then the undertakers locked the casket down, and they rolled it away.

So her friend said,

"Girl, I know you weren't fool enough to put all that money in there with your husband!"

She said, "Listen, I'm a Christian. I can't go back on my word. I promised him that I would put that money in that casket with him."

"You mean to tell me you really put that money in the casket with him!?

"I sure did," said the wife. "I wrote him a cheque."

Little Johnny is approached by the lifeguard at the public swimming pool. "You're not allowed to pee in the pool," says the lifeguard. "I'm going to report you."

"But everyone pees in the pool," says little Johnny.

"Maybe," says the lifeguard. "But not from the diving board."

One trade union is now demanding that unskilled men get paid more than skilled men because the work is harder if people are not skilled to do it.

Mr Smith to judge: "Your Honour, my wife is being ridiculous. Most women would love to have a chivalrous husband. Who could object to having a car door opened for them?"

Judge to Mr Smith: "It might be chivalrous to open a car door for your wife, but not when you're driving at 65 miles an hour."

"Mummy, why do fairytales always start 'Once upon a time …'?"

"They don't always, my dear. The ones your father tells usually start with 'I got caught up at the office. Sorry I'm late, love …'."

A German jumps into a river to save a dog from drowning. "Are you a vet?" asks a passer-by.

"A vet!" says the German. "I'm bloody zoaking."

Harry and Tom go to the theatre, but Harry gets up to leave after the curtain closes for the first interval. "Where are you going?" asks Tom.

"It's not worth the wait," says Harry. "Look in the programme – 'Act Two – one month later'."

It was a cold winter day, when an old man walked out onto a frozen lake, cut a hole in the ice, dropped in his fishing line and began waiting for a fish to bite.

He was there for almost an hour without even a nibble when a young boy walked out onto the ice, cut a hole in the ice not too far from the old man and dropped in his fishing line. It only took about a minute and WHAM! a huge fish hit his hook and the boy pulled it in.

The old man couldn't believe it but figured it was just

luck. But, the boy dropped in his line and again within just a few minutes pulled in another one.

This went on and on until finally the old man couldn't take it any more since he hadn't caught a thing all this time.

He went to the boy and said, "Son, I've been here for over an hour without even a nibble. You have been here only a few minutes and have caught about half a dozen fish! How do you do it?"

The boy responded, "Roo raf roo reep ra rums rrarm."

"What was that?" the old man asked.

Again the boy responded, "Roo raf roo reep ra rums rarrm."

"Look," said the old man, "I can't understand a word you are saying."

So, the boy spat a mouthful of something into his hand and said, "You have to keep the worms warm!"

A salesman, tired of his job, gives it up to become a policeman. Several months later a friend asks him how he likes it. "Well," he replies. "The pay is good and the hours aren't bad, but what I like best is that the customer is always wrong."

An old lady sits on her front porch, rocking away the last days of her long life, when, all of a sudden, a fairy godmother appears and informs her that she will be granted three wishes.

"Well, now," says the old lady, "I guess I would like to be really rich."

*** POOF *** Her rocking chair turns to solid gold.

"And I wouldn't mind being a young, beautiful princess."

*** POOF *** She turns into a beautiful young woman.

"Your third wish?" asks the fairy godmother.

Just then the old woman's cat wanders across the porch in front of them. "Ooh - can you change him into a handsome prince?" she asks.

*** POOF ***

There before her stands a young man more handsome than anyone could possibly imagine. She stares at him, smitten. With a smile that makes her knees weak, he saunters across the porch and whispers in her ear, "Bet you're sorry you had me neutered."

My small son went with some friends to the local ice rink. When he returned he told me: "I still don't know if I can skate. I can't seem to stand upright long enough to find out."

An elderly patient needs a heart transplant and discusses his options with his doctor. The doctor says, "We have three possible donors. One is a young, healthy athlete. The second is a middle-aged businessman who never drank or smoked, and the third is an attorney, who just died after practising law for thirty years."

"I'll take the lawyer's heart," says the patient.

"Why?" asks the doctor.

The patient replies, "It's never been used."

It's a Man's World

How many men does it take to open a beer?

None. It should be opened by the time she brings it.

Why is a Laundromat a really bad place to pick up a woman?

Because a woman who can't even afford a washing machine will probably never be able to support you.

Why do women have smaller feet than men?

It's one of those "evolutionary things" that allows them to stand closer to the kitchen sink.

How do you know when a woman is about to say something smart?

When she starts her sentence with: "A man once told me..."

How do you fix a woman's watch?

You don't. There is a clock on the oven.

Why do men break wind more than women? Because women can't shut up long enough to build up the required pressure.

Why do men die before their wives?

They want to.

If your dog is barking at the back door and your wife is yelling at the front door, who do you let in first?

The dog, of course. He'll shut up once you let him in.

I married Miss Right.

I just didn't know her first name was Always.

I haven't spoken to my wife for 18 months:

I don't like to interrupt her.

Scientists have discovered a food that diminishes a woman's sex drive by 90%.

It's called a Wedding Cake.

Our last fight was my fault:

My wife asked me, "What's on the TV?"

I said, "Dust!"

Marriage is a 3-ring circus:
Engagement Ring, Wedding Ring, Suffering.

What's worse than a Male Chauvinist Pig?
A woman that won't do what she's told.

In the beginning, God created the Earth and rested. Then God created Man and rested. Then God created Woman. Since then, neither God nor Man has rested.

A beggar walked up to a well-dressed woman out shopping and said,

"I haven't eaten anything for days."

She looked at him and said, "God, I wish I had your willpower."

A drunken man staggers into a Catholic church, sits down in the Confessional and says nothing. The priest is waiting and waiting and waiting.

The priest coughs to attract the drunk man's attention, but still the man says nothing.

The priest then knocks on the wall three times in a final attempt to get the man to speak.

Finally the drunk replies, "No use knockin', pal. There's no paper."

An aspiring young actor asks his girlfriend's father if he can have her hand in marriage. The father says, "I would never let my daughter marry an actor."

The actor replies, "Sir, I think you may change your mind if you see me perform. Won't you at least come and see the play?"

So the father goes to see the play and calls the actor the next day. "You were right. I did change my mind. Go ahead and marry my daughter. You're certainly no actor."

Young son: "Is it true, Dad, I heard that in some parts of Africa a man doesn't know his wife until he marries her?"

Dad: "That happens in every country, son."

A man inserted an advertisement in the classifieds: "Wife Wanted."

The next day he received a hundred letters. They all said the same thing:

"You can have mine."

A guy escapes from prison and goes home. His wife says, "Where have you been? You escaped eight hours ago."

Why don't witches like to ride their brooms whey they're angry? They're afraid of flying off the handle.

One woman paid a genealogist £5,000 to trace her family tree. Then she had to pay another £5,000 to have it hushed up.

A woman finds her house has been robbed, so she calls the police and demands that they send a patrol car immediately. The dispatcher tells her that the only patrol car near her home is a canine car.

She yells, "I don't care. Just send him over!" The car stops by, but when the woman sees the officer get out of the car with his alsatian, she wails, "Just my luck! My house gets robbed and they send me a blind policeman."

I rang up my local swimming baths and said, "Is that the local swimming baths?"

They said, "Well, that depends on where you're calling from."

Advice for teenagers: leave home now, while you still know everything.

A young girl visits a clairvoyant, who, looking into her crystal ball, bursts out laughing. With a crack like a pistol shot the girl slaps the medium hard across the jaw.

"*Ouch*! What was *that* for?" protests the fortune-teller.

"My mother always insists that I should strike a happy medium!" the girl explains.

The sports car came hurtling down the narrow, winding country lane, narrowly avoiding an elderly lady in an old car.

"Pig!" shouted the elderly lady as the sports car driver scraped past her car.

"Bitch!" shouted back the sports car driver as he drove on and around the corner – and hit a pig in the middle of the road.

An old man is given 25 years for murder. "Twenty-five years?" he complains. "I'll never live that long!"

"Well, never mind, old chap," replies the judge. "Just do what you can."

I once saw a man eat a pocket watch. Then he swallowed two wristwatches. He said I could stay and see him swallow even more watches – but I said I thought it was very time consuming.

A hole has appeared in the ladies' changing rooms at the sports club. The police are looking into it.

A man is in a public toilet but soon discovers there's no toilet paper. He calls into the next cubicle, "Do you have any tissue paper in there?"

"No," comes the reply.

"Do you have any newspaper?" asks the man.

"Sorry," is the reply.

"OK," says the man. "So could you give me two fives for a ten?"

After having a big operation a lawyer slowly comes out of anaesthesia. He looks round his room and says, "Doctor, why are all the blinds drawn in my room?"

"There's a big fire across the street," replies the doctor. "We didn't want you to think the operation had been a failure."

Judge to defendant: "You have been found not guilty of robbery and can leave this court without a stain on your character."

Defendant: "Great! Does that mean I can keep the money?"

My father taught me to swim the hard way – he threw me out into the middle of the lake! Learning to swim that way wasn't easy, but the really hard part was getting out of the sack.

"I bet I can make you talk like a Red Indian."
"How?"
"Voila!"

A passenger train is creeping along, slowly. Finally it creaks to a halt. A passenger sees a guard walking by outside.

"What's going on?" she yells out the window.

"Cow on the track!" replies the guard.

Ten minutes later, the train resumes its slow pace.

Within five minutes, however, it stops again.

The woman sees the same guard walk by again.

She leans out the window and yells, "What happened? Did we catch up with the cow again?"

If you're American when you enter the bathroom, and you're American when you leave the bathroom, what are you while you're in the bathroom? European.

Last year the children and I had a lot of fun on holiday burying my husband in the sand on the beach. Next year we might go back and dig him up.

Some tortoises are playing cards when they run out of beer. They pick one of their number, Billy, to go to the off-licence. Billy goes off, but after waiting two days the others start to get a bit impatient. "Billy is getting really slow," says one.

"He's not what he used to be," says another.

A voice shouts back from behind the door, "Oi, if you're going to talk about me behind my back I'm not going."

If a lawyer and a tax official were both drowning and you could save only one of them, what would you do? Go to lunch or read the paper?

Susie Guv dyed her hair blonde when she became a policewoman so that when she made an arrest people could say, "It's a fair cop, Guv."

Detective's assistant: "Sir, I have found a box of vestas with your name on it."

Detective: "Ah! So at last I have met my match."

A little old man is in a toyshop when he spots a fantastic train set with a red locomotive that whistles and blows real steam. "I'll have one of those," he says to the sales assistant.

"Excellent choice," says the assistant. "They're very popular with grandchildren."

"You're right," says the old man. "Billy would love one. In that case, I'd better have two."

Robert goes golfing every Saturday. One Saturday, he comes home three hours late. His wife asks him, "What took you so long?"

The guy says, "That was the worst game of golf I've ever had. We got up to the first tee, and Charlie hit a hole-in-one and immediately dropped dead of a heart attack."

The guy's wife says, "That's terrible!"

The guy says, "I know. Then, for the rest of the game, it was hit the ball, drag Charlie, hit the ball, drag Charlie, hit the ball, drag Charlie..."

I always know if it's a wrong number when my wife answers the phone – the conversation only lasts for twenty minutes.

Heard the one about the bloke who was so unmusical he didn't know his brass from his oboe?

People who cough loudly never go to the doctor – they go to the cinema.

Advantages Of Being A Woman

1. We got off the Titanic first.

2. We get to flirt with systems support men who always return our calls, and are nice to us when we blow up our computers.

3. Our boyfriend's clothes make us look elfin & gorgeous. Guys look like complete idiots in ours.

4. We can be groupies. Male groupies are stalkers.

5. We can cry and get off speeding fines.

6. We've never lusted after a cartoon character or the central female figure in a computer game.

7. Taxis stop for us.

8. Men die earlier, so we get to cash in on the life insurance.

9. We don't look like a frog in a blender when dancing.

10. Free drinks, free dinners, free movies ... (you get the point).

11. We can hug our friends without wondering if she thinks we're gay.

12. We can hug our friends without wondering if WE'RE gay.

13. New lipstick gives us a whole new lease on life.

14. It's possible to live our whole lives without ever taking a group shower.

15. We don't have to fart to amuse ourselves.

16. If we forget to shave, no one has to know.

17. We can congratulate our team-mate without ever touching her butt.

18. If we have a zit, we know how to conceal it.

19. We never have to reach down every so often to make sure our privates are still there.

20. If we're dumb, some people will find it cute.

21. We don't have to memorize any stupid songs to fit in.

22. We have the ability to dress ourselves.

23. We can talk to people of the opposite sex without having to picture them naked.

24. If we marry someone 20 years younger, we're aware that we look like an idiot.

25. Our friends won't think we're weird if we ask whether there's spinach in our teeth.

26. There are times when chocolate really can solve all your problems.

27. We'll never regret piercing our ears.

28. We can fully assess a person just by looking at their shoes.

29. We know which glass was ours by the lipstick mark.

30. We have enough sense to realize that the easiest way to get out of being lost is to ask for directions.

Paddy and his two friends are talking at a bar.

His first friend says: "I think my wife is having an affair with the electrician. The other day I came home and found wire cutters under our bed and they weren't mine."

His second friend says: "I think my wife is having an affair with the plumber. The other day I found a wrench under the bed and it wasn't mine."

Paddy says: "I think my wife is having an affair with a horse."

Both his friends look at him with utter disbelief.

"No, I'm serious. The other day I came home and found a jockey under our bed."

A Republican, a Democrat and Bill Clinton are travelling in a car when a tornado suddenly comes along and whirls them into the air. When they eventually come down they realise they're in the land of Oz. They decide to go to see the Wizard.

"I'm going to ask the Wizard for a brain," says the Democrat.

"I'm going to ask the Wizard for a heart," says the Republican.

Clinton says, "Where's Dorothy?"

A vasectomy is never having to say you're sorry.

Santa Claus, the tooth fairy, an honest lawyer and a drunk are in a bar when they spot a hundred pounds on the floor. Who gets it? The drunk, of course. The other three are mythical creatures.

Two men get talking on a train. "I'm originally from Minnesota," says one. "I'm sure glad I left. The only people you'll find in Minnesota are whores and hockey players."

"I'll have you know that my wife is from Minnesota," says the second man.

"Really?" replies the first. "Which team did she play for?"

A friend of mine is a poet and he's almost starving. He says that rhyme doesn't pay.

I knew it was going to be a plane flight with a difference when a naked man rushed down the aisle shouting, "This is your captain streaking...."

A man drives to a garage and has his tank filled up. The attendant spots two penguins sitting in the back seat of the car.

He asks the driver, "What's with the penguins in the back seat?"

The man in the car says, "I found them. I asked myself what to do with them, but I haven't had a clue."

The bloke ponders a bit then says, "You should take them to the zoo."

"Hey, that's a good idea," says the man in the car and drives away.

The next day the man with the car is back at the same

garage. The attendant sees the penguins are still in the back seat of the car.

"Hey, they're still here! I thought you were going to take them to the zoo."

"Oh, I did," says the driver, "And we had a great time. Today I'm taking them to the beach."

Jerry is charged with stealing a Mercedes Benz, but after a long trial the jury acquits him. Later that day Jerry comes back to speak to the judge who tried his case.

"Your Honour," he says. "I want to get out a warrant for that dirty lawyer of mine."

"Why?" says the judge. "He won your acquittal. Why do you want to have him arrested?"

Jerry replies, "I don't have the money to pay his fee, so the bugger went and took the car I stole."

What do you get if you cross a chicken with a clock?
An alarm cock.

Ninety-nine per cent of lawyers give the rest a bad name.

Old lawyers never die, they just lose their appeal.

Late one night a little old lady rings her vet and asks the best way to separate two mating dogs. "Try prising them apart with a stick," says the vet. A few minutes later the old lady rings back. The stick hasn't worked so can the vet suggest something else. "Oh, I dunno," says the vet. "Chuck some water over them." A few minutes later the old lady rings again. The water hasn't done anything. What else can she try? The irritated vet says, "Go and tell one of the dogs that it's wanted on the phone."

"Will that work?" asks the old lady.

"Well," the vet replies. "It's already worked three times with me."

A Scotsman takes a huge jar of urine to a clinic and pays to have it tested. When the results come back he discovers that there is absolutely no sign of any illness. He gets on the phone and says, "It's me, Willie. Tell your Auntie Mary that there's nothing wrong with you, her, me, grandpa or the dog."

Success doesn't always go to the head – more often it goes to the mouth.

A group of soldiers takes a first aid course. After they've finished they're given a test by their instructor. The instructor points to one of the soldiers and says, "The sergeant major sustains a head injury during a cross-country march. What do you do about it?"

The soldier replies, "I wrap a tourniquet around his neck and tighten it until the bleeding stops."

Three men are travelling in the countryside when their car breaks down. They go to a farmhouse to seek shelter. The farmer only has two spare beds but says that one of the men can sleep in the barn. The first man, a rabbi, volunteers to sleep outside, but a few minutes after he leaves, there's a knock on the door. It's the rabbi. It turns out there's a pig in the barn, and the rabbi doesn't feel comfortable sleeping there. To get round the problem the second man, a Hindu, volunteers to take the rabbi's place. He leaves for the barn, but a few minutes later there's a knock at the door. It's the Hindu. It turns out there's also a cow in the barn, and the Hindu doesn't feel comfortable sleeping near it. The third man, a lawyer, says he doesn't have any religious hang-ups and walks out to sleep in the barn. A few minutes later the rabbi and the Hindu hear a knock on the door. The rabbi opens the door. Standing outside are the pig and the cow.

A man walks into a bar with a giraffe and they proceed to get blitzed. The giraffe drinks so much it passes out on the floor. The man gets up and heads for the door to leave when the bartender yells, "Hey! You can't leave that lyin' there!"

The drunk replies, "That's not a lion! It's a giraffe."

A short history of medicine:
I have an earache.
2000 B.C. - Here, eat this root
1000 A.D. - That root is heathen, say this prayer.
1850 A.D. - That prayer is superstition, drink this potion.
1940 A.D. - That potion is snake oil, swallow this pill.
1985 A.D. - That pill is ineffective, take this antibiotic.
2005 A.D. - That antibiotic is artificial. Here, eat this root.

The local bar was so sure that its bartender was the strongest man around that they offered a standing £500 bet. The bartender would squeeze a lemon until all the juice ran into a glass, and hand the lemon to a patron. Anyone who could squeeze one more drop of juice out would win the money. Many people had tried over time but nobody could do it. One day this scrawny little man came into the bar, wearing thick glasses and a grey suit, and said in a tiny squeaky voice, "I'd like to try the bet."

After the laughter had died down, the bartender said, "OK," grabbed a lemon, and squeezed away. Then he handed the wrinkled remains of the rind to the little man.

The crowd's laughter turned to total silence as the man clenched his fist around the lemon and six drops fell into the glass. As the crowd cheered, the bartender paid the £500, and asked the little man, "What do you do for a living? Are you a lumberjack, a weight-lifter, or what?"

The man replied, "I'm a tax inspector."

Two crooks try to hold up a lawyers' club but the lawyers put up such a fight they have to flee before they manage to take much money. In the getaway car they count their loot.

"I've got good news and bad news," says one of the crooks.

"What do you mean?" asks the second crook.

"We got away with £50," replies the first crook. "But we went into there with £75."

If at first you don't succeed you're just like 99.99 per cent of the population.

Sherlock Holmes and Dr. Watson go on a camping trip, set up their tent, and fall asleep. Some hours later, Holmes wakes his faithful friend.

"Watson, look up at the sky and tell me what you see."

Watson replies, "I see millions of stars."

"What does that tell you?"

Watson ponders for a minute. "Astronomically speaking,

it tells me that there are millions of galaxies and potentially billions of planets. Astrologically, it tells me that Saturn is in Leo. Time-wise, it appears to be approximately a quarter past three. Theologically, it's evident the Lord is all-powerful and we are small and insignificant. Meteorologically, it seems we will have a beautiful day tomorrow. What does it tell you?"

Holmes is silent for a moment, then speaks. "Watson, you idiot, someone has stolen our tent."

Helpful advice if you have vegetarians coming to dinner: just serve them a nice bit of steak or veal. Since they're always going on about how tofu and quorn taste like the real thing they shouldn't notice the difference.

Two lawyers make a suicide pact and plan to jump from the top of their office block. The building is twenty storeys high, each lawyer has the same body type, and they weigh the same. One is wearing a brown suit; the other is wearing a blue suit. Question: which of them hits the street first? Answer: who cares?

The less people know, the more stubbornly they know it.

A woman walks into a bar with her tiny Chihuahua and sits down next to this man, whom she notices is feeling a little bit queasy. A few minutes go by and the man is suddenly sick all over the floor. He looks down and sees the little dog struggling in a pool of vomit and says, "Blimey! I don't remember eating that!"

Eighty-year-old Bessie bursts into the recreation room of the men's retirement home. She holds her clenched fist in the air and says, "Anyone who can guess what's in my hand can make wild passionate love to me all night!"

An elderly gentleman at the rear calls out, "An elephant."

Bessie thinks for a moment then replies, "Close enough!"

❖

If it wasn't for Venetian blinds it would be curtains for all of us.

❖

A couple were driving to a church to get married. On the way, they got into a car accident and died. When they arrive in heaven, they see St. Peter at the gate. They ask him if he could arrange it so they could marry in heaven.

St. Peter tells them that he'll do his best to work on it for them.

Three months pass by and the couple hear nothing. They bump into St. Peter and ask him about the marriage.

He says, "I'm still working on it."

Two years pass by and no marriage.

St. Peter again assures them that he's working on it.

Finally after twenty long years, St. Peter comes running with a priest and tells the couple it's time for their wedding.

The couple marry and live happily for a while. But after a few months the couple go and find St. Peter and tell him things are not working out, and that they want to get a divorce.

"Can you arrange it for us?" they ask.

St. Peter replies, "Are you kidding?! It took me twenty years to find a priest up here. How am I going to find you a lawyer?"

This guy walks into a bar with this really great shirt on. The bartender goes, "Where'd you get the great shirt, mate?"

The man replies, "David Jones."

This second guy walks into the bar with really good pants on and the bartender goes "Where'd you get the great pants, mate?"

The man replies, "David Jones."

This third guy walks into the bar with really great shoes and socks on. The bartender goes, "Where'd you get the great shoes and socks, mate?"

The man replies, "David Jones."

Then this fourth guy runs in naked and the bartender goes, "Who the hell are you, mate?"

And the naked guy says, "I'm David Jones!"

A group of US marines is stranded on a Pacific island after the war. After a few months the sergeant decides he has to do something to boost morale. "Good news, men," he says. "We're going to have a change of underwear." It's not much, but the marines are cheered up. The sergeant continues, "Johnson, you change with Kropowlski. Kropowlski you change with Peterson…"

A man walks into a bar, and orders a beer. As he sits there, the jar of nuts on the bar tells him what a nice shirt he is wearing. Disturbed by this, he goes to the cigarette vending machine to buy a pack of smokes. As he approaches the machine, it starts screaming and shouting at him. He runs to the bar and explains this to the barman. The barman apologizes and says, "The peanuts are complimentary, but the cigarette machine is out of order!"

There was once a man who was in a bar, terribly drunk. The bartender noticed this, and when he asked for another beer, the bartender politely told him that he was too drunk to be served another drink. The man leaves. He walks in the side door and asks the bartender for a beer. A little frustrated, the bartender repeats the answer he said before. The man leaves. He then comes in the other side door, walks to the bartender and asks for a beer. The bartender is annoyed, and tells the man he is too drunk and to get a ride home and leave his bar. He leaves. He then comes in the BACK door, comes to the bartender, and before he can say a word, the bartender explodes at him. "I told you already, you are way too drunk, you can not have another beer! Get out of my bar!"

Disgruntled, the man looks at the bartender and asks, "Man, how many bars do you work at?"

A girl asks her boyfriend to come over Friday night and have dinner with her parents. This being a big event, the girl tells her boyfriend that after dinner, she would like to go out and "do it" for the first time. Well, the boy is ecstatic, but he has never done it before, so he takes a trip to the chemists to get some protection. The chemist helps the boy for about an hour. He tells the boy everything there is to know about protection and doing it. At the register, the chemist asks the boy how many he'd like to buy: a 3-pack, a 10-pack, or a family pack. The boy insists on the family pack because he thinks he will be very busy, it being his first time and all.

That night, the boy shows up at the girl's parent's house

and meets his girlfriend at the door. "Oh, I'm so excited for you to meet my parents; come on in." The boy goes inside and is taken to the dinner table where the girl's parents are seated. The boy quickly offers to say grace and bows his head. A minute passes, and the boy is still deep in prayer with his head down. Ten minutes pass and there's still no movement from the boy. Finally, after 20 minutes with his head down, the girlfriend leans over and whispers to her boyfriend, "I had no idea you were so religious."

The boy turns and whispers back, "I had no idea your father was a chemist."

A priest goes into a bar and says, "Anybody who wants to go to heaven, stand up." Everybody stands up except for a drunk in the corner. The preacher says, "My son, don't you want to go to heaven when you die?"

The drunk says, "When I die? Sure. I thought you were taking a load up right now."

He was a very keen lawyer. He even named his daughter Sue.

"I'm not saying that the customer service in my bank is bad, but when I went in the other day and asked the clerk to check my balance ... she leaned over and pushed me."

A knight and his men return to their castle after a hard day of fighting. "How are we faring?" asks the king.

"Sire," replies the knight. "I have been robbing and pillaging on your behalf all day, burning the towns of your enemies in the west."

"What?" shrieks the king. "I don't have any enemies to the west."

"Oh," says the knight. "Well, you do now."

What happens to plants in the maths teacher's room?
They grow square roots.

What two letters of the alphabet hurt teeth?
D.K.

Young King Arthur was ambushed and imprisoned by the monarch of a neighbouring kingdom. The monarch could have killed him but was moved by Arthur's youthful happiness. So he offered him freedom so long as he could answer a very difficult question. Arthur would have a year to figure out the answer. If, after a year, he still had no answer, he would be killed. The question was, "What do women really want?"

Such a question would perplex even the most knowledgeable man, and, to young Arthur, it seemed an impossible query. Since it was better than death, he accepted the monarch's proposition to have an answer by the year's end. Arthur returned to his kingdom and began to poll everybody: the princess, the prostitutes, the priests, the wise men, the court jester. He spoke with everyone, but no one could give him a satisfactory answer. What most people told him was to consult the old witch, as only she would know the answer. The price would be high, since the witch was famous throughout the kingdom for the exorbitant prices she charged.

The last day of the year arrived, and Arthur had no alternative but to talk to the witch. She agreed to answer his question, but he'd have to accept her price first: The old witch wanted to marry Gawain, the most noble of the Knights of the Round Table and Arthur's closest friend! Young Arthur was horrified. The witch was hunchbacked and awfully hideous, she had only one tooth, she smelled like sewage water, and she often made obscene noises. He had never run across such a repugnant creature. He refused to force his friend to marry her and have to endure such a burden.

Gawain, upon learning of the proposal, spoke with Arthur. He told him that nothing was too big a sacrifice compared with Arthur's life and the preservation of the Round Table. Hence, their wedding was proclaimed, and the witch answered Arthur's question: "What a woman really wants is to be able to be in charge of her own life."

Everyone instantly knew that the witch had uttered a great truth and that Arthur's life would be spared. And so it went. The neighbouring monarch spared Arthur's life and granted him total freedom. What a wedding Gawain and the witch had! Arthur was torn between relief and anguish. Gawain was proper as always, gentle and courteous. The old witch put her worst manners on display. She ate with her hands, belched and farted, and made everyone uncomfortable.

The wedding night approached. Gawain, steeling himself for a horrific night, entered the bedroom. What a sight awaited! The most beautiful woman he'd ever seen lay before him! Gawain was astounded and asked what had happened. The beauty replied that since he had been so kind to her (when she had been a witch), half the time she would be her horrible, deformed self, and the other half, she would be her beautiful maiden self. Which, she asked, would he want her to be during the day and which during the night?

What a cruel question. Gawain began to think of his predicament: During the day, he could have a beautiful woman to show off to his friends, but at night, in the privacy of his home, he would be with an old spooky witch. Or would he prefer having by day a hideous witch but by night a beautiful woman to enjoy many intimate moments? What would you do? What Gawain chose follows below, but don't read until you've made your own choice.

...

Noble Gawain replied that he would let the witch choose for herself. Upon hearing this, she announced that she would be beautiful all the time because he had respected her and had let her be in charge of her own life.

What is he moral of this story? The moral is that it doesn't matter if your woman is pretty or ugly; underneath it all, she could still be a witch.

There are only two things wrong with my wife's dancing – her left foot and her right foot.

A man walks into a bar in New Orleans and asks the bartender, "If I show you a really good trick, will you give me a free drink?" The bartender considers it, then agrees. The man reaches into his pocket and pulls out a tiny rat. He reaches into his other pocket and pulls out a tiny piano. The rat stretches, cracks his knuckles, and proceeds to play the blues.

After the man finished his drink, he asked the bartender, "If I show you an even better trick, will you give me free drinks for the rest of the evening?" The bartender agrees, thinking that no trick could possibly be better than the first. The man reaches into another pocket and pulls out a small bullfrog, who begins to sing along with the rat's music.

While the man is enjoying his beverages, a stranger

confronts him and offers him $100,000 for the bullfrog.

"Sorry," the man replies, "he's not for sale."

The stranger increases the offer to $250,000 cash up front.

"No," the man insists, "he's not for sale."

The stranger again increases the offer, this time to $500,000 cash. The man finally agrees, and turns the frog over to the stranger in exchange for the money.

"Are you insane?" the bartender demanded. "That frog could have been worth millions to you, and you let him go for a mere $500,000!"

"Don't worry about it," the man answered. "The frog was really nothing special. You see, the rat's a ventriloquist."

A bear walks into a bar and says to the bartender, "I would like a bourbon and ...... a coke."

The bar tender says, "Why the big pause?"

The bear says, "I was born with them."

Why can't a bicycle stand up?
Because it's two tyred.

Why do bees have sticky hair?
Because they use honeycombs

A man loses his donkey and gets down on his knees to thank God. A passer-by asks, "Why are you thanking God when you've lost your donkey?"

The man replies, "Well, thank goodness I wasn't on it at the time or I'd be lost too."

What fish races through the water at ninety miles an hour?

A motor pike.

What did the vampire doctor shout out in his waiting room?

"Necks please!"

After a heavy night at the pub, a drunken man decides to sleep off his drunkenness at a local hotel. He approaches the reception desk, takes care of the formalities and heads off to his suite. Several minutes later, the drunk staggers back to the reception desk and demands his room be changed.

"But, sir," said the clerk, "you have the best room in the hotel."

"I insist on another room!!!" said the drunk.

"Very good, sir. I'll change you from 502 to 525. Would you mind telling me why you don't like 502?" asked the clerk.

"Well, for one thing," said the drunk, "it's on fire."

Two little boys come home with a football. "Where did you get that from?" asks their mother.

"We found it," they say.

"Are you absolutely sure it was lost?" says Mum.

"Yes," say the kids. "We saw the people looking for it."

A man asks a judge to let him off jury service. The judge says, "But surely your firm can manage without you for a few weeks."

"Certainly," the man replies. "They can manage without me altogether – and I don't want them to find out."

What do rich turtles wear?
People-necked sweaters.

What do you get when you cross some grass seed with a cow?
A lawn moo-er.

A businessman gets into an elevator in his office building. A woman already inside greets him, saying, "T-G-I-F."

He smiles at her and replies, "S-H-I-T."

The woman looks at him, puzzled, and again says, "T-G-I-F." Again the man answers her with S-H-I-T. The woman says, "Do you know what I'm saying. T-G-I-F means 'Thank God it's Friday'."

"I know," replies the man. "But S-H-I-T means 'Sorry, Honey, it's Thursday'."

What do you call a man who breaks into a house and steals ham?
A ham burglar.

Where does Friday come before Tuesday?
In a dictionary

Why are rivers lazy?
Because they never leave their beds.

❖

How do you make a witch itch?
Remove the w.

A military cargo plane, flying over a populated area, suddenly loses power and starts to nose down. The pilot tries to pull up, but with all their cargo, the plane is too heavy. So he yells to the soldiers in back to throw things out to make the plane lighter. They throw out a pistol. "Throw out more!" shouts the pilot. So they throw out a rifle. "More!" he cries again. They heave out a missile, and the pilot regains control.

He pulls out of the dive and lands safely at an airport. They get into a jeep and drive off. Pretty soon they meet a boy on the side of the road who's crying. They ask him why he's crying and he says, "A pistol hit me on the head!"

They drive more and meet another boy who's crying even harder. Again they ask why and the boy says, "A rifle hit me on the head!"

They apologize and keep driving. They meet a boy on the sidewalk who's laughing hysterically. They ask him, "Kid, what's so funny?"

The boy replies, "I sneezed and a house blew up!"

❖

Terrorists have hijacked a planeload of lawyers bound for a legal convention. They've threatened to start releasing the lawyers one by one until their demands are met.

❖

There was a boy standing on a corner selling fish.
He was saying, "Dam fish for sale, dam fish for sale."

358

A preacher walked up and asked why he was calling them dam fish.

The kid said, "I caught them at the dam, so they're dam fish."

The preacher bought some, took them home and asked his wife to cook the dam fish.

His wife looked at him in bewilderment and said, "Preachers aren't supposed to talk like that."

The preacher explained why they were dam fish, and she agreed to cook them. When dinner was ready and everyone was sitting down, the preacher asked his son to pass him the dam fish.

His son replied, "That's the spirit, dad. Pass the effing potatoes!"

When I told the Irish decorators that I wanted a matt finish on the walls they nailed the carpets to them.

The geography teacher was lecturing on map reading. He spent the class explaining about latitude, longitude, degrees, and minutes. Towards the end of class, the teacher asked his students, "Suppose I asked you to meet me for lunch at 23 degrees, 4 minutes north latitude and 45 degrees, 15 minutes east longitude..."

A student's voice broke the confused silence, and volunteered, "I guess you'd be eating alone, sir."

A policeman pulls over a driver for swerving in and out of lanes on the highway. He tells the guy to blow a breath into a breathalyser.

"I can't do that, officer."

"Why not?"

"Because I'm an asthmatic. I could get an asthma attack if

I blow into that tube."

"Okay, we'll just get a urine sample down at the station."

"Can't do that either, officer."

"Why not?"

"Because I'm a diabetic. I could get low blood sugar if I pee in a cup."

"Alright, we could get a blood sample."

"Can't do that either, officer."

"Why not?"

"Because I'm a haemophiliac. If I give blood I could die."

"Fine then, just walk this white line."

"Can't do that either, officer."

"Why not?"

"Because I'm drunk."

An 80-year-old couple were having problems remembering things, so they decided to go to their doctor to get checked out to make sure nothing was wrong with them.

When they arrived at the doctor's, they explained to the doctor about the problems they were having with their memories. After checking the couple out, the doctor told them that they were physically okay but might want to start writing things down and making notes to help them remember things.

The couple thanked the doctor and left. Later that night while watching TV, the man got up from his chair and his wife asked, "Where are you going?"

He replied, "To the kitchen."

She asked, "Will you get me a bowl of ice cream?"

He replied, "Sure."

She then asked him, "Don't you think you should write it down so you can remember it?"

He said, "No, I can remember that."

She then said, "Well I would also like some strawberries

on top. You had better write that down because I know you'll forget that."

He said, "I can remember that; you want a bowl of ice cream with strawberries."

She replied, "Well, I also would like whipped cream on top. I know you will forget that so you better write it down."

With irritation in his voice, he said, "I don't need to write that down! I can remember that." He then stormed into the kitchen. After about 20 minutes he returned from the kitchen and handed her a plate of bacon and eggs.

She stared at the plate for a moment and said angrily, "I TOLD you to write it down! You forgot my toast!"

A man goes to his bank manager for advice. "How do I set up a small business?"

"Easy," replies the bank manager. "Buy a big one and wait."

First girl: "What would you give a man who has everything?"

Second girl: "Encouragement."

A cowboy rode into town and stopped at a saloon for a drink. Unfortunately, the locals always had a habit of picking on strangers, which he was. When he finished his drink, he found his horse had been stolen. He went back into the bar, handily flipped his gun into the air, caught it above his head without even looking and fired a shot into the ceiling.

"Which one of you sidewinders stole my horse?!?!?" he yelled with surprising forcefulness. No one answered. "Alright, I'm going to have another beer, and if my horse ain't back outside by the time I finish, I'm going to do what

I did in Texas! And I don't want to have to do what I did in Texas!" Some of the locals shifted restlessly. The man, true to his word, had another beer, walked outside, and found his horse had been returned to the post.

He saddled up and started to ride out of town. The bartender wandered out of the bar and asked, "Say, partner, before you go...what happened in Texas?"

The cowboy turned back and said, "I had to walk home."

A man takes the ferry to work every day, but one day he oversleeps. He hurries to the docks and sees the ferry ten feet from the quayside. Determined not to miss it, he take a running jump and, by the skin of his teeth, just manages to grab hold the ferry's passenger rail. One of the crew helps pull him up over the side. "Y'know," he says. "If you'd waited another second or two we'd have docked."

How many nuclear engineers does it take to change a light bulb?

Seven. One to install the new bulb and six to figure out what to do with the old one for the next 10,000 years.

How many straight San Franciscans does it take to change a light bulb?

Both of them.

How many Freudian analysts does it take to change a light bulb?

Two. One to change the bulb and one to hold the penis ... ladder, I mean ladder.

How many politicians does it take to change a light bulb?
Two. One to change it and one to change it back again.

How many stockbrokers does it take to change a light bulb?
Two. One to take out the bulb and drop it and one to try and sell it before it crashes (knowing that it's already burned out).

How many systems programmers does it take to change a light bulb?
None. You'll never find one who'll admit it went down in the first place.

How many gay men does it take to screw in a light bulb?
Two. One to screw it in and the other to say "Fabulous".

How many Real Men does it take to change a light bulb?
None. Real Men aren't afraid of the dark.

How many pessimists does it take to change a light bulb?
None. The old one is probably screwed in too tight.

How many Marxists does it take to change a light bulb?
None. The seeds of revolution and change are within the light bulb itself.

How many nihilists does it take to change a light bulb?
There is nothing to change.

How many Hollywood directors does it take to change a light bulb?

One, but he'll want to do it nineteen times.

How many punk rockers does it take to change a light bulb?

Two. One to change the bulb and one to eat the old one.

How many telesales people does it take to change a light bulb?

One, but he has to do it while you're having dinner.

How many surrealists does it take to change a light bulb?

Two. One to hold the giraffe and one to fill the bathtub with brightly coloured machine tools.

How many philosophers does it take to change a light bulb?

Three. One to change it and two to argue about whether the light bulb really exists.

How many managers does it take to change a light bulb?

Three. One to get the bulb and two to get the phone number to dial one of the subordinates to actually change it.

❖

How many psychiatrists does it take to change a light bulb?

Only one, but the light bulb has really got to want to change.

How many male chauvinists does it take to change a light bulb.

None – she can do it when she's finished the dishes.

How many poets does it take to change a light bulb?

Three. One to curse the darkness, one to light a candle and one to change the bulb.

How many preservation society members does it take to change a light bulb.

One, but it takes a year to find an antique Edison bulb so it'll be aesthetically accurate.

How many lawyers does it take to change a light bulb?

How many can you afford?

How many programmers does it take to change a light bulb?

None. That's a hardware problem.

How many MPs does it take to change a light bulb?

It depends on how many it took under the previous government.

A man goes to an auction and bids for a parrot. He starts the bidding at £10, then another bidder goes to £20. The man bids to £40, and the other bidder raises it to £60. The man is running out of cash but puts in a final bid of £70 and wins the parrot.

"For all that money I hope the damn parrot can talk," he says to the auctioneer.

The auctioneer replies, "Of course, it can. Who d'you think you were bidding against?"

A woman's husband had been slipping in and out of a coma for several months, yet she stayed by his bedside every single day. When he came to, he motioned for her to come nearer. As she sat by him, he said,

"You know what? You have been with me all through the bad times. When I got fired, you were there to support me. When my business failed, you were there. When I got shot, you were by my side. When we lost the house, you gave me support. When my health started failing, you were still by my side... You know what?"

"What, dear?" she asked gently.

"I think you bring me bad luck."

❖

A magician works on a cruise ship. The audience is different each week, so he does the same tricks over and over again. However, the captain's parrot sees the same show every week and starts to get bored. It even starts heckling and giving away the magician's secrets. "Look, it's not the same hat. He's hiding the flowers under the table. Hey, why are all the cards the ace of spades?" and so on.

The magician is furious but can't do anything, and the

situation continues until the ship hits a reef and sinks. The magician finds himself floating on a piece of wreckage with, as fate would have it, the parrot. They stare at each other in hatred but don't utter a word. This goes on for a whole day, then another, then another. On the fourth day the parrot can't contain itself any longer. "OK," it says. "I give up. What *did* you do with the bloody ship?"

A new employee is called into the personnel manager's office. "What's the meaning of this?" asks the manager. "When you applied for the job you told us you had five years' experience. Now we discover this is the first job you've ever had."

"Yes," replies the young man. "But your ad also said you wanted somebody with imagination."

A man was driving down a quiet country lane when out into the road strayed a rooster.

Whack! The cock disappeared under the car in a cloud of feathers. Shaken, the man pulled over at the farmhouse and rang the doorbell. A farmer appeared.

The man somewhat nervously said, "I think I killed your cockerel. Please allow me to replace him."

"Suit yourself," the farmer replied, "the hens are round the back."

Scientists suggest that men should take a look at their alcohol consumption considering recent experimental results that revealed the presence of female hormones in beer. The theory is that drinking beer makes men turn into women. To test the finding, 100 men were fed 6 pints of beer each. It was then observed that 100% of the men gained weight, talked excessively without making sense, became overly emotional, couldn't drive, failed to think rationally, argued over nothing, and refused to apologize when wrong. No further testing is planned.

A couple go to see a magic show in Las Vegas. After one especially amazing feat, the man yells, "How'd you do that?"

"I could tell you, sir," replies the magician, "but then I'd have to kill you."

After a pause the man yells back, "OK then, just tell my wife."

A musical director was having a lot of trouble with one drummer. He talked and talked and talked with the drummer, but his performance simply didn't improve.

Finally, before the whole orchestra, he said, "When a musician just can't handle his instrument and doesn't improve when given help, they take away the instrument, and give him two sticks, and make him a drummer."

A stage whisper was heard from the percussion section: "And if he can't handle even that, they take away one of his sticks and make him a conductor."

A man walks into a post office one day to see a middle-aged, balding man standing at the counter methodically placing "Love" stamps on bright pink envelopes with hearts all over them.

He then takes out a perfume bottle and starts spraying scent all over them.

His curiosity getting the better of him, he goes up to the balding man and asks him what he is doing. The man says, "I'm sending out 1,000 Valentine cards signed, 'Guess who?'"

"But why?" asks the man.

"I'm a divorce lawyer."

A small child asks a businessman, "What does two and two make?"

The businessman replies, "Are you buying or selling?"

A man visits his aunt in the nursing home. It turns out that she is taking a nap, so he just sits down in a chair in her room, flips through a few magazines, and munches on some peanuts sitting in a bowl on the table.

Eventually, the aunt wakes up, and her nephew realizes he's absentmindedly finished the entire bowl. "I'm so sorry, auntie, I've eaten all of your peanuts!"

"That's okay, dear," the aunt replied. "After I've sucked the chocolate off, I don't care for them anyway."

When I first went out with my girlfriend she made me lay all my cards on the table – Barclaycard, American Express …

Customer: "Have you got asparagus?"

Waiter: "No, we don't serve sparrows and my name is *not* Gus."

A prospector in the Wild West is crossing the mountains in a horse and wagon. With him are his daughter and $10,000 in cash. Suddenly the pair are stopped by a bandit, who searches the wagon then rides off with it.

"Dang it!" says the prospector. "There goes my $10,000."

"No, Pa," says his daughter. "Look, I managed to hide the money in my mouth."

"Jeepers," says the prospector. "If only your Ma were here we could have saved the horse and wagon too."

❖

Paddy finds an old lamp and starts to polish it. Poof! A genie appears and grants Paddy three wishes.

"Well now," says Paddy. "I've always liked my Guinness in bottles, so I'd like a bottle of Guinness that will never be empty."

Poof! There it is. Paddy opens the bottle and takes a drink. "Oh, that's grand," says Paddy. "Did you say I get three of these wishes?"

"Yes, indeed," says the genie.

"Great," says Paddy. "I'll take two more of these."

❖

A young man goes for a job interview and is asked what sort of employment package he expects. "What I expect is a starting salary of £30,000 a year, six weeks' annual holiday and a Jaguar for a company car."

"All right," says the interviewer. "How about this? We pay you £40,000 a year, rising to £60,000 after two years. You get eight weeks' annual leave, your own secretary and PA, and we'll promote you to board level after four years."

"Wow!" says the young man. "You've got to be joking!"

"I am," replies the interviewer. "But you started it."

A couple come across a wishing well. The husband leans over, makes a wish and throws in a penny. The wife makes a wish too, but she leans over too far, falls into the well and drowns. The husband says, "Wow! It really works!"

An Englishwoman and her young son were travelling in a taxi in New York, USA. As the taxi passed a particularly seedy part of the city, the small boy was fascinated by the garishly made-up ladies who were walking along the streets, accosting some of the male passers-by.

"What are those ladies doing?" asked the boy.

His mother blushed and said, somewhat embarrassed, "I expect they are lost and are asking people for directions."

The taxi driver overheard this and said in a loud voice, "Why don't you tell the boy the truth? In other words they're prostitutes."

The woman blushed an even deeper red, and her son asked, "What are p ... p ... pros ... what the driver said? Are they like other women? Do they have children?"

"Of course," replied his mother. "That's where New York taxi drivers come from."

An elderly couple were killed in an accident and found themselves being given a tour of heaven by Saint Peter. "Here is your seaside villa; over there are the tennis courts, swimming pool, and two golf courses. If you need any refreshments, just stop by any of the many bars located throughout the area."

"Blimey, Gloria," the old man hissed when Saint Peter walked off, "we could have been here ten years ago if you hadn't heard about all that stupid oat bran, wheat germ, and low-fat diet stuff!"

What would Shakespeare be doing if he was alive today? Shouting and scratching at the lid on his coffin.

An applicant for a job with the US federal government is filling out the application form. He comes to the question: "Do you favour the overthrow of the United States government by force, subversion or violence?" After thinking about it, he ticks "violence".

An applicant is being interviewed for admission to a prominent medical school. "Tell me," inquires the interviewer. "Where do you expect to be ten years from now?"

"Well, let's see," replies the student. "It's Wednesday afternoon, so I suppose I'll be on the golf course."

A third-year teacher is getting to know her pupils on the first day of school. She turns to one little girl and says, "And what does your daddy do?"

The girl replies, "Whatever mummy tells him."

A man's boss asks him why he's been for a haircut when he should have been at work.

"Why shouldn't I get it cut in office hours?" says the man.

"It grows while I'm at work."

"It doesn't all grow while you're at work," says the boss.

"Yes," replies the man. "And I don't have it all cut."

Customer: "I want a pen that writes underwater."

Shop assistant: "Wouldn't you like it to write other words, too?"

I don't believe in luck, but then how else do you explain other people doing so well?

The company personnel department had carefully interviewed thirty-eight people for the job of assistant to the financial director. The chief executive thought that one candidate, Charles, seemed ideal. Charles had been to a major public school. Not only was he a qualified accountant, but he also had a masters degree in business administration. He seemed fully aware of the latest creative accountancy techniques.

"Charles," said the chief executive. "We've decided to offer you the job. And as you're so well qualified we've decided to start you off on a slightly higher salary than the one advertised. We'll pay you £48,000 a year."

"Thank you," replied Charles. "How much is that a month?"

Harry goes for a job interview. Sitting next to him is a well-spoken applicant wearing a Cambridge University tie. After a moment the applicant notices Harry's apparel. "I say," says the well-spoken man. "I see you're wearing a Cambridge tie as well."

"Yup," replies Harry.

"I hope you don't mind my saying," observes the applicant, "that you don't look the sort of chap who'd have gone to Cambridge."

"Nope," says Harry.

"Tell me," says the applicant. "When you were at Cambridge, what did you do there?"

"I bought a tie."

A man walks up to a house and says, "Hello, I'm looking for the people who live here."

"Well," says the man at the door. "You've come to the right place."

Of course, the thing you've lost is going to turn up in the last place you look. You're not going to carry on looking for it once you've found it, are you?

A man is walking down the street when he hears a voice shouting, "Stop! Take one more step and you'll be killed!" The man stops, and a brick crashes on to the path in front of him. The man looks around but can't see who shouted the warning. A few moments later the man is about to cross a road when the same voice yells, "Stop! Don't step off the kerb!" A car jumps a red light and zooms past, just missing the man. Again, he looks round but can't see who shouted. An hour later the man is getting on a ferry when the voice yells, "Don't do it! You'll drown!" The man steps off the ferry then watches it sink in midstream a few minutes later. The man looks round but still can't see who shouted.

He calls out, "Who's there?"

"It's me. Your guardian angel," replies the voice. "I watch over everything you do."

"You rotten bastard," shouts the man.

"What do you mean?" replies the voice. "I've just saved your life three times."

"Yes," replies the man, "but where were you on my wedding day?"

An executive is interviewing a nervous young woman for a position in his company. "If you could have a conversation with someone, living or dead, who would it be?" asks the executive.

The woman replies, "The living one."

A man is stranded alone on a desert island for ten years. One day, he sees a speck on the horizon. He thinks to himself, *It's not a ship*. The speck gets a little closer and he thinks, *It's not a boat*. The speck gets even closer and he thinks, *It's not a raft*.

Then, out of the surf comes this gorgeous blonde woman, wearing a wet suit and scuba gear. She comes up to the guy and says, "How long has it been since you've had a cigarette?"

"Ten years!" he says.

She reaches over and unzips a waterproof pocket on her left sleeve and pulls out a pack of fresh cigarettes.

He takes one, lights it, takes a long drag, and says, "Man, oh man! Is that good!"

Then she asks, "How long has it been since you've had a drink of whisky?"

He replies, "Ten years!"

She reaches over, unzips her waterproof pocket on her right sleeve, pulls out a flask and gives it to him.

He takes a long swig and says, "Wow, that's fantastic!"

Then she starts unzipping a longer zipper that runs down the front of her wet suit and she says to him, "And how long has it been since you've had some real fun?"

And the man replies, "Wow! Don't tell me that you've got golf clubs in there!"

A shopkeeper was held up by a man waving a bunch of flowers at him in a threatening manner. It was robbery with violets.

A man rushes into his house and yells to his wife, "Martha, pack up your things! I just won the lottery!"

Martha shouts back, "Shall I pack for warm weather or for cold?"

The man replies, "I don't care, just as long as you're out of the house by noon!"

Mr Smith was fed up with his wife's insistence on absolute tidiness. He was not allowed to smoke cigarettes or cigars or a pipe at home. He had to take off his shoes before he entered the house. His wife even made him comb his hair in the garden in case a speck of dandruff fell on the floor.

When he died Mr Smith managed to get some revenge. His will stipulated that his ashes were to be scattered on the lounge carpet.

The boss, Mr Perkins, is showing a new employee around the office. "Some people might find me old-fashioned," says Mr Perkins, "but I don't believe in first names. They encourage over-familiarity, slackness and a lowering of standards. You will refer to me as Mr Perkins, and I will address you by your last name. What is your name, by the way?"

"Stuart Darling," replies the employee.

"Welcome on board, Stuart."

Employer to applicant: "Do you think you can handle a variety of work?"

Applicant: "I ought to, I've had ten different jobs in four months."

The Pope met with the College of Cardinals to discuss a proposal from Shimon Peres, the former leader of Israel. "Your Holiness," said one of the Cardinals, "Mr. Peres wants to determine whether Jews or Catholics are superior by challenging you to a golf match."

The Pope was greatly disturbed, as he had never held a golf club in his life.

"Not to worry," said the Cardinal, "we'll call America and talk to Jack Nicklaus. We'll make him a Cardinal and he can play Shimon Peres... We can't lose!" Everyone agreed it was a good idea. The call was made and, of course, Jack was honoured and agreed to play.

The day after the match, Nicklaus reported to the Vatican to inform the Pope of his success in the match. "I came in second, Your Holiness," said Nicklaus.

"Second?!!" exclaimed the surprised Pope. "You came in second to Shimon Peres?!!"

"No," said Nicklaus, "second to Rabbi Woods."

A lady was picking through the frozen turkeys, but couldn't find one big enough for her family.

377

She asked an assistant, "Do these turkeys get any bigger?"

The boy replied, "No, madam, they're dead."

"Do you believe in life after death?" the boss asked one of his employees.

"Yes, sir," the new recruit replied.

"Well, then, that makes everything just fine," the boss went on. "After you left early yesterday to go to your grandmother's funeral, she popped in to see you."

Four job applicants are told that they have to answer a single question and the one who gives the best answer will get the job. The question is: "What's the fastest thing in the world?"

The first applicant comes in and gives his answer. "Thought is the fastest thing," he says. "It's instantaneous."

The second applicant comes in and says, "A blink is the fastest thing. It's a reflex that you don't even have to think about."

The third applicant comes in and says, "It must be electricity. You can throw a switch and 20 miles away a light will come on."

Finally, the fourth applicant shuffles in, looking very ill. "I guess the fastest thing in the world must be diarrhoea," he says. "Last night in bed I had terrible cramps in my guts and before I could think, blink or put on the light ..."

"Doctor, doctor! I keep thinking I'm a ball of string."
"Well, go and get knotted."

A blonde gets on an airplane and sits down in the first class section of the plane. The stewardess rushes over to her and tells her she must move to coach because she doesn't have a first class ticket. The blonde replies, "I'm blonde, I'm smart, I have a good job, and I'm staying in first class until we reach Jamaica."

The disgusted stewardess gets the head stewardess who asks the blonde to leave. The blonde yet again repeats, "I'm blonde, I'm smart, I have a good job and I'm staying in first class until we reach Jamaica." The head stewardesses doesn't even know what to do at this point because they still have to get the rest of the passengers seated to take off; the blonde is causing a problem with boarding now, so the stewardess gets the co-pilot.

The co-pilot goes up to the blonde and whispers in her ear. She immediately gets up and goes to her seat in the coach section. The head stewardess asks the co-pilot in amazement what he said to get her to move to her correct seat. The co-pilot replies, "I told her the front half of the airplane wasn't going to Jamaica."

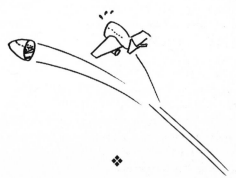

A pheasant is standing in a field talking to a bull. "I would love to be able to get to the top of that tree," sighs the pheasant, "but I haven't got the energy."

"Why don't you nibble on my droppings?" suggests the bull. "They're packed with nutrients." So the pheasant pecks at the dung and finds that he has the strength to fly to the first branch of the tree. The next day he eats some more dung and reaches the second branch, and so on. A week later he's eaten so much dung that he can perch on the very top of the tree, at which point the farmer shoots him dead. The moral of the story is that bullshit might get you to the top but it won't keep you there.

The schoolteacher was taking her first golfing lesson.

"Is the word spelt p-u-t or p-u-t-t?" she asked the instructor.

"P-u-t-t is correct," he replied.

"P-u-t means to place a thing where you want it. P-u-t-t means merely a vain attempt to do the same thing."

A lion is roaming around the jungle looking for something to eat. He comes across two men, one sitting under a tree reading a book and the other typing away at his typewriter. The lion quickly pounces on the man reading the book and eats him – because even the King of the Jungle knows that readers digest and writers cramp.

After a particularly poor game of golf, a popular club member skipped the clubhouse and started to go home. As he was walking to the parking lot to get his car, a policeman stopped him and asked, "Did you tee off on the sixteenth hole about twenty minutes ago?"

"Yes," the golfer responded.

"Did you happen to hook your ball so that it went over the trees and off the course?"

"Yes, I did. How did you know?" he asked.

"Well," said the policeman very seriously, "your ball flew out onto the road and crashed through a driver's windscreen. The car went out of control, crashing into five other cars and a fire engine. The fire engine couldn't make it to the fire, and the building burned down. So, what are you going to do about it?"

The golfer thought it over carefully and responded,"I think I'll close my stance a little bit, tighten my grip and lower my right thumb."

I wouldn't say my sister was an ugly baby, but it was almost a year before my mother realised she had been putting the nappy on the wrong end.

A man is on his deathbed. "Grant me one last wish, my dear," he gasps pitifully to his wife. "Six months after I die I want you to marry Joe."

"But I thought you hated Joe," says his wife.

"I do," says the man.

"You've all heard my arguments," says the managing director to the board. "Now let's vote on it. Anyone who doesn't agree with me should raise their right hand and say 'I resign'."

A man went to a brain store to get some brain to complete a study. He sees a sign remarking on the quality of professional brain offered at this particular brain store. He begins to question the butcher about the cost of these brains.

"How much does it cost for engineer brain?"

"Three pounds an ounce."

"How much does it cost for programmer brain?"

"Four pounds an ounce."

"How much for lawyer brain?"

"£1,000 an ounce."

"Why is lawyer brain so much more?"

"Do you know how many lawyers we had to kill to get one ounce of brain?"

A husband and wife visit a marriage guidance counsellor. The wife complains that her husband doesn't pay her enough attention, so the counsellor decides on some shock treatment. He leans over the desk and gives the woman a long, passionate kiss. He then turns to the husband and says, "Your wife needs that kind of attention at least twice a week."

"OK," replies the husband, "but I can only get her here on Tuesdays and Thursdays."

❖

Two strangers, a man and a woman, find themselves in the same sleeping carriage of a train. They both go to sleep, the man on the top bunk, the woman on the bottom. In the middle of the night the man leans over and says, "I'm sorry to bother you, but I'm awfully cold and I wondered if you could possibly get me another blanket?"

"I have a better idea," replies the woman with a glint in her eye. "Just for tonight, let's pretend that we're married."

"Sounds good to me," says the man.

"Great," says the woman. "Now go and get your own damn blanket!"

My printer's type began to grow faint, so I called a local repair shop. A friendly man informed me that the printer probably needed to be cleaned. Because the store charged £50 for this service, the man told me I might be better off trying the job myself. Pleasantly surprised by his candour, I asked, "Does your boss know that you discourage business?"

"Actually, it's my boss's idea," replied the man. "We usually make more money on repairs if we let people try to fix things themselves first."

A man goes up to his boss and says, "Here! My wage packet was empty last week."

"I know," says the boss, "but I pay people what they're worth, and in your case it turned out they don't make money in small enough denominations."

A golfer, playing a round by himself, is about to tee off, and a greasy little salesman runs up to him, and yells, "Wait! Before you tee off, I have something really amazing to show you!"

The golfer, annoyed, says, "What is it?"

"It's a special golf ball," says the salesman. "You can never lose it!"

"What do you mean," scoffs the golfer, "you can never lose it? What if you hit it into the water?"

"No problem," says the salesman. "It floats, and it detects where the shore is, and spins towards it."

"Well, what if you hit it into the woods?"

"Easy," says the salesman. "It emits a beeping sound, and

you can find it with your eyes closed."

"Okay," says the golfer, impressed. "But what if your round goes late and it gets dark?"

"No problem, sir, this golf ball glows in the dark! I'm telling you, you can never lose this golf ball!"

The golfer buys it at once. "Just one question," he says to the salesman. "Where did you get it?"

"I found it."

Four married men go golfing on Sunday. During the 3rd hole the following conversation ensued:

First man: "You have no idea what I had to do to be able to come out golfing this weekend. I had to promise my wife that I will paint every room in the house next weekend."

Second man: "That's nothing. I had to promise my wife that I will build her a new deck for the pool."

Third man: "You both have it easy! I had to promise my wife that I will remodel the kitchen for her."

They continue to play the hole when they realized that the fourth man has not said a word. So they ask him, "You haven't said anything about what you had to do to be able to come golfing this weekend. What's the deal?"

"I don't want to talk about it. Let's just say that the foundation for the new house is being poured next Tuesday."

The captain called the sergeant in. "Sarge, I just got a telegram that Private Jones' mother died yesterday. Better go tell him and send him in to see me."

So the sergeant calls for his morning formation and lines up all the troops. "Listen up, men," says the sergeant. "Johnson, report to the mess hall for KP. Smith, report to personnel to sign some papers. The rest of you men report to the motor pool for maintenance. Oh, by the way, Jones, your mother died. Report to the commander."

Later that day the captain called the sergeant into his office. "Hey, Sarge, that was a pretty cold way to inform Jones his mother died. Couldn't you be a bit more tactful next time?"

"Yes, sir," answered the sergeant.

A few months later, the captain called the sergeant in again with, "Sarge, I just got a telegram that Private McGrath's mother died. You'd better go tell him and send him in to see me. This time be more tactful."

So the Sergeant calls for his morning formation. "OK, men, fall in and listen up. Everybody with a mother, take two steps forward. Not so fast, McGrath!"

An Israeli soldier who had just enlisted asked the commanding officer for a 3-day pass.

The CO said, "Are you crazy? You've just joined the Israeli army, and you already want a 3-day pass? You must do something spectacular for that recognition!"

So the soldier came back a day later in an Arab tank!

The CO was so impressed, he asked, "How did you do it?"

"Well, I jumped in a tank, and went toward the border with the Arabs. I approached the border, and saw an Arab tank. I put my white flag up, the Arab tank put his white flag up. I said to the Arab soldier, 'Do you want to get a three-day pass?' He nodded and we exchanged tanks!"

A man jumps out of an airplane with a parachute on his back. As he's falling, he realises his 'chute is broken. He doesn't know anything about parachutes, but as the earth rapidly approaches, he realizes his options are limited; he takes off the parachute and tries to fix it himself on the way down. The wind is ripping past his face, he's dropping like a rock, and at 5,000 feet, another man goes shooting up past him. In desperation, the man with the 'chute looks up and yells, "Hey do you know anything about parachutes?"

The man flying up looks down and yells, "No, do you know anything about gas stoves?"

❖

Two women meet on the street. One asks the other about her husband.

"Well, liquor doesn't agree with him, and he doesn't know how to play poker," says the first.

"That's wonderful," says her friend.

"It would be," says the first woman, "if he didn't drink and play poker."

❖

A research scientist drops a piece of buttered toast on the floor and is astonished to find that it lands butter-side up. He takes the toast to a colleague and asks him how on earth the toast landed butter-side up when, according to experience, it always lands butter-side down. The colleague thinks for a moment then comes up with answer. "It's easy," he says. "You must have buttered the wrong side."

❖

The general went out to find that none of his GIs were there. One finally ran up, panting heavily.

"Sorry, sir! I can explain. You see I had a date and it ran a little late. I ran to the bus but missed it, I hailed a cab but it broke down, found a farm, bought a horse but it dropped dead, ran 10 miles, and now I'm here."

The general was very sceptical about this explanation but at least he was here so he let the GI go. Moments later, eight more GIs came up to the general panting, he asked them why they were late.

One by one they replied, "Sorry, sir! I had a date and it ran a little late. I ran to the bus but missed it, I hailed a cab but it broke down, found a farm, bought a horse but it dropped dead, ran 10 miles, and now I'm here."

The general eyed them, feeling very sceptical but since he let the first guy go, he let them go, too. A ninth GI jogged up to the general, panting heavily.

"Sorry, sir! I had a date and it ran a little late. I ran to the bus but missed it, I hailed a cab but..."

"Let me guess," the general interrupted, "it broke down."

"No," said the GI, "there were so many dead horses in the road, it took forever to get around them."

❖

A man goes into a magic shop and sees a pair of 'nudie' glasses for sale. "What do they do?" asks the man.

"They let you see everyone in the nude," says the shopkeeper. "Why not try them on?"

So the man tries on the glasses and straight away everyone

he looks at is in the nude. The shopkeeper is nude, his assistant is nude, even a passer-by looking in the window is nude. The man buys the glasses and goes out into the street to look at everyone in the nude. After an hour of fun he decides to sneak home and surprise his wife with his new toy. He gets back, creeps to the living room and finds his wife and neighbour nude on the couch.

"Surprise!" he shouts, coming into the room. "What do you think of my new glasses?" He takes them off and is surprised to see that his wife and neighbour are still naked. "Damn!" he says. "I've only had them an hour and they're broken already."

Two men were boasting to each other about their old army days.

"Why, my outfit was so well drilled," declared one, "that when they presented arms all you could hear was slap, slap, click."

"Very good," conceded the other, "but when my company presentèd arms you'd just hear slap, slap, jingle."

"What was the jingle?" asked the first.

"Oh," replied the other offhand, "just our medals."

I can't help admiring my boss. If I don't, he'll fire me.

A boss approaches his four employees and tells them he has to fire one of them. The black employee replies, "I'm a protected minority."

The female employee says, "And I'm a woman."

The oldest employee says, "Fire me, buster, and I'll hit you with an age discrimination suit."

Everyone turns to look at the young white guy. He thinks for a moment, then says, "I think I might be gay …"

This is the transcript of an actual radio conversation of a US naval ship with Canadian authorities off the coast of Newfoundland in October, 1995.

Radio conversation released by the Chief of Naval Operations on November 10, 1995.

Americans: Please divert your course 15 degrees to the North to avoid a collision.

Canadians: Recommend you divert YOUR course 15 degrees to the South to avoid a collision.

Americans: This is the Captain of a US Navy ship. I say again, divert YOUR course.

Canadians: No. I say again, you divert YOUR course.

Americans: THIS IS THE AIRCRAFT CARRIER USS LINCOLN, THE SECOND LARGEST SHIP IN THE UNITED STATES' ATLANTIC FLEET. WE ARE ACCOMPANIED BY THREE DESTROYERS, THREE CRUISERS, AND NUMEROUS SUPPORT VESSELS. I DEMAND THAT YOU CHANGE YOUR COURSE 15 DEGREES NORTH, THAT'S ONE FIVE DEGREES NORTH, OR COUNTER-MEASURES WILL BE UNDERTAKEN TO ENSURE THE SAFETY OF THIS SHIP.

Canadians: This is a lighthouse. Your call…

"Doctor, doctor! How can I get this ugly mole off my face?"

"Get your dog to chase it back into its hole."

Dick is introduced to an author at a party. "My last book was terribly difficult," the author says. "It took me over six years to complete."

"I can sympathise," replies Dick. "I'm a slow reader myself."

A man going to India for his summer holidays asked his doctor how he could avoid getting a disease from biting insects. He just told him not to bite any.

A hunter hires a cabin and a gun dog for the season and catches lots of game. Next year he returns and asks for the same cabin and the same dog.

"Was that the dog called 'Salesman'?" asks the cabin owner.

"It sure was," replies the hunter. "He's the best dog I ever worked with."

"Not any more," says the owner. "Some jerk came by and started calling him 'Sales Manager'. Now all he does is sit around all day and bark."

Of course Vincent Van Gogh was notoriously vague. Whatever you said to him just went in one ear – and straight out of the same ear.

❖

A Texan farmer goes to Australia for a vacation. There he meets an Aussie farmer and gets talking. The Aussie shows off his big wheat field and the Texan says, "Oh! We have wheat fields that are at least twice as large."

Then they walk around the ranch a little and the Aussie shows off his herd of cattle. The Texan immediately says, "We have longhorns that are at least twice as large as your cows."

The conversation has, meanwhile, almost died when the Texan sees a herd of kangaroos hopping through the field. He asks, "And what are those?"

The Aussie asks with an incredulous look, "Don't you have grasshoppers in Texas?"

❖

My father came home and told us that he'd been fired. His company had replaced him with a machine that was able to do everything he could, but do it much, much better. The tragic thing was, my mother went out and bought one too.

A software manager, a hardware manager and a sales manager are driving to a meeting when a tyre blows. They get out of the car and look at the problem. The software manager says, "I can't do anything about this – it's a hardware problem."

The hardware manager says, "Maybe if we turned the car off and on again, it would fix itself."

The sales manager says, "Hey, 75 per cent of it is working – let's ship it."

A general had sent some of his men off to fight for their country in the Falkland Islands Crisis.

Upon returning to England, three soldiers who had distinguished themselves in battle were summoned to the general's office. "Since we weren't actually at war," the general began, "I can't give out any medals. We did, however, want to let each of you know your efforts were appreciated.

What we've decided to do is to let each of you choose two points on your body. You will be given two pounds for each inch of distance between those parts. We'll start on the left, boys, so what'll it be?"

Soldier 1: "The tip of my head to my toes, sir!"

General: "Very good, son, that's 70 inches, which comes to 140 pounds."

Soldier 2: "The tip of the finger on one outstretched hand to the tip of the other, sir!"

General: "Even better, son, that's 72 inches, which comes to 144 pounds."

Soldier 3: "The palm of my hand to the tip of my left little finger, sir!"

General: "That's a strange but fair request, son!"

As the general began the measurement he said, "What! Son, where is your left little finger?"

Soldier 3: "Falkland Islands, sir!"

Dick has just started his own firm and leased a new office. On his first day he sees a man come into the outer office and, wanting to look like a hot-shot, picks up the phone and pretends he's in the middle of a huge business deal. After a few minutes of animated conversation, Dick concludes his business, puts down the receiver and turns to the man. "Can I help you?" he asks.

"Yeah," replies the man. "I'm here to connect your phone."

The US Air Force has an ultra-high-security, super-secret base in Nevada, known simply as Area 51. Well, late one afternoon, the Air Force folks out at Area 51 were very surprised to see a Cessna landing at their secret base. They immediately impounded the aircraft and hauled the pilot into an interrogation room. The pilot's story was that he took off from Las Vegas, got lost, and spotted the base just as he was about to run out of fuel. The Air Force started a full FBI background check on the pilot and held him overnight during the investigation.

By the next day, they were finally convinced that the pilot really was lost and wasn't a spy. They fuelled up his airplane, gave him a terrifying "you-did-not-see-a-base" briefing, complete with threats of spending the rest of his life in prison, told him Vegas was that-a-way on such-and-such a heading, and sent him on his way. The day after that though, to the total disbelief of the Air Force, the same Cessna showed up again. Once again, the MPs surrounded the plane...only this time there were two people in the plane. The same pilot jumped out and said, "Do anything you want to me, but my wife is in the plane and you have to tell her where I was last night!"

"I say, your dog is very clever being able to play the trombone."

"Not really – he can't read a single note of music."

"What is your dog's name?"

"I don't know. He refuses to tell me."

First soldier: "Pass me the chocolate pudding, would you?"

Second soldier: "No way, Jose!"

First soldier: "Why ever not?"

Second soldier: "It's against regulations to help another soldier to dessert!"

Tom and Dick are playing a round of golf when they get stuck behind a pair of female players. Eventually Tom gets tired of waiting and walks over to ask if they can play through. However, he soon scuttles back. "When I got closer

393

I realised it was my wife and mistress," says Tom. "You go and ask them instead."

Dick walks over to the women, but he too soon hurries back. "Small world," he says.

A man is sitting reading his paper when his wife sneaks up behind him and whacks him with a frying pan.

"What was that for?" says the man.

"I found a piece of paper in your pocket with the name Mary Lou written on it," says his wife. "You're having an affair!"

"Of course I'm not," says the man. "Mary Lou is the name of a horse I bet on last week." The wife apologises and calm is restored. Next day the man's wife sneaks up on him and again and again swats him with a frying pan.

"What's the matter this time?" says the man.

His wife replies, "Your horse phoned!"

Philosophy of a skunk: I stink, therefore I am.

There's an important meeting at the corporation, and one by one each of the directors and executives are summoned for an interview with the managing director. Finally, only the most junior executive is left. He enters the MD's office and sits down. "Young man," says the MD. "Have you had sexual relations with Miss Jones, my secretary."

"No, sir," says the executive.

"Not even a quick fling at an office party?" queries the MD.

"No, sir. Never," replies the executive.

"So you've never laid a finger on her?" says the MD.

"Not once," replies the executive.

"Excellent," says the MD. "In that case, you can be the one who tells her she's fired."

Officer: "Soldier, do you have change for five pounds?"

Soldier: "Sure, mate."

Officer: "That's no way to address an officer! Now let's try it again."

"Do you have change for five pounds?"

Soldier: "No, SIR!"

A Canadian park ranger is giving some ramblers a warning about bears. "Brown bears are usually harmless. They avoid contact with humans so we suggest that you attach small bells to your rucksacks and give the bears time to get out of your way. However, grizzly bears are extremely dangerous. If you see any grizzly bear droppings leave the area immediately."

"So how do we know if they're grizzly bear droppings?" asks one of the ramblers.

"It's easy," replies the ranger. "They're full of small bells."

There was a young soldier, who, just before battle, told his sergeant that he didn't have a rifle.

"That's no problem, son," said the sergeant. "Here, take this broom. Just point it at the Germans, and go 'Bangety Bang Bang'."

"But what about a bayonet, Sarge?" asked the young (and gullible) recruit.

The sergeant pulls a piece of straw from the end of the broom, and attaches it to the handle end. "Here, use this... just go, 'Stabity Stab Stab'."

The recruit ends up alone on the battlefield, holding just his broom. Suddenly, a German soldier charges at him. The recruit points the broom. "Bangety Bang Bang!" The German falls dead.

More Germans appear. The recruit, amazed at his good luck, goes, "Bangety Bang Bang! Stabity Stab Stab!" He mows down the enemy by the dozens. Finally, the battlefield is clear, except for one German soldier walking slowly toward him.

"Bangety Bang Bang!" shouts the recruit. The German keeps coming. "Bangety Bang Bang!" repeats the recruit, to no avail. He gets desperate. "Bangety Bang Bang! Stabity Stab Stab!"

It's no use.

The German keeps coming. He stamps the recruit into the ground, and says, "Tankety Tank Tank."

Research shows that most men sleep on the right side of the bed. Even when they're asleep they have to be right.

The Crist family worked at a zoo. At the same time each year they predicted the general luck and overall mood of the forthcoming year by watching the gnu. If the gnu's ears were forward, it meant a successful, joyous year was almost certain to happen. But if its ears were laid back flat against its head, it meant that an unlucky or very unhappy year was sure to happen. One year it was Mary's turn to "survey" the animal and come up with the prediction, and it was the first time she'd done this alone. In her excitement, she forgot to take the key to the cage and was late in coming to check on the gnu. Then she saw the wrong ear position and predicted a bad year, when, in fact, it was quite good. To explain the error, the local newspaper ran the following headline twelve months later: MARY CRIST MISSES A HAPPY GNU'S EAR.

A new soldier was on sentry duty at the main gate. His orders were clear. No car was to enter unless it had a special sticker on the windshield. A big army car came up with a general seated in the back. The sentry said, "Halt, who goes there?"

The chauffeur, a corporal, says, "General Wheeler."

"I'm sorry, I can't let you through. You've got to have a sticker on the windshield."

The general said, "Drive on!"

The sentry said, "Hold it! You really can't come through. I have orders to shoot if you try driving in without a sticker."

The general repeated, "I'm telling you, son, drive on!"

The sentry walked up to the rear window and said, "General, I'm new at this. Do I shoot you or the driver?"

Tom comes home to his wife looking very concerned. "I've just been told our milkman has made love to every woman in this street apart from one."

"Really," says his wife. "I bet it's that snooty cow at number 27."

A sixty-year-old couple are celebrating their fortieth wedding anniversary. During the celebration a fairy appears and says that, since they have been such a loving couple, she'll give them each one wish. The wife wishes to travel around the world. The fairy waves her wand and poof!

She has a handful of plane tickets. Next, it's the husband's turn. He pauses for a moment, then says, "I'd like to have a woman thirty years younger than me." So the fairy picks up her wand and poof! He's ninety.

Jill hears that milk baths will make her beautiful so she leaves a note for her milkman asking for 15 gallons of milk. When the milkman reads the note he thinks there must be a mistake, so he knocks on the door. Jill answers, and the milkman says, "I found your note to leave 15 gallons of milk. Did you mean 1.5 gallons?"

Jill replies, "No. I want 15 gallons. I'm going to fill my bathtub with milk."

"Pasteurised?" asks the milkman.

"No," says Jill. "Just up to my boobs."

A woman is chatting with her friend. "My husband bought me a mood ring the other day," she says. "It lets him monitor my emotional state."

"Oh yes?" says the friend. "How does it work?"

The woman replies, "When I'm in a good mood it turns green, and when I'm in a bad mood it leaves a big red mark on his forehead."

A young naval student was being put through his paces by an old sea captain.

"What would you do if a sudden storm sprang up to starboard?"

"Throw out an anchor, sir," the student replied.

"What would you do if another storm sprang up aft?"

"Throw out another anchor, sir."

"And if another terrific storm sprang up forward, what would you do then?" asked the captain.

"Throw out another anchor, sir."

"Hold on," said the captain. "Where are you getting all those anchors from?"

"From the same place you're getting your storms, sir."

Boss to new secretary: "Will you file these papers for me?"

Secretary: "Wouldn't it be easier to trim them with scissors?"

Two men went bear hunting. While one stayed in the cabin, the other went out looking for a bear.

He soon found a huge bear, shot at it but only wounded it. The enraged bear charged toward him, he dropped his rifle and started running for the cabin as fast as he could.

He ran pretty fast but the bear was just a little faster and gained on him with every step.

Just as he reached the open cabin door, he tripped and fell flat.

Too close behind to stop, the bear tripped over him and went rolling into the cabin.

The man jumped up, closed the cabin door and yelled to his friend inside, "You skin this one while I go and get another!"

This is how regimental training methods develop:

Start with a cage containing five apes. In the cage, hang a banana on a string and put stairs under it. Before long, an ape will go to the stairs and start to climb towards the banana. As soon as he touches the stairs, spray all of the apes with cold water. After a while, another ape makes an attempt with the same result - all the apes are sprayed with cold water.

Continue until, when another ape tries to climb the stairs, the other apes try to prevent it.

Now, turn off the cold water.

Now, remove one ape from the cage and replace it with a new one. The new ape sees the banana and wants to climb the stairs. To his horror, all of the other apes attack him. After another attempt and attack, he knows that if he tries to climb the stairs, he will be assaulted.

Next, remove another of the original five apes and replace it with a new one. The newcomer goes to the stairs and is attacked. The previous newcomer takes part in the punishment with enthusiasm.

Again, replace a third original ape with a new one. The new one makes it to the stairs and is attacked as well. Two of the four apes that beat him have no idea why they were not permitted to climb the stairs, or why they are participating in the beating of the newest ape.

After replacing the fourth and fifth original apes, all the apes which have been sprayed with cold water have been replaced. Nevertheless, no ape ever again approaches the stairs. Why not?

"Because that's the way it's always been around here."

This is how regimental training methods develop.

A zookeeper sees a visitor throwing £5 notes into the monkey enclosure. "What are you doing that for?" he asks.

"The sign says it's OK," replies the visitor.

"No, it doesn't," says the keeper.

"Yes, it does," replies the visitor. "It says, 'Do not feed. £5 fine.'"

Scientists have just discovered something that can do the work of five men – a woman.

"Mummy," said the small boy. "Can I have a saluki or a dachshund for Christmas?"

"No," replied his mother. "You'll have turkey like everyone else."

The British Military writes OFR's (officer fitness reports). The form used for Royal Navy and Marines' fitness reports is the S206. The following are actual excerpts taken from people's 206s....

- His men would follow him anywhere, but only out of curiosity.

- I would not breed from this officer.

- This officer is really not so much of a has-been, but more of a definitely won't-be.

- When she opens her mouth, it seems that this is only to change whichever foot was previously in there.

- He has carried out each and every one of his duties to his entire satisfaction.

- He would be out of his depth in a car park puddle.

- Technically sound, but socially impossible.

- This officer reminds me very much of a gyroscope - always spinning around at a frantic pace, but not really going anywhere.

- This young lady has delusions of adequacy.

- When he joined my ship, this officer was something of a granny; since then he has aged considerably.

- This medical officer has used my ship to carry his genitals from port to port, and my officers to carry him from bar to bar.

- Since my last report he has reached rock bottom, and has started to dig.

- She sets low personal standards and then consistently fails to achieve them.

- He has the wisdom of youth, and the energy of old age.

- This officer should go far - and the sooner he starts, the better.

- In my opinion this pilot should not be authorized to fly below 250 feet.

- The only ship I would recommend this man for is citizenship.

- Works well when under constant supervision and cornered like a rat in a trap.

- This man is depriving a village somewhere of an idiot.

Patrick has ten children and swears to hang himself if his wife has another. Sure enough, his wife gets pregnant, and one of his friends reminds him of his suicide oath. "I almost did hang myself," explains Patrick. "I made the noose and tied it to the rafter, then got on a stool. I was just about to jump when I stopped and said to myself, 'Hang on, Paddy. Perhaps we're hanging the wrong man here.'"

When the professor of mathematics was involved in a car crash he was asked by a policeman if he could remember the other car's registration number.

"Not exactly," replied the professor, "but the total of the numbers divided by the last digit was equal to the square root of the second number."

A Freudian slip is when you say one thing but mean your mother.

❖

After examining a 3,000-year-old mummy an archaeologist announces that it's the body of a man who died of a heart attack.

"How can you tell?" asks one of his students.

"I examined a piece of parchment in the mummy's hand," replies the archaeologist. "It was a betting slip that said '5,000 on Goliath'."

❖

A woman worked for a psychiatrist but in the end she had to give up the job. If she was late he said she was hostile. If she was early he said she had an anxiety complex. And if she was on time he called her a compulsive.

At the bar last night was a man who demanded to be served a drink called Less.

"I've never heard of it," said the barmaid.

"But you *must* have," insisted the man.

"We don't have it. Is Less a new foreign beer or something? Where did you hear about it?" asked the barmaid.

"I don't exactly know what it is," replied the man, "but my doctor insists that I should drink Less."

Harry hears that a zoo has managed to train a lion to live in the same cage as a lamb. He pays a visit and finds that the two animals are indeed sitting next to each other in a cage. Harry approaches the keeper in charge. "It's incredible," says Harry. "How do you manage it?"

"Well, it hasn't been easy," replies the keeper, "and most mornings we do have to buy a new lamb."

A famous admiral and an equally famous general were fishing together when a sudden squall came up. When it died down both eminent warriors were struggling helplessly in the water.

The admiral floundered his way back to the boat and pulled himself painfully in. Then he fished out the general, using an oar.

Catching his breath, he puffed: "Please don't say a word about this to anyone. If the Navy found I can't swim I'd be disgraced."

"Don't worry," the general said. "Your secret is safe. I'd hate to have my men find out I can't walk on water."

The physical training instructor was drilling a platoon of soldiers.

"I want every man to lie on his back, put his legs in the air and move them as though he were riding a bicycle," he explained. "Now begin!"

After a few minutes, one of the men stopped.

"Why did you stop, Smith?" demanded the officer.

"If you please, sir," said Smith, "I'm freewheeling for a while."

A man buys a budgie but is disappointed when it doesn't speak. He goes back to the pet shop where the owner suggests getting the budgie a mirror to play with. This doesn't make the budgie any more talkative, so the pet shop owner next suggests buying it a cuttlefish bone. The bone has no effect either, so the owner suggests that the man buys the budgie a bell and a ladder. Finally, the man returns to the pet shop and announces he's had success. "The budgie looked in the mirror," says the man. "It pecked at the cuttlefish, climbed the ladder, rang the bell, then said a few words and fell dead off its perch."

"Oh dear," said the pet shop owner. "What did it say?"

"It said, 'Hasn't that shop got any bloody bird seed?'"

As the plane was flying low over some hills near Athens, a lady asked the stewardess: "What's that stuff on those hills?"

"Just snow," replied the stewardess.

"That's what I thought," said the lady, "but this fellow in front of me said it was Greece."

A man in a plane is surprised to see a parrot strapped in next to him. He asks the stewardess for a coffee whereupon the parrot squawks, "And get me a whisky, you cow!" The stewardess, flustered, brings back a whisky for the parrot and forgets the coffee.

When this omission is pointed out to her the parrot drains its glass and bawls, "And get me another whisky, you idiot".

Quite upset, the girl comes back shaking with another whisky but still no coffee.

Unaccustomed to such slackness the man tries the parrot's approach, "I've asked you twice for a coffee; go and get it now or I'll kick you."

The next moment, both he and the parrot have been wrenched up and thrown out of the emergency exit by two burly stewards. Plunging downwards the parrot turns to him and says, "For someone who can't fly, you sure complain a lot!"

Emily-Sue gets sick and Billy-Bob calls for an ambulance. The operator asks Billy-Bob where he lives. "1132 Eucalyptus Drive," replies Billy-Bob.

"Can you spell that for me," asks the operator.

There's a long pause. Finally, Billy-Bob says, "How 'bout if I drag her over to Oak Street?"

After years in an asylum a patient is tested to see if he's be able to function in the outside world. The patient is taken to the cinema and shown a number of seats, half of which have 'wet paint' signs on them. The doctors are disappointed to see the patient pick one of the 'wet paint' seats but are pleased when the patient puts down a sheet of paper before sitting down. Later they ask him why he chose one of the seats.

"I like paint," replies the man.

"So why did you put down a sheet of paper before you sat down?" asks a doctor.

The patient replies, "I thought I'd have a better view if I was sitting higher up."

Nature has a way of compensating for weaknesses, which is why stupid people have big mouths.

Did you hear about the dwarf psychic who escaped from prison? The newspaper headline read, "Small medium at large".

An instructor in chemical warfare asked soldiers in his class: "Anyone know the formula for water?"

"Sure. That's easy," said one man.

"What is it?"

"H, I, J, K, L, M, N, O."

"What, what?" asked the instructor.

"H to O," explained the chemistry expert.

A man walks into a psychiatrist's office dressed in a tutu, a diving mask and flippers. "Doctor," he says. "I'm worried about my brother."

Private Lloyd was brought up before the unit CO for some offence.

"You can take your choice, Private - one month's restriction or twenty days' pay," said the officer.

"All right, sir," said the bright soldier, "I'll take the money."

A farmer buys a new cockerel to replace the elderly bird that's been ruling the roost in the hen house. The new bird struts up to the old cockerel and tells him to pack his bags.

"Give me a chance," says the old bird. "Tell you what, let's have a race, and if I lose I'll go without any trouble. All I ask is a five foot start to make up for my bad knee."

The young cockerel agrees, and they both dash round the farmyard, with the old cockerel in front by a nose. The farmer sees this, pulls out a shotgun and shoots the young bird dead. "Damn it!" he shouts. "That's the third gay cockerel I've been sold this month."

Q: What is the difference between an Uzi and an accordion?

A: The Uzi stops after 20 rounds.

Q: How do you get your viola section to sound like the horn section?

A: Have them miss every other note.

Q: What is the difference between a banjo and an anchor?

A: You tie a rope to an anchor before you throw it overboard.

Q: What do you call someone who hangs around with musicians?

A: A drummer.

Q: How many bass players does it take to change a light bulb?

A: Only one - but the guitarist has to show him first.

Q: Why is a bassoon better than an oboe?
A: The bassoon burns longer.

Q: What is perfect pitch on a flute?
A: When it misses the rim of the toilet as you throw it in.

Q: What is the difference between a guitar and a tuna?
A: You can tune a guitar but you can't tuna fish.

Q: Why are harps like elderly parents?
A: Both are unforgiving and hard to get into and out of cars.

Q: Why are a organist's fingers like lightning?
A: Because they rarely strike the same place twice.

Q: What is the range of a tuba?
A: Twenty yards if you've got a good arm.

Q. If you were lost in the woods, who would you trust for directions, an in-tune bagpipe player, an out of tune bagpipe player, or Santa Claus?
A. The out of tune bagpipe player. The other two indicate you have been hallucinating.

Q: What do you get when you drop a piano down a mine shaft?
A: A flat minor.

Q: Two musicians are walking down the street, and one says to the other, "Who was that piccolo I saw you with last night?"
A: The other replies, "That was no piccolo, that was my fife."

Q: What's the definition of a gentleman?
A: One who knows how to play the saxophone, but doesn't!

Q: What is the difference between a trombone and a trumpet?

A: A trombone will bend before it breaks

Q: What is the difference between grapes and a viola?

A: You take off your shoes to stamp on grapes.

Q: Why are orchestra intermissions limited to 20 minutes?

A: So you don't have to retrain the cellists.

Q: What is the difference between a clarinet and an onion?

A: Nobody cries when you chop an clarinet into little pieces.

I used to be schizophrenic, but we're all right now.

There once was a blind man who decided to visit Texas. When he arrived on the plane, he felt the seats and said, "Wow, these seats are big!"

The person next to him answered, "Everything is big in Texas."

When he finally arrived in Texas, he decided to visit a bar. Upon arriving in the bar, he ordered a beer and got a mug placed between his hands. He exclaimed, "Wow these mugs are big!"

The bartender replied, "Everything is big in Texas."

After a couple of beers, the blind man asked the bartender where the bathroom was located. The bartender replied, "Second door to the right." The blind man headed for the bathroom, but accidentally tripped over and skipped the second door. Instead, he entered the third door, which lead to the swimming pool and fell into the pool by accident.

Scared to death, the blind man started shouting, "Don't flush, don't flush!"

Bob is throwing a party. He decides that, to break the ice he'll ask his guests what their I.Q. is.

The day of Bob's party rolls around, and when the first guest knocks on the door, Bob asks the person what her I.Q. is.

"200," replies the first guest.

"Well, that's great," says Bob, let's talk about advanced astrophysics.

Later in the party, someone else is at the door. "Hi, my name is Bob, welcome to my party; what's your I.Q.?"

The new guest responds with, "250."

"Great," says Bob. "Lets talk about advanced maths. Bob and his new guest talk about calculus and statistics for a while.

Much later in the party, after many more guests had arrived and been spoken to by Bob, another guest arrives at the door. "Hi, my name's Bob, welcome to my party; what's your I.Q.?"

This time the guest replies after putting some thought into it, "five."

"Well, that's great," says Bob, "what kind of drumsticks do you use?"

An old man is in the street shouting into thin air. "Why's he doing that?" asks a passer-by.

"That's old Mr Fosdyke," says a woman. "But he's just talking to himself again."

"So why is he shouting?" asks the passer-by.

The woman replies, "He has to. He's deaf."

A farmer was milking his cow. He was just starting to get a good rhythm going when a wasp flew into the barn and started circling his head. Suddenly, the wasp flew into the cow's ear. The farmer didn't think much about it, until the wasp squirted out into his bucket. It went in one ear and out the udder.

Two old men are sitting in an old people's home when one of the female residents runs past completely naked. "What was that she was wearing?" asks the first.

"Don't know," replies the second, "but it sure needed ironing."

A doctor examines a woman and takes her husband aside. "I don't want to alarm you," he says, "but I don't like the way your wife looks."

"Me neither, doctor," says the husband. "But she's a great cook and real good with the kids."

Secretary to boss: "Excuse me, sir, but the Invisible Man is waiting outside."

Boss: "Tell him I can't see him."

❖

A blonde sees a sign reading 'Press bell for night watchman'. She does so, and after a few seconds she hears the watchman clomping down the stairs. He then proceeds to unlock first one gate, then another, then shut down the alarm system and finally make his way through the revolving door.

"Well," he says. "What do you want?"

The blonde replies, "I just wanted to know why you can't ring the bell yourself?"

A woman comes home from psychic fair with a crystal ball she's just bought. "How much was that?" asks her husband.

"Thirty pounds," replies his wife.

"Thirty pounds!" says her husband. "They must have seen you coming."

A big-city lawyer was representing the railroad in a lawsuit filed by an old rancher in Texas. The rancher's prize bull was missing from the field through which the railroad passed. The rancher only wanted to be paid the fair value of the bull.

The case was scheduled to be tried before the justice of the peace in the back room of the general store. The attorney for the railroad immediately cornered the rancher and tried to get him to settle out of court. The lawyer did his best selling job, and finally the rancher agreed to take half of what he was asking.

After the rancher had signed the settlement and taken the cheque, the young lawyer couldn't resist gloating a little over his success, telling the rancher, "You know, I hate to tell you this, old man, but I put one over on you in there. I couldn't have won the case. The driver was asleep when the train went through your ranch that morning. I didn't have one witness to put on the stand. I bluffed you!"

The old rancher replied, "Well, I'll tell you, young feller, I was a little worried about winning that case myself, because that old bull came home this morning."

An army fort in the Wild West is about to be attacked by renegades. The captain sends for his trustiest Indian scout. "Use all your tracking skills to estimate the sort of war party we're up against," the captain orders.

The scout lies down and puts his ear to the ground. "Big war party," he says. "One hundred braves in war paint. Two chiefs, one on a black horse, one on a white horse. Also a medicine man with a limp."

"Good God!" exclaims the captain. "You can tell all that just by listening to the ground?"

"No, sir," replies the scout. "I'm looking under the gate."

The manager of the orchestra comes across an oboe player and a viola player having a fight.

He breaks the fight up and asks what it was about.

The oboe player says, "He broke my reed! I was just about to play my big solo when he broke my reed!"

"Well?" says the stage manager to the viola player. "What do you say to that?"

In umbrage, the viola player replies, "He loosened two of my strings but he won't tell me which ones!"

A soprano died and went to Heaven. St. Peter stopped her at the gate asking, "Well, how many false notes did you sing in your life?"

The soprano answers, "Three."

"Three times, fellows!" says St Peter, and along comes an angel and pricks the soprano three times with a needle.

"Ow! What was that for?" asks the soprano.

St Peter explains, "Here in heaven, we stick you once for

each false note you've sung down on Earth."

"Oh," says the soprano, and is just about to step through the gates when she suddenly hears a horrible screaming from behind a door. "Oh my goodness, what is that?" asks the soprano, horrified.

"Oh," says St Peter, "that's a tenor we got some time back. He's just about to start his third week in the sewing machine."

Therapy is expensive. Popping bubblewrap is cheap. You choose.

A tourist is sightseeing in a European city. She comes upon the grave of Beethoven, and begins reading the plaque, only to be distracted by a low scratching noise.

She asks a passer-by what the scratching sound is. The local replies, "Oh, that is Beethoven. He's decomposing."

A lone tourist passing through the countryside on the way to town by car, unfortunately experiences mechanical problems. The car stalls and the tourist parks by the side of the road and waits for help.

Not much later, a farmer happens to pass by with a truck full of farm animals. The farmer offers the tourist a lift to town and proceeds to explain that he is bringing his farm animals to the town market, where they will be auctioned off to the highest bidders.

Well, it so happens that on the way to the town, the farmer being so engrossed in his story, unintentionally wanders into the other side of road where another vehicle is approaching in the other direction.

The farmer realizes his absent-mindedness and attempts to avoid the possible collision with the other vehicle. He just misses the other car, but unfortunately crashes the truck into the side of the road. The tourist winds up thrown into a ditch and suffers broken ribs and a broken arm and leg and is obviously in extreme pain. The farm animals are all messed up very badly and the farmer, although remaining inside the vehicle, suffers cuts and scrapes.

The farmer gets out of the truck and looks at his farm animals.

The chickens all have broken limbs and can barely move. "These chickens are all useless! Nobody will want to buy these chickens anymore!" bellows the farmer. With that, he grabs and loads his shotgun and blows away the chickens.

Next, he sees the pigs and they are all lame and bleeding profusely. "These pigs are all worthless now! I'll get nothing for them!" yells the farmer. With great rage, the farmer reloads his shotgun and blows away the pigs.

The farmer looks at the sheep and they all have broken limbs and their wool is all bloodied. "Worthless sheep!" screams the farmer and with that, he reloads his shotgun and blows away the sheep.

Meanwhile, the injured tourist witnesses all of this carnage in great horror.

The farmer then moves over to the side of the ditch and looks at the tourist. "Are you okay down there?" he asks.

"NEVER FELT BETTER IN MY ENTIRE LIFE!!!"

The farmer's son was returning from the market with the crate of chickens his father had entrusted to him, when all of a sudden the box fell and broke open. Chickens scurried off in different directions, but the determined boy walked all over the neighbourhood scooping up the wayward birds and returning them to the repaired crate. Hoping he had found them all, the boy reluctantly returned home, expecting the worst.

"Dad, the chickens got loose," the boy confessed sadly, "but I managed to find all twelve of them."

"Well, you did well, son," the farmer beamed. "You left with seven."

A woman rushes to see her doctor, looking very much worried and all strung out.

She rattles off, "Doctor, take a look at me. When I woke up this morning, I looked at myself in the mirror and saw my hair all wiry and frazzled up, my skin was all wrinkled and pasty, my eyes were blood-shot and sticking out, and I had this corpse-like look on my face! What's wrong with me, Doctor?"

The doctor looks her over for a couple of minutes, then calmly says, "Well, I can tell you one thing... there's nothing wrong with your eyesight."

On a rural road a policeman pulled this farmer over and said: "Sir, do you realize your wife fell out of the car several miles back?"

"Thank God, I thought I had gone deaf!"

"Haven't I seen your face before?" a judge demanded, looking down at the defendant.

"You have, Your Honour," the man answered hopefully. "I gave your son violin lessons last winter."

"Ah, yes," recalled the judge. "Twenty years!"

❖

A young vicar came upon a farmer working in his field. Being concerned about the farmer's soul he asked the man, "Are you labouring in the vineyard of the Lord my good man?"

Not even looking at the preacher and continuing his work the farmer replied, "No, these are beans."

"You don't understand," said the preacher. "Are you a Christian?"

With the same amount of interest as his previous answer the farmer said, "Nope, my name is Jones. You must be looking for Jimmy Christian. He lives a mile south of here."

The young determined priest tried again asking the farmer, "Are you lost?"

"No! I've lived here all my life," answered the farmer.

"Are you prepared for the resurrection?" the frustrated preacher asked.

This caught the farmer's attention and he asked, "When's it going to be?"

Thinking he had accomplished something the young vicar replied, "It could be today, tomorrow, or the next day."

Taking a handkerchief from his back pocket and wiping his brow, the farmer remarked, "Well, don't mention it to my wife. She don't get out much and she'll want to go all three days."

A retiring farmer in preparation for selling his land, needed to rid his farm of animals. So he went to every house in his town.

To the houses where the man is the boss, he gave a horse. To the houses where the woman is the boss, a chicken was given.

He got toward the end of the street and saw a couple outside gardening. "Who's the boss around here?" he asked.

"I am," said the man.

"I have a black horse and a brown horse," the farmer said.

"Which one would you like?"

The man thought for a minute and said, "The black one."

"No, no, no, get the brown one," the man's wife said.

"Here's your chicken," said the farmer.

❖

A clergyman walking down a country lane sees a young farmer struggling to load hay back onto a cart after it had fallen off.

"You look hot, my son," said the cleric. "Why don't you rest a moment, and I'll give you a hand."

"No thanks," said the young man.

"Why not?"

"My father wouldn't like it."

"Don't be silly," the minister said. "Everyone is entitled to a break. Come and have a drink of water."

Again the young man protested that his father would be upset. Losing his patience, the clergyman said, "Your father must be a real slave driver. Tell me where I can find him and I'll give him a piece of my mind!"

"Well," replied the young farmer, "he's under that load of hay."

❖

A newlywed farmer and his wife were visited by her mother, who immediately demanded an inspection of the place. The farmer had genuinely tried to be friendly to his new mother-in-law, hoping that it could be a friendly, non-antagonistic relationship. All to no avail though, as she kept nagging them at every opportunity, demanding changes, offering unwanted advice, and generally making life unbearable to the farmer and his new bride.

While they were walking through the barn, during the forced inspection, the farmer's mule suddenly reared up and kicked the mother-in-law in the head, killing her instantly. It was a shock to all no matter their feelings toward her demanding ways.

At the funeral service a few days later, the farmer stood

near the casket and greeted folks as they walked by. The vicar noticed that whenever a woman would whisper something to the farmer, he would nod his head yes and say something. Whenever a man walked by and whispered to the farmer, however, he would shake his head no, and mumble a reply.

Very curious as to this bizarre behaviour, the pastor later asked the farmer what that was all about.

The farmer replied, "The women would say, 'What a terrible tragedy' and I would nod my head and say, 'Yes, it was.' The men would then ask, 'Can I borrow that mule?' and I would shake my head and say, 'Can't. It's all booked up for a year.'"

A bus load of politicians were driving down a country road one afternoon, when all of a sudden, the bus ran off the road and crashed into a tree in an old farmer's field.

Seeing what happened, the old farmer went over to investigate. He then proceeded to dig a hole and bury the politicians.

A few days later, the local constable came out, saw the crashed bus, and asked the old farmer, "Were they all dead?"

The old farmer replied, "Well, some of them said they weren't, but you know how politicians lie."

A man's car stalled on a country road one morning. When the man got out to fix it, a cow came along and stopped beside him. "Your trouble is probably in the distributor," said the cow.

Startled, the man jumped back and ran down the road until he met a farmer. The amazed man told the farmer his story.

"Was it a large red cow with a brown spot over the right eye?" asked the farmer.

"Yes, yes," the man replied.

"Oh! I wouldn't listen to Bessie," said the farmer. "She doesn't know a thing about cars."

The owner of a chemists arrives at work to find a man leaning heavily against a wall.

The owner goes inside and asks his assistant what's up.

"He wanted something for his cough, but I couldn't find the cough syrup," the assistant explains. "So I gave him a laxative and told him to take it all at once."

"Laxatives won't cure a cough, you idiot," the owner shouts angrily.

"Sure it will," the assistant says, pointing at the man leaning on the wall. "Look at him. He's afraid to cough."

A farmer in the country has a watermelon patch and upon inspection he discovers that some of the local kids have been helping themselves to a feast.

The farmer thinks of ways to discourage this profit-eating situation. So he puts up a sign that reads: "WARNING! ONE OF THESE WATERMELONS CONTAINS CYANIDE!"

He smiled smugly as he watched the kids run off the next night without eating any of his melons.

The farmer returns to the watermelon patch a week later to discover that none of the watermelons have been eaten, but finds a sign underneath his own that reads: "NOW THERE ARE TWO!"

A townie moved to the country and bought a piece of land. He went to the local feed and livestock store and talked to the proprietor about how he was going to take up chicken farming. He then asked to buy 100 chicks.

"That's a lot of chicks," commented the proprietor.

"I mean business," the city slicker replied.

A week later the yuppie was back again. "I need another 100 chicks," he said.

"My, you are serious about this chicken farming," the man said.

"Yeah," the yuppie replied. "If I can iron out a few problems."

"Problems?" asked the proprietor.

"Yes," replied the yuppie, "I think I planted that last batch too close together."

Three men were standing in line to get into heaven one day. Apparently it had been a pretty busy day, though, so Peter had to tell the first one, "Heaven's getting pretty close to full today, and I've been asked to admit only people who have had particularly horrible deaths. So what's your story?"

So the first man replies, "Well, for a while I suspected my wife was been cheating on me, so today I came home early to try to catch her red-handed. As I came into my 25th floor apartment, I could tell something was wrong, but all my searching around didn't reveal where this other guy could have been hiding. Finally, I went out to the balcony, and sure enough, there was this man hanging off the railing, 25 floors above ground! By now I was really mad, so I started beating him and kicking him, but wouldn't you know it, he wouldn't fall off. So finally I went back into my apartment and got a hammer and starting hammering on his fingers. Of course, he couldn't stand that for long, so he let go and fell, but even after 25 stories, he fell into the bushes, stunned but okay. I couldn't stand it anymore, so I ran into the kitchen, grabbed the fridge and threw it over the edge where it landed on him, killing him instantly. But all the stress and anger got to me, and I had a heart attack and died there on the balcony."

"That sounds like a pretty bad day to me," said Peter, and let the man in.

The second man comes up and Peter explains to him about heaven being full, and again asks for his story.

"It's been a very strange day. You see, I live on the 26th floor of my apartment building, and every morning I do my exercises out on my balcony. Well, this morning I must have slipped or something, because I fell over the edge. But I got lucky, and caught the railing of the balcony on the floor below me. I knew I couldn't hang on for very long, when suddenly this man burst out onto the balcony. I thought for sure I was saved, when he started beating me and kicking me. I held on the best I could until he ran into the apartment and grabbed a hammer and started pounding on my hands. Finally I just let go, but again I got lucky and fell into the bushes below, stunned but all right. Just when I was thinking I was going to be okay, this refrigerator comes falling out of the sky and crushes me instantly, and now I'm here."

Once again, Peter had to concede that that sounded like a pretty horrible death.

The third man came to the front of the line, and again Peter explained that heaven was full and asked for his story.

"Picture this," says the third man, "I'm hiding inside a refrigerator..."

A townie drove his car into a ditch in the country. Luckily, a local farmer came to help with his big strong horse named Buddy.

He hitched Buddy up to the car and yelled, "Pull, Nellie, pull." Buddy didn't move.

Then the farmer hollered, "Pull, Bobby, pull." Buddy didn't respond.

Once more the farmer commanded, "Pull, Jennie, pull." Nothing.

Then the farmer nonchalantly said, "Pull, Buddy, pull." And the horse easily dragged the car out of the ditch.

The motorist was most appreciative and very curious. He asked the farmer why he called his horse by the wrong name three times.

The farmer said, "Oh, Buddy is blind, and if he thought he was the only one pulling, he wouldn't even try!"

In most offices, the photocopier is out of order every now and then. One copy repairman had answered question after question for the employees. Finally one day, he just smiled and handed them this sheet.

1 The copier is out of order!

2 Yes, we have called the service man.

3 Yes, he will be in today.

4 No, we cannot fix it.

5 No, we do not know how long it will take.

6 No, we do not know what caused it.

7 No, we do not know who broke it.

8 Yes, we are keeping it.

9 No, we do not know what you are going to do now.

10 Thank You

A New York divorce lawyer died and arrived at the pearly gates. Saint Peter asks him, "What have you done to merit entrance into heaven?"

The Lawyer thought a moment, then said, "A week ago, I gave a quarter to a homeless person on the street."

Saint Peter asked Gabriel to check this out in the record, and after a moment Gabriel affirmed that this was true.Saint Peter said, "Well, that's fine, but it's not really quite enough to get you into heaven."

The Lawyer said, "Wait, wait! There's more! Three years ago I also gave a homeless person a quarter."

Saint Peter nodded to Gabriel, who after a moment nodded back, affirming this, too, had been verified.Saint Peter then whispered to Gabriel, "Well, what do you suggest we do with this fellow?"

Gabriel gave the lawyer a sidelong glance, then said to Saint Peter,"Let's give him back his 50 cents and tell him to go to hell."

Three friends die in a car crash, and they go to heaven to an orientation.

They are all asked, "When you are in your casket and friends and family are mourning upon you, what would you like to hear them say about you?"

The first one says, "I would like to hear them say that I was a great doctor of my time, and a great family man."

The second one says, "I would like to hear that I was a wonderful husband and school teacher who made a huge difference in the children of tomorrow."

The last one replies, "I would like to hear them say, 'Look! He's moving!'"

A man walks into the doctor's surgery and asks to be examined. The doctor gives him a once-over and is astonished to find money stuffed into his ear. The money is taken out, and the doctor counts it. "There's exactly £1,950 in there," says the doctor.

"That sounds about right," says the patient. "I knew I wasn't feeling two grand."

A reporter outside a courtroom asked a defendant without his shirt: "Oh, I see you lost the case!"

The defendant answered: "No, we won."

❖

There once was a rich man who was near death. He was worried because he had worked so hard for his money and wanted to be able to take it with him to heaven. So he began to pray that he might be able to take some of his wealth with him.

An angel hears his plea and appears to him. "Sorry, but you can't take your wealth with you." The man implores the angel to speak to God to see if He might bend the rules.

The man continues to pray that his wealth might follow him. The angel appears and informs the man that God has decided to allow him to take one suitcase with him. Overjoyed, the man gathers his largest suitcase and fills it with gold bars and places it beside his bed.

Soon afterward the man dies and shows up at the gates of heaven to greet St. Peter.

St. Peter, seeing the suitcase, says, "Hold on, you can't bring that in here!"

But the man explains to St. Peter that he has permission and asks him to verify his story with the Lord. Sure enough, St. Peter checks and comes back saying, "You're right. You are allowed one carry-on bag, but I'm supposed to check its contents before letting it through."

St. Peter opens the suitcase to inspect the worldly items that the man found too precious to leave behind and exclaims, "You brought paving stones with you!?"

"Waiter! Please bring me a coffee without cream."

"I'm sorry, madam, but we've run out of cream. Would you like it without milk instead?"

There were 3 men who died and before God would let them into heaven, he gave them a chance to come back as anything they wanted.

The first said, "I want to come back as myself, but 100 times smarter."

So God made him 100 times smarter.

The second said, "I want to be better than that guy. Make me 1000 times smarter."

So God made him 1000 times smarter.

The last one decided he would be the best. So he said, "God, make me better than both of them. Make me 1,000,000 times smarter."

So God made him a woman ...

An American lawyer's dog, running around town unleashed, heads for a butcher shop and steals a piece of meat. The butcher goes to the lawyer's office and asks, "if a dog running unleashed steals a piece of meat from my store, do I have a right to demand payment for the meat from the dog's owner?"

The lawyer answers, "Absolutely."

"Then you owe me $8.50. Your dog was loose and stole a roast from me today."

The lawyer, without a word, writes the butcher a cheque for $8.50. The butcher, having a feeling of satisfaction, leaves.

Three days later, the butcher finds a bill from the lawyer: $100 due for a consultation.

A lawyer died and arrived at the Pearly Gates. To his dismay, there were thousands of people ahead of him in line to see St. Peter. But, to his surprise, St. Peter left his desk at the gate and came down the long line to where the lawyer was standing. St. Peter greeted him warmly. Then St. Peter and one of his assistants took the lawyer by the hands and guided him up to the front of the line into a comfortable chair by his desk.

The lawyer said, "I don't mind all this attention, but what makes me so special?"

St. Peter replied, "Well, I've added up all the hours for which you billed your clients, and by my calculation you must be about 193 years old!"

A doctor, an engineer, and a lawyer were discussing who among them belonged to the oldest of the three professions represented.

The doctor said, "Remember, on the sixth day God took a rib from Adam and fashioned Eve, making him the first surgeon. Therefore, medicine is the oldest profession."

The engineer replied, "But, before that, God created the heavens and earth from chaos and confusion, and thus he was the first engineer. Therefore, engineering is an older profession than medicine."

Then, the lawyer spoke up. "Yes," he said, "but who do you think created all of the chaos and confusion?"

A man walks into a bar and orders a drink, then discovers that he has to go to the bathroom. To stop anyone stealing his drink he puts a note on it saying, "I spat in this beer". When he returns he finds another note saying, "So did I!"

NASA was interviewing professionals to be sent to Mars. Only one could go and couldn't return to Earth.

The first applicant, an engineer, was asked how much he wanted to be paid for going. "A million dollars," he answered, "because I want to donate it to my university."

The next applicant, a doctor, was asked the same question. He asked for two million dollars. "I want to give a million to my family," he explained, "and leave the other million for the advancement of medical research."

The last applicant was a lawyer. When asked how much money he wanted, he whispered in the interviewer's ear, "Three million dollars."

"Why so much more than the others?" asked the interviewer.

The lawyer replied, "If you give me three million, I'll give you one million, I'll keep one million, and we'll send the engineer to Mars."

A golfer hooked his tee shot over a hill and onto the next fairway. Walking toward his ball, he saw a man lying on the ground, groaning with pain.

"I'm a lawyer," the wincing man said, "and this is going to cost you £5000."

"I'm sorry, I'm really sorry," the concerned golfer replied. "But I did yell 'fore'."

"I'll take it," the lawyer said.

❖

A navy psychiatrist is interviewing a potential recruit. The psychiatrist says, "What would you do if you looked out of that window and saw a battleship coming down the street?"

The recruit replies, "I'd grab a torpedo and sink it."

"Really," says the psychiatrist. "And where would you get a torpedo?"

The recruit replies, "The same place you got your battleship."

❖

A barber gave a haircut to a priest one day. The priest tried to pay for the haircut, but the barber refused, saying, "You do God's work." The next morning the barber found a dozen bibles at the door to his shop.

A policeman came to the barber for a haircut, and again the barber refused to pay, saying, "You protect the public." The next morning the barber found a dozen doughnuts at the door to his shop.

A lawyer came to the barber for a haircut, and again the barber refused payment, saying, "You serve the justice system." The next morning the barber found a dozen lawyers waiting for a free haircut.

Satan was complaining bitterly to God, "You made the world so that it was not fair, and you made it so that most people would have to struggle every day, fight against their innate wishes and desires, and deal with all sorts of losses, grief, disasters, and catastrophes. Yet people worship and adore you. People fight, get arrested, and cheat each other, and I get blamed, even when it is not my fault. Sure, I'm evil, but give me a break. Can't you do something to make them stop blaming me?"

And so God created lawyers.

The Devil visited a lawyer's office and made him an offer. "I can arrange some things for you," the Devil said. "I'll increase your income five-fold. Your partners will love you; your clients will respect you; you'll have four months of vacation each year and live to be a hundred. All I require in return is that your wife's soul, your children's souls, and their children's souls rot in hell for eternity."

"What's the catch?" the lawyer asked.

A lawyer died and was delivered into the Devil's hands. "You will be spending eternity here, but I'll let you pick your own room from three I'll show you," the Devil said.

In the first room were thousands of people standing on

their heads on a brick floor. "I don't like that," said the man. "Show me the second."

In the second room were thousands of people standing on their heads on a wood floor. "Well, that's better than brick," the man said, "but show me the third."

In the third, thousands of people were standing ankle-deep in a room full of maggot infested garbage, all drinking coffee.

"I'll choose this room," he said.

Into the room he went and the door slammed behind him.

Immediately, the voice of a minor demon rang out, "OK, coffee break is over, back on your heads."